Lecture Notes in Computer Science

Commenced Publication in 1973
Founding and Former Series Editors:
Gerhard Goos, Juris Hartmanis, and Jan van Leeuwen

Walter Dosch   Roger Y. Lee
Chisu Wu (Eds.)

Software Engineering Research, Management and Applications

Second International Conference, SERA 2004
Los Angeles, CA, USA, May 5-7, 2004
Selected Revised Papers

 Springer

Volume Editors

Walter Dosch
University of Lübeck
Institute of Software Technology and Programming Languages
Ratzeburger Allee 160, 23538 Lübeck, Germany
E-mail: dosch@isp.uni-luebeck.de

Roger Y. Lee
Central Michigan University
Software Engineering and Information Technology Institute
Mt.Pleasant,MI 48858, P.O. Box , USA
E-mail: lee@cps.cmich.edu

Chisu Wu
Seoul National University
School of Computer Science and Engineering
Seoul 151-742, South Korea
E-mail: wuchisu@selab.snu.ac.kr

Library of Congress Control Number: 2005939044

CR Subject Classification (1998): D.2, I.2.11, C.2.4, H.5.2-3, K.6

LNCS Sublibrary: SL 2 – Programming and Software Engineering

ISSN   0302-9743
ISBN-10   3-540-32133-0 Springer Berlin Heidelberg New York
ISBN-13   978-3-540-32133-0 Springer Berlin Heidelberg New York

Springer is a part of Springer Science+Business Media

springer.com

© Springer-Verlag Berlin Heidelberg 2005
Printed in Germany

Typesetting: Camera-ready by author, data conversion by Scientific Publishing Services, Chennai, India
Printed on acid-free paper   SPIN: 11668855   06/3142   5 4 3 2 1 0

Foreword

It was our great pleasure to extend a welcome to all who participated in SERA 2004, the second International Conference on Software Engineering Research, Management and Applications, held at the Omni Hotel, Los Angeles, California, USA. The conference would not have been possible without the cooperation of Seoul National University, Korea, the University of Lübeck, Germany, and Central Michigan University, USA. SERA 2004 was sponsored by the International Association for Computer and Information Science (ACIS).

The conference brought together researchers, practitioners, and advanced graduate students to exchange and share their experiences, new ideas, and research results in all aspects (theory, applications, and tools) of Software Engineering Research and Applications. At this conference, we had keynote speeches by Barry Boehm, C.V. Ramamoorthy, Raymond Yeh, and Con Kenney.

We would like to thank the publicity chairs, the members of our program committees, and everyone else who helped with the conference for their hard work and time dedicated to SERA 2004. We hope that SERA 2004 was enjoyable for all participants.

Barry Boehm

May 2004

Preface

The 2nd ACIS International Conference on Software Engineering – Research, Management and Applications (SERA 2004) was held at the Omni Hotel in Los Angeles, California, during May 5–7, 2004. The conference particularly welcomes contributions at the junction of theory and practice disseminating basic research with immediate impact on practical applications. The SERA conference series has witnessed a short, but successful history:

SERA 2003	San Francisco, California	June 25–27, 2003
SERA 2004	Los Angeles, California	May 5–7, 2004
SERA 2005	Mt. Pleasant, Michigan	August 11–13, 2005

The conference covers a broad range of topics from the field of software engineering including theory, methods, applications, and tools. The conference received 103 submissions from the scientific community in 18 different countries all over the world. Each paper was evaluated by three members of the International Program Committee and additional referees judging the originality, significance, technical contribution, and presentation style. After the completion of the review process 46 papers were selected for presentation at the conference which gave us an acceptance rate of about 45%.

The conference was structured into 14 sessions running in two parallel tracks. The conference sessions covered the following topics: formal methods and tools, data mining and knowledge discovery, requirements engineering, component-based software engineering, object-oriented technology and software architectures, Web engineering and Web-based applications, software reuse and software metrics, agent technology and information engineering, reverse engineering, communication systems and middleware design, XML applications and multimedia computing, parallel and distributed computing, and cost modelling and analysis.

Based on the opinion of the Program Committee and the recommendations of the session chairs, authors of selected papers were invited to submit a substantially revised and extended version for inclusion in the postconference proceedings. The submissions were subject to a second refereeing process. With great pleasure, we finally present 18 papers that were accepted for publication in Springer's LNCS as the post-conference proceedings.

We would like to express our sincere thanks to the Honorary General Chair Dr. Barry Boehm and to the Conference Chair Dr. Con Kenney. We appreciate the dedication of Dr. Barry Boem, Dr. C.V. Ramamoorthy, Dr. Raymond T. Yeh, and Dr. Con Kenney in contributing keynote speeches. We gratefully acknowledge the professional work of the International Program Committee and the subreviewers. We thank the Publicity Chairs for their commitment and, finally, the editorial staff at Springer for the smooth cooperation.

June 2005

Walter Dosch,
Roger Y. Lee,
Chisu Wu

Organizing Committee

Honorary General Chair

Dr. Barry Boehm
Directory, USC Center for Software
Engineering
University of Southern California
(USA)

Conference Chair

Dr. Con Kenney
Chief IT Enterprise Architect Federal
Aviation Administration (USA)

Program Co-chairs

Prof. Roger Lee
Computer Science Department Central
Michigan University (USA)

Prof. Chisu Wu Computer Science &
Engineering National University
(Seoul, Korea)

Prof. Dr. Walter Dosch Institute of
Software Technology & Programming
Languages University of Lubeck
(Germany)

Publicity Chairs

Canada
Sylvanus Ehikioya
University of Manitoba

Korea
Haeng-Kon Kim
Catholic University of Daegu

France
Pascale Minet
INRIA, France

Lebanon
Ramzi Haraty
Lebanese American University

Hong Kong, China
Pak Lok Poon
   Hong Kong Polytechnic University

Spain
Ana Moreno
Universidad Politecnica de Madrid

Italy
Susanna Pelagatti
University of Pisa

USA
Lawrence Chung University of Texas-
Dallas

Japan
Naohiro Ishii
Aichi Institute of Technology

International Program Committee

Doo-Hwan Bae
(KAIST, Korea)

Jongmoon Baik
(Motorola Labs, USA)

Ken Barker
(Univ. of Calgary, Canada)

Chia-Chu Chiang
(University of Arkansas-Little Rock,
USA)

Byoungju Choi
(Ewha Womans University, Korea)

Lawrence Chung
(University of Texas-Dallas, USA)

Jozo Dujmovic
(San Francisco State University,
USA)

Sylvanus Ehikioya
(University of Manitoba, Canada)

Paul Garratt
(University of Southampton, UK)

Gonzhu Hu
(Central Michigan University, USA)

Chih Cheng Hung
(Southern Polytechnic State Univ.,
USA)

Naohiro Ishii
(Aichi Institute of Technology, Japan)

Taewoong Jeon
(Korea University, Korea)

Lianxing Jia
(Univ. of Manchester, UK)

Soo-Dong Kim
(Soongsil University, Korea)

Tai-Hoon Kim
(Korea Information Security Agency,
Korea)

Juhnyoung Lee
(IBM T.J. Watson Research Center, USA)

Jun Li
(University of Oregon, USA)

Brian Malloy
(Clemson University, USA)

Pascale Minet
(INRIA, France)

Ana Moreno
(Universidad Politecnica de Madrid,
Spain)

Nohpill Park
(Oklahoma State University, USA)

Susanna Pelagatti
(University of Pisa, Italy)

Frantisek Plasil
(Charles University, Czech Republic)

Vinod Prasad
(Bradley University, USA)

David Primeaux
(Virginia Commonwealth University,
USA)

Stuart Rubin
(SPAWAR, USA)

Laura Simini
(University of Pisa, Italy)

Table of Contents

Web Engineering and Web-Based Applications

Parallel and Distributed Computing

Software Reuse and Metrics

Object-Oriented Technology and Information Technology

Communications Systems and Networks

Transforming Stream Processing Functions into State Transition Machines

Walter Dosch and Annette Stümpel

Institute of Software Technology and Programming Languages,
University of Lübeck, Germany
http://www.isp.uni-luebeck.de

Abstract. The black-box view of an interactive component in a distributed system concentrates on the input/output behaviour based on communication histories. The glass-box view discloses the component's internal state with inputs effecting an update of the state. The black-box view is modelled by a stream processing function, the glass-box view by a state transition machine. We present a formal method for transforming a stream processing function into a state transition machine with input and output. We introduce states as abstractions of the input history and derive the machine's transition functions using history abstractions. The state refinement is illustrated with three applications, viz. an iterator component, a scan component, and an interactive stack.

1 Introduction

A distributed system consists of a network of components that communicate asynchronously via unidirectional channels. The communication histories are modelled by sequences of messages, called streams. Streams abstract from discrete or continuous time, since they record only the succession of messages. The input/output behaviour of a communicating component is described by a stream processing function [14,15] mapping input histories to output histories.

During the development of a component, the software designer employs different points of view. On the specification level, a component is considered as a black box whose behaviour is determined by the relation between input and output histories. The external view is relevant for the service provided to the environment.

On the implementation level, the designer concentrates on the component's internal state where an input is processed by updating the internal state. The internal view, also called glass-box view, is described by a state transition machine with input and output.

A crucial design step amounts to transforming the specified behaviour of a communicating component into a state-based implementation. In our approach, we conceive machine states as abstractions of the input history. The state stores information about the input history that influences the component's output on future input. In general, there are different abstractions of the input history which lead to state spaces of different granularity [10].

W. Dosch, R.Y. Lee, and C. Wu (Eds.): SERA 2004, LNCS 3647, pp. 1–18, 2005.

This paper presents a formal method, called *state refinement*, for transforming stream processing functions into state transition machines. The transformation is grounded on history abstractions which identify subsets of input histories as the states of the machine. The state refinement preserves the component's input/output behaviour, if we impose two requirements. Upon receiving further input, a history abstraction must be compatible with the state transitions and with the generation of the output stream. The formal method supports a top-down design deriving the state-based implementation from a behavioural specification in a safe way.

The paper is organized as follows. In Section 2 we summarize the basic notions for the functional description of interactive components with communication histories. Section 3 introduces state transition machines with input and output. Section 4 presents the systematic construction of a state transition machine that implements a stream processing function in a correctness preserving way. History abstractions relate input histories to machine states. With their help, the transition functions of the machine can be derived involving the output extension of the stream processing function.

In the subsequent sections, we demonstrate the state refinement for different types of applications. In Section 5, the transformation of an iterator component leads to state transition machines with a trivial state space resulting from the constant history abstraction. Section 6 presents a general implementation scheme for scan components based on the reduce function as a history abstraction. Section 7 discusses the state-based implementation of an interactive stack. The history abstraction leading to a standard implementation results from combining a control state and a data state in a suitable way.

2   Streams and Stream Processing Functions

In this section we briefly summarize the basic notions about streams and stream processing functions to render the paper self-contained. The reader is referred to [24] for a survey and to [25] for a comprehensive treatment. Streams constitute a basic concept for describing different types of interactive systems [19].

2.1   Finite Streams

A stream models the communication history of a channel which is determined by the sequence of data transferred. Untimed streams record only the succession of messages and provide no further information about the timing.

Given a non-empty set $\mathcal{A}$ of data, the set $\mathcal{A}^\star$ of finite *communication histories*, for short *streams*, over $\mathcal{A}$ is the least set with respect to set inclusion defined by the recursion equation

$$\mathcal{A}^\star = \{\langle\rangle\} \cup \mathcal{A} \times \mathcal{A}^\star. \tag{1}$$

A stream is either the *empty stream* $\langle\rangle$ or it is constructed by the prefix operation $\vartriangleleft : \mathcal{A} \times \mathcal{A}^\star \to \mathcal{A}^\star$ attaching an element to the front of a stream. We denote streams by capital letters and elements of streams by small letters. A stream $X = x_1 \triangleleft x_2 \triangleleft \ldots \triangleleft x_n \triangleleft \langle \rangle$ $(n \geq 0)$ is denoted by $\langle x_1, x_2, \ldots, x_n \rangle$ for short.

The *concatenation* $X \& Y$ of two streams $X = \langle x_1, \ldots, x_k \rangle$ and $Y = \langle y_1, \ldots, y_l \rangle$ over the same set $\mathcal{A}$ of data yields the stream $\langle x_1, \ldots, x_k, y_1, \ldots, y_l \rangle$ of length $k + l$. The concatenation $X \& \langle x \rangle$ appending an element x at the rear of a stream X is abbreviated as $X \triangleright x$.

2.2   Prefix Order

Operational progress is modelled by the prefix order. The longer stream forms an extension of the shorter history, and, vice versa, the shorter stream is an initial segment of the longer stream.

A stream X is called a *prefix* of a stream Y, denoted $X \sqsubseteq Y$, iff there exists a stream R with $X \& R = Y$. The set of finite streams over a data set forms a partial order under the prefix relation with the empty stream as the least element. Monotonic functions on finite streams possess unique continuous extensions to infinite streams [18].

2.3   Stream Processing Functions

The sequence of data passing along a communication channel between two components is captured by the notion of a stream. Thus, a deterministic component which continuously processes data from its input ports and emits data at its output ports can be considered as a function mapping input histories to output histories.

A *stream processing function* $f : \mathcal{A}^\star \rightarrow \mathcal{B}^\star$ maps an input stream to an output stream. The input type $\mathcal{A}$ and the output type $\mathcal{B}$ determine the syntactic *interface* of the component.

We require that a stream processing function is *monotonic* with respect to the prefix order:

$$f(X) \sqsubseteq f(X \& Y) \tag{2}$$

This property ensures that a prolongation of the input history leads to an extension of the output history. A communicating component cannot change the past output when receiving future input.

A stream processing function describes the *(input/output) behaviour* of a component.

2.4   Output Extension

A stream processing function characterizes the behaviour of a component on entire input streams. A finer view reveals the causal relationship between single elements in the input stream and corresponding segments of the output stream.

The output extension isolates the effect of a single input on the output stream after processing a prehistory, compare Fig. 1.

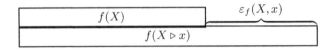

Fig. 1. Output extension of a stream processing function f

Definition 1. *The output extension $\varepsilon_f : \mathcal{A}^\star \times \mathcal{A} \to \mathcal{B}^\star$ of a stream processing function $f : \mathcal{A}^\star \to \mathcal{B}^\star$ is defined by*

$$f(X \triangleright x) \;=\; f(X) \;\&\; \varepsilon_f(X, x) \; . \tag{3}$$

The output extension completely determines the behaviour of a stream processing function apart from its result for the empty input history.

3   State Transition Machines with Input and Output

The operational behaviour of distributed systems is often formalized by labelled state transition systems specifying a transition relation between states associated with labels [27]. The transitions denote memory updates, inputs, outputs, or other actions. For the purposes of modelling communicating components, we associate a state transition with receiving an element on the input channel and sending data to the output channel.

3.1   Architecture of the Machine

A state transition machine reacts on input with an update of the internal state generating a sequence of outputs.

Definition 2. *A state transition machine with input and output,* for short a state transition machine, *$M = (\mathcal{Q}, \mathcal{A}, \mathcal{B}, next, out, q_0)$ consists of*

- *a non-empty set $\mathcal{Q}$ of states,*
- *a non-empty set $\mathcal{A}$ of input data,*
- *a non-empty set $\mathcal{B}$ of output data,*
- *a (single-step) state transition function $next : \mathcal{Q} \times \mathcal{A} \to \mathcal{Q}$,*
- *a (single-step) output function $out : \mathcal{Q} \times \mathcal{A} \to \mathcal{B}^\star$, and*
- *an initial state $q_0 \in \mathcal{Q}$.*

The types $\mathcal{A}$ and $\mathcal{B}$ determine the interface *of the state transition machine.*

Given a current state and an input, the single-step state transition function determines a unique successor state. The single-step output function yields a finite sequence of elements, not just a single element.

The single-step functions can naturally be extended to finite input streams.

Definition 3. *The* multi-step state transition function $next^\star : Q \to [A^\star \to Q]$ *yields the state reached after processing a finite input stream:*

$$next^\star(q)(\langle\rangle) \;=\; q \tag{4}$$

$$next^\star(q)(x \triangleleft X) \;=\; next^\star(next(q,x))(X) \tag{5}$$

The multi-step output function $out^\star : Q \to [A^\star \to B^\star]$ *accumulates the output stream for a finite input stream:*

$$out^\star(q)(\langle\rangle) \;=\; \langle\rangle \tag{6}$$

$$out^\star(q)(x \triangleleft X) \;=\; out(q,x) \,\&\, out^\star(next(q,x))(X) \tag{7}$$

The multi-step output function describes the (input/output) *behaviour of the state transition machine.*

The multi-step state transition function cooperates with concatenation:

$$next^\star(q)(X \& Y) \;=\; next^\star(next^\star(q)(X))(Y) \tag{8}$$

Moreover, the multi-step output function is prefix monotonic as shown by the following decomposition property:

$$out^\star(q)(X \& Y) \;=\; out^\star(q)(X) \,\&\, out^\star(next^\star(q)(X))(Y) \tag{9}$$

Hence, for each state $q \in Q$, the multi-step output function $out^\star(q) : A^\star \to B^\star$ constitutes a stream processing function. It abstracts from the individual state transitions and offers a history-based view of the component.

3.2   Output Equivalence

We aim at transforming a state transition machine into a more compact one with a reduced number of states without changing the input/output behaviour. To this end, we are interested in states which induce an equal behaviour when the state transition machine receives further input.

Definition 4. *Two states $p, q \in Q$ of a state transition machine $M = (Q, A, B, next, out, q_0)$ are called* output equivalent, *denoted $p \approx q$, iff they generate the same output for all input streams:*

$$out^\star(p) \;=\; out^\star(q) \tag{10}$$

An observer of the state transition machine cannot distinguish output equivalent states, as they produce the same output stream for every input stream.

Successor states of output equivalent states are also output equivalent:

$$p \approx q \;\Longrightarrow\; next^\star(p)(X) \approx next^\star(q)(X) \tag{11}$$

In [1] special properties of Mealy machines are investigated which ease the recognition of output equivalent states.

3.3   Related Models

State transition machines with input and output are closely related to other state-based computing devices used to specify, verify, and analyse the behaviour of distributed systems.

Most of the models describing the behaviour of components with input and output originate in *finite state machines* distinguishing between machines of Mealy type and machines of Moore type.

The widely used *Mealy machines* produce exactly one output datum with each transition. Moreover, they operate on a finite set of states with finite input and output alphabets.

HAREL's *statecharts* [13] are built upon Mealy machines. They allow a distributed system to be hierarchically decomposed into state machines where communication is conducted via a broadcast mechanism. μ-Charts [22] are a derivative of statecharts which employ multicast communication and rectify some semantic problems of statecharts. *UML state diagrams* [21,20] are based on statecharts. The inputs are events, and outputs are actions; state diagrams also may have final states.

A transition of a *port input/output automaton* [16] is labelled with either an input, or an output or an internal action. Transitions may depend on a condition. Moreover, in each state each input action is enabled. Consequently, there is no direct connection between an input and the corresponding output. The input stream is not processed step by step, and output can be arbitrarily delayed.

Stream X-machines [2] are automata with input and output which distinguish between states and memory values.

State transition systems were used in [3] for specifying the behaviour of components and in [5] for verifying safety and liveness properties. In order to ease verification, these state transition systems carry as much information as possible: states are labelled with the previous and the future content of the channels and additional attributes.

More recently, *persistent Turing machines* [12] formalized the intuitive notion of sequential interactive computation endowing classical Turing machines with a dynamic stream semantics.

In summary, there exist many similar state-based devices; nevertheless none of them is identical to the type of state transition machines presented here. Our state transition machines with input and output [9] are tailored for asynchronous systems. They support a smooth transition from a component's black-box view based on communication histories to a glass-box view based on abstract state transitions.

4   From Stream Processing Functions to State Transition Machines

In this section, we implement stream processing functions by state transition machines using history abstractions. Given a stream processing function, we construct a state transition machine with the same interface and the same behaviour. The crucial design decision amounts to choosing an appropriate set of states. In our approach, the states of the machine represent subsets of input histories that have the same effect on the output for all future input streams.

4.1   History Abstractions

A history abstraction extracts from an input history certain information that influences the component's future behaviour.

Definition 5. *For a stream processing function $f : A^\star \to B^\star$ and a set Q of states, a function $\alpha : A^\star \to Q$ is called a* history abstraction *for f, if it is* output compatible

$$\alpha(X) = \alpha(Y) \implies \varepsilon_f(X, x) = \varepsilon_f(Y, x) \tag{12}$$

and transition closed*:*

$$\alpha(X) = \alpha(Y) \implies \alpha(X \triangleright x) = \alpha(Y \triangleright x) \tag{13}$$

The output compatibility guarantees that a history abstraction identifies at most those input histories which have the same effect on future output. The transition closedness ensures that extensions of identified streams are identified as well:

$$\alpha(X) = \alpha(Y) \implies \alpha(X \& Z) = \alpha(Y \& Z) \tag{14}$$

The transition closedness constitutes a general requirement, whereas the output compatibility refers to the particular stream processing function.

4.2   Construction of the State Transition Machine

When implementing a stream processing function with a state transition machine, the history abstraction determines the state space, the transition functions, and the initial state.

Definition 6. *Given a stream processing function $f : A^\star \to B^\star$ and a surjective history abstraction $\alpha : A^\star \to Q$ for f, we construct a state transition machine $M[f, \alpha] = (Q, A, B, next, out, q_0)$ with the same interface as follows:*

$$next(\alpha(X), x) = \alpha(X \triangleright x) \tag{15}$$
$$out(\alpha(X), x) = \varepsilon_f(X, x) \tag{16}$$
$$q_0 = \alpha(\langle\rangle) \tag{17}$$

The state transition function and the output function are well-defined, since the history abstraction is surjective, transition closed, and output compatible.

The following proposition establishes the correctness of the implementation step.

Theorem 1. *Under the assumptions of Def. 6, the stream processing function and the multi-step output function of the state transition machine agree:*

$$f(X) \; = \; f(\langle\rangle) \; \& \; out^\star(q_0)(X) \tag{18}$$

In particular, for a strict stream processing function we have

$$f \; = \; out^\star(q_0) \; . \tag{19}$$

In general, a stream processing function possesses various history abstractions identifying different subsets of input histories as states.

The finest history abstraction is given by the identity function $\alpha(X) = X$ keeping all input histories distinct. The associated state transition machine is called the *canonical state transition machine*. Its states correspond to input histories, the state transition function extends the input history input by input, the output function is the output extension.

The coarsest history abstraction $\alpha(X) = [X]_\approx$ maps every input history to the class of output equivalent input histories. The associated state transition machine possesses a minimal state space.

We can generalize the construction of the state transition machine to history abstraction functions that are not surjective. In this case, the state transition functions are uniquely specified only on the subset $next^\star(q_0)(\mathcal{A}^\star)$ of reachable states. The transition functions can be defined in an arbitrary way on the subset of unreachable states; this will not influence the input/output behaviour of the machine starting in the initial state.

4.3   State Refinement

Every stream processing function can be transformed into a state transition machine with the same input/output behaviour using a history abstraction.

This universal construction lays the foundations for a formal method for developing a correct state-based implementation of a communicating component from its input/output-oriented specification. We call the formal method *state refinement*, since it transforms a component's communication-oriented black-box description into a state-based glass-box description. The history abstraction documents the essential design decisions for the state space. The state refinement complements other methods of refinement for communicating components such as interface refinement [4], property refinement [6], and architecture refinement [23].

We presented the state refinement transformation $f \mapsto M[f, \alpha]$ for unary stream processing functions f only. The transformation generalizes to stream processing functions with several arguments in a natural way [25].

5   History Independent Components

This section applies the state refinement transformation to the class of components whose behaviour does not dependent on the previous input history. We uniformly describe the set of history independent stream processing functions by a higher-order function. A constant history abstraction leads to an associated state transition machine with a singleton set as state space.

5.1 Iterator Components

An iterator component repeatedly applies a basic function to all elements of the input stream, compare Fig. 2.

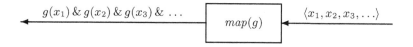

$$g(x_1) \& g(x_2) \& g(x_3) \& \ldots \quad \boxed{map(g)} \quad \langle x_1, x_2, x_3, \ldots \rangle$$

Fig. 2. Input/output behaviour of an iterator component

Iterator components are uniformly described by the higher-order function $map : [\mathcal{A} \to \mathcal{B}^\star] \to [\mathcal{A}^\star \to \mathcal{B}^\star]$ with

$$map(g)(\langle\rangle) = \langle\rangle \tag{20}$$
$$map(g)(x \triangleleft X) = g(x) \& map(g)(X) \ . \tag{21}$$

The higher-order function map concatenates the sequences generated by the single input elements to form the output stream. For every basic function g, the function $map(g)$ distributes over concatenation:

$$map(g)(X \& Y) = map(g)(X) \& map(g)(Y) \tag{22}$$

Therefore the function $map(g)$ is prefix monotonic. The output extension

$$\varepsilon_{map(g)}(X, x) = g(x) \tag{23}$$

depends only on the current input, but not on the previous input history.

5.2 State Transition Machine of an Iterator Component

The history abstraction of an iterator component need not preserve any information of the previous input history. Thus any transition closed function forms a proper history abstraction, in particular, any constant function.

For constructing the state transition machine $M[map(g), const]$, we choose a singleton state space $\mathcal{Q} = \{q_0\}$ and a constant history abstraction $const(X) = q_0$. The resulting state transition machine is shown in Fig. 3. The history independent behaviour of an iterator component is reflected by a "state-free" machine whose singleton state is irrelevant.

Vice versa, any state transition machine $M = (\{q_0\}, \mathcal{A}, \mathcal{B}, next, out, q_0)$ with a singleton state implements the behaviour of an iterator component $map(g)$ where the basic function $g : \mathcal{A} \to \mathcal{B}^\star$ is defined as $g(x) = out(q_0, x)$.

Iterator components are frequently used in various application areas, among others in transmission components, processing units, and control components.

$M[map(g), const]$	$=$	$(\{q_0\}, \mathcal{A}, \mathcal{B}, next, out, q_0)$
$next(q_0, x)$	$=$	q_0
$out(q_0, x)$	$=$	$g(x)$

Fig. 3. State transition machine of an iterator component

6   Scan Components

Many components such as counters accumulate their input with a dyadic operation, compare Fig. 4.

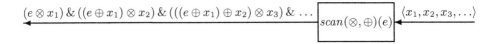

$$(e \otimes x_1) \& ((e \oplus x_1) \otimes x_2) \& (((e \oplus x_1) \oplus x_2) \otimes x_3) \& \ldots \quad \boxed{scan(\otimes, \oplus)(e)} \quad \langle x_1, x_2, x_3, \ldots \rangle$$

Fig. 4. Input/output behaviour of a scan component

The history abstraction for such components reduces the input stream with this operation. In this section, we present the systematic state refinement of scan components using the reduce function as a history abstraction.

6.1   Specification

We uniformly describe scan components by a higher-order function and explore its algebraic properties.

The higher-order function

$$scan : [[\mathcal{C} \times \mathcal{A} \to \mathcal{B}^\star] \times [\mathcal{C} \times \mathcal{A} \to \mathcal{C}]] \to [\mathcal{C} \to [\mathcal{A}^\star \to \mathcal{B}^\star]]$$

constructs its output stream by applying the outer combining operation $\otimes :$ $\mathcal{C} \times \mathcal{A} \to \mathcal{B}^\star$ to the proper prefixes of its input stream reduced under the inner combining operation $\oplus : \mathcal{C} \times \mathcal{A} \to \mathcal{C}$ with an initial value $e \in \mathcal{C}$:

$$scan(\otimes, \oplus)(e)(\langle\rangle) = \langle\rangle \tag{24}$$
$$scan(\otimes, \oplus)(e)(x \triangleleft X) = (e \otimes x) \& scan(\otimes, \oplus)(e \oplus x)(X) \tag{25}$$

6.2   History Abstraction

We can find a suitable history abstraction by exploring the decomposition property of scan components. This property reveals the information to be abstracted from the input history for specifying the future behaviour.

The result of the scan component for a composite input stream can be inferred from the results of the two substreams:

$$scan(\otimes, \oplus)(e)(X \& Y) = scan(\otimes, \oplus)(e)(X) \& scan(\otimes, \oplus)(red(\oplus)(e)(X))(Y) \tag{26}$$

The auxiliary function $red : [\mathcal{C} \times \mathcal{A} \to \mathcal{C}] \to [\mathcal{C} \to [\mathcal{A}^\star \to \mathcal{C}]]$ reduces an input stream under a dyadic operation $\oplus : \mathcal{C} \times \mathcal{A} \to \mathcal{C}$ with initial value $e \in \mathcal{C}$:

$$red(\oplus)(e)(\langle\rangle) = e \qquad (27)$$

$$red(\oplus)(e)(x \triangleleft X) = red(\oplus)(e \oplus x)(X) \qquad (28)$$

The reduce function is transition closed, since it validates the equation

$$red(\oplus)(e)(X \triangleright x) = red(\oplus)(e)(X) \oplus x \ . \qquad (29)$$

The output extension of the scan component

$$\varepsilon_{scan(\otimes,\oplus)(e)}(X, x) = red(\oplus)(e)(X) \otimes x \qquad (30)$$

depends only on the reduced value of the input history; thus $red(\oplus)(e)$ is a suitable history abstraction for $scan(\otimes, \oplus)(e)$.

6.3   State Transition Machine of a Scan Component

We construct the state transition machine for scan components in a schematic way. We choose the set $\mathcal{Q} = \mathcal{C}$ of states and the history abstraction $red(\oplus)(e) : \mathcal{A}^\star \to \mathcal{C}$. We calculate the initial state

$$q_0 = red(\oplus)(e)(\langle\rangle) = e \ . \qquad (31)$$

We derive the state transition function $next : \mathcal{C} \times \mathcal{A} \to \mathcal{C}$ for states that are reductions of an input history with the initial value e:

$$next(red(\oplus)(e)(X), x) = red(\oplus)(e)(X \triangleright x) = red(\oplus)(e)(X) \oplus x \qquad (32)$$

The results of the state transition function on the set of unreachable states in $\mathcal{C}$ can be chosen in an arbitrary way. We achieve a uniform description by setting $next(q, x) = q \oplus x$.

Similarly, we derive the single-step output function $out : \mathcal{C} \times \mathcal{A} \to \mathcal{B}^\star$ as

$$out(red(\oplus)(e)(X), x) = \varepsilon_{scan(\otimes,\oplus)(e)}(X, x) = red(\oplus)(e)(X) \otimes x \qquad (33)$$

and extend it to all states by setting $out(q, x) = q \otimes x$. The resulting state transition machine is summarized in Fig. 5.

Note that scan components comprise the general class of stream processing functions [25]. Therefore the state transition machine for scan components provides a universal method for the iterative implementation of stream processing functions.

$M[scan(\otimes, \oplus)(e), red(\oplus)(e)] = (\mathcal{C}, \mathcal{A}, \mathcal{B}, next, out, e)$
$next(q, x) = q \oplus x$
$out(q, x) = q \otimes x$

Fig. 5. State transition machine of a scan component

7   Interactive Stack

As a final application we construct the implementation of an interactive stack
[7]. The application shows how to combine a control abstraction and a data
abstraction into an overall history abstraction.

7.1   Specification

An interactive stack is a communicating component that stores and retrieves
data following a last-in/first-out strategy. The component reacts on requests
outputting the last datum which has previously been stored, but was not requested yet, compare Fig. 6.

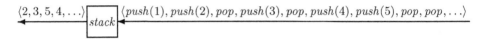

Fig. 6. Input/output behaviour of an interactive stack

We assume that the interactive stack is fault-sensitive. A pop command to
the empty stack causes a stack underflow: the component breaks and provides
no further output whatsoever future input arrives.

Let $\mathcal{D}$ denote the non-empty set of data to be stored in the stack. The
component's input consists of pop commands or push commands along with the
datum to be stored:

$$\mathcal{I} = \{pop\} \cup push(\mathcal{D}) \tag{34}$$

The component's behaviour forms a stream processing function $stack : \mathcal{I}^\star \to \mathcal{D}^\star$
defined by the following equations $(Push \in push(\mathcal{D})^\star)$:

$$stack(Push) = \langle\rangle \tag{35}$$

$$stack(Push \& \langle push(d), pop \rangle \& X) = d \lhd stack(Push \& X) \tag{36}$$

$$stack(pop \lhd X) = \langle\rangle \tag{37}$$

A sequence of push commands generates no output (35). A pop command outputs the datum stored most recently (36). After an erroneous pop command,
the interactive stack breaks (37).

The behaviour of the interactive stack leads to the output extension ε_{stack} :
$\mathcal{I}^\star \times \mathcal{I} \to \mathcal{D}^\star$ defined by $(Push \in push(\mathcal{D})^\star)$:

$$\varepsilon_{stack}(X, push(d)) = \langle\rangle \tag{38}$$

$$\varepsilon_{stack}(Push \rhd push(d), pop) = \langle d \rangle \tag{39}$$

$$\varepsilon_{stack}(\langle\rangle, pop) = \langle\rangle \tag{40}$$

$$\varepsilon_{stack}(pop \lhd X, pop) = \langle\rangle \tag{41}$$

$$\varepsilon_{stack}(Push \& \langle push(d), pop \rangle \& X, pop) = \varepsilon_{stack}(Push \& X, pop) \tag{42}$$

A push command generates no output after any input history (38). A pop command yields the datum stored most recently which was not requested yet (39) unless the stack contains no datum (40) or there was a stack underflow (41).

7.2   Control Abstraction

The future behaviour of a fault-sensitive stack is influenced by the occurrence of an illegal pop command in the preceding input history.

We discriminate between regular and erroneous input histories using a binary control state $Control = \{reg, err\}$. The control abstraction $control : \mathcal{I}^\star \rightarrow Control$ classifies input histories as regular or erroneous ($Push \in push(\mathcal{D})^\star$):

$$control(Push) = reg \tag{43}$$
$$control(Push\&\langle push(d), pop\rangle \& X) = control(Push\& X) \tag{44}$$
$$control(pop \triangleleft X) = err \tag{45}$$

A sequence of push commands forms a regular input history (43), whereas a pop command without a preceding push command gives rise to an erroneous input history (45).

The control abstraction is neither transition closed nor output compatible, since it identifies all regular input histories, but forgets the data stored in the component.

7.3   Data Abstraction

The future behaviour of the interactive stack will be influenced by the collection of data stored in the component from the previous input history.

As a second abstraction, we explore the state $Data = \mathcal{D}^\star$ representing a stack of data. The data abstraction $data : \mathcal{I}^\star \rightarrow Data$ extracts from the input history the stack of data retained in the component after processing the input stream ($n \geq 0$, $Push \in push(\mathcal{D})^\star$):

$$data(\langle push(d_1), \ldots, push(d_n)\rangle) = \langle d_1, \ldots, d_n\rangle \tag{46}$$
$$data(Push\&\langle push(d), pop\rangle \& X) = data(Push\& X) \tag{47}$$
$$data(pop \triangleleft X) = \langle\rangle \tag{48}$$

The data abstraction is neither output compatible nor transition closed. It identifies regular input histories leading to the empty stack with erroneous input histories resulting in a broken stack.

7.4   History Abstraction

We integrate the control abstraction and the data abstraction into a joint history abstraction.

This design decision leads to a composite state space $\mathcal{Q} = Control \times Data$ combining a control part and a data part. The abstraction function $\alpha : \mathcal{I}^\star \rightarrow Control \times Data$ pairs the control and the data abstraction ($n \geq 0$, $Push \in push(\mathcal{D})^\star$):

$$\alpha(\langle push(d_1), \dots, push(d_n) \rangle) \;=\; (reg, \langle d_1, \dots, d_n \rangle) \tag{49}$$

$$\alpha(Push \& \langle push(d), pop \rangle \& X) \;=\; \alpha(Push \& X) \tag{50}$$

$$\alpha(pop \lhd X) \;=\; (err, \langle \rangle) \tag{51}$$

The abstraction function keeps all required information from the input history which determines the component's future behaviour. The abstraction function is indeed a history abstraction and supports the transition to a state-based implementation.

7.5   State Transition Machine of an Interactive Stack

The implementation of the interactive stack is derived from the input/output behaviour using the combined history abstraction for control and data states. The resulting state transition machine is summarized in Fig. 7. In a regular

$M[stack, \alpha] \;=\; (Control \times Data, \mathcal{I}, \mathcal{D}, next, out, (reg, \langle \rangle))$	
$next((reg, Q), push(d)) \;=\; (reg, Q \rhd d)$	(7.1)
$next((reg, Q \rhd q), pop) \;=\; (reg, Q)$	(7.2)
$next((reg, \langle \rangle), pop) \;=\; (err, \langle \rangle)$	(7.3)
$next((err, \langle \rangle), x) \;=\; (err, \langle \rangle)$	(7.4)
$out((reg, Q), push(d)) \;=\; \langle \rangle$	(7.5)
$out((reg, Q \rhd q), pop) \;=\; \langle q \rangle$	(7.6)
$out((reg, \langle \rangle), pop) \;=\; \langle \rangle$	(7.7)
$out((err, \langle \rangle), x) \;=\; \langle \rangle$	(7.8)

Fig. 7. State transition machine of an interactive stack

state, a push command attaches an element to the stack (7.1) and produces no output (7.5). Moreover, a pop command delivers the top of a non-empty stack (7.6); for an empty stack it leads to the error state (7.3). This state cannot be left any more by further input (7.4) which produces no output in the error state (7.8).

The subset of states reachable from the initial state $(reg, \langle \rangle)$ is isomorphic to the direct sum of the data stack and an error state:

$$\{reg\} \times \mathcal{D}^\star \;\cup\; \{(err, \langle \rangle)\} \;\simeq\; \mathcal{D}^\star + \{err\} \tag{52}$$

The transition functions defined on the subset of reachable states can simply be extended to the set of all states by setting $next((err, Q), x) = (err, Q)$ and $out((err, Q), x) = \langle \rangle$.

7.6   State Transition Table of an Interactive Stack

For practical purposes, state transition machines are often described by *state transition tables* displaying the different transition rules in a clear way.

Control	Data	Input	Control'	Data'	Output
reg	Q	$push(d)$	reg	$Q \triangleright d$	$\langle \rangle$
reg	$Q \triangleright q$	pop	reg	Q	$\langle q \rangle$
reg	$\langle \rangle$	pop	err	$\langle \rangle$	$\langle \rangle$
err	$\langle \rangle$	x	err	$\langle \rangle$	$\langle \rangle$

Fig. 8. State transition table of an interactive stack

Fig. 8 describes the interactive stack by a state transition table. The four *transition rules* relate current states and inputs to new states and outputs. The transition rules tabulate the transition functions *next* and *out*. We use the notational convention that the constituents of the successor state are designated by a prime. For an empty input stream, the state transition table produces no output which agrees with Equation (35).

7.7 State Transition Diagram of an Interactive Stack

A state transition machine with input and output may be visualized by a *state transition diagram* having the set of states as vertices. Each directed edge from one state to a successor state is labelled by a corresponding pair naming input and output:

$$q \xrightarrow{(x,\, out(q,x))} next(q, x) \tag{53}$$

In general, the graph will be infinite and can only be displayed in fragments or in a symbolic way.

The state transition diagram of an interactive stack is infinite, but quite regular. Fig. 9 shows an initial part of the state transition diagram for a binary data type $\mathcal{D} = \{0, 1\}$. Following Equation (52), we display states either by the stack of data or the error state. The error state is a trap state which can only be reached from the empty stack.

8 Conclusion

Nowadays interaction [26] is consider as an important paradigm. Therefore the specification and the systematic design of interactive components belongs to the central challenges of modern software technology. The software design must safely bridge component descriptions on different levels of abstraction.

The component's specification reflects a communication-oriented view concentrating on input and output histories. History-based specifications raise the abstraction level of initial descriptions. The black-box view provides a functional model of the component important for constructing networks in a compositional way.

The component's implementation decisively depends on the internal state supporting an efficient realization of the transition functions. The glass-box view

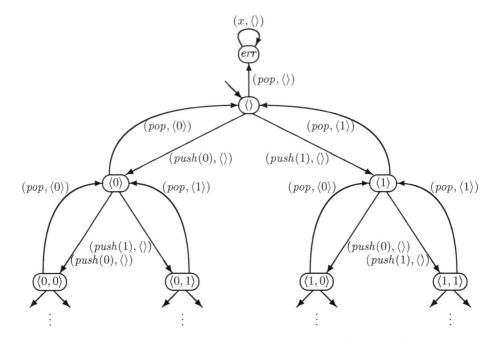

Fig. 9. Initial part of the state transition diagram of an interactive stack of binary values

discloses the component's internal state which is in general composed from various control and data parts [11].

This paper contributes to a better understanding how to relate communication-oriented and state-based descriptions. We presented a formal method for transforming a stream processing function into a state transition machine. The state refinement employs history abstractions to bridge the gap between input histories and machine states. The transition functions can be derived from the defining equations using the Lübeck Transformation System [8,17].

Yet, the crucial design decision consists in discovering a suitable history abstraction which determines the state space. In general, the state of a component must store at least the information which is needed to process further inputs in a correct way. The particular information depends on the area of application. For example, the state of a counter records the sum of all elements which passed the component; so it depends on the entire prehistory. The state of a memory cell remembers the datum of the last write command which is the only decisive event in the prehistory. The state of a shift register stores a final segment of the input stream that is withheld from the output stream. The state of a transmission component may record the active channel, the successful transmission or the failure of acknowledge.

The state refinement presents a standard transformation from a denotational to an operational description of interactive components. The refinement step can be prepared by calculating the output extension of the stream processing function. This step localizes the component's reaction in response to a single input wrt. a previous input history.

Among the candidates for an implementation, we identified the canonical state transition machine whose state records the complete input history. State transition machines with a reduced state space originate from the canonical machine by identifying states as input histories under history abstractions. By construction, all resulting state transition machines correctly implement the specified behaviour.

The history-oriented and the state-based descriptions of software or hardware components allow complementary insights. Both formalisms show advantages and shortcomings with respect to compositionality, abstractness, verification, synthesis, and tool support. In long term, proven design methods must flexibly bridge the gap between functional behaviour and internal realization following sound refinement rules.

References

1. I. Babcsányi and A. Nagy. Mealy-automata in which the output-equivalence is a congruence. *Acta Cybernetica*, 11(3):121–126, 1994.
2. T. Bălănescu, A. J. Cowling, H. Georgescu, M. Gheorghe, M. Holcombe, and C. Vertan. Communicating stream X-machines systems are no more than X-machines. *Journal of Universal Computer Science*, 5(9):494–507, 1999.
3. M. Breitling and J. Philipps. Diagrams for dataflow. In J. Grabowski and S. Heymer, editors, *Formale Beschreibungstechniken für verteilte Systeme*, pages 101–110. Shaker Verlag, 2000.
4. M. Broy. (Inter-)action refinement: The easy way. In M. Broy, editor, *Program Design Calculi*, volume 118 of *NATO ASI Series F*, pages 121–158. Springer, 1993.
5. M. Broy. From states to histories: Relating state and history views onto systems. In T. Hoare, M. Broy, and R. Steinbrüggen, editors, *Engineering Theories of Software Construction*, volume 180 of *Series III: Computer and System Sciences*, pages 149–186. IOS Press, 2001.
6. M. Broy and K. Stølen. *Specification and Development of Interactive Systems: Focus on Streams, Interfaces, and Refinement*. Monographs in Computer Science. Springer, 2001.
7. W. Dosch. Designing an interactive stack. *WSEAS Transactions on Systems*, 1(2):296–302, Apr. 2002.
8. W. Dosch and S. Magnussen. The Lübeck Transformation System: A transformation system for equational higher order algebraic specifications. In M. Cerioli and G. Reggio, editors, *Recent Trends in Algebraic Development Techniques (WADT 2001)*, number 2267 in Lecture Notes in Computer Science, pages 85–108. Springer, 2002.
9. W. Dosch and A. Stümpel. From stream transformers to state transition machines with input and output. In N. Ishii, T. Mizuno, and R. Lee, editors, *Proceedings of the 2nd International Conference on Software Engineering, Artificial Intelligence, Networking and Parallel/Distributed Computing (SNPD'01)*, pages 231–238. International Association for Computer and Information Science (ACIS), 2001.

10. W. Dosch and A. Stümpel. History abstractions of a sequential memory component. In B. Gupta, editor, *Proceedings of the 19th International Conference on Computers and their Applications (CATA-2004)*, pages 241–247. International Society for Computers and their Applications (ISCA), 2004.
11. W. Dosch and A. Stümpel. Introducing control states into communication based specifications of interactive components. In H. Arabnia and H. Reza, editors, *Proceedings of the International Conference on Software Engineering Research and Practice (SERP'04)*, volume II, pages 875–881. CSREA Press, 2004.
12. D. Q. Goldin, S. A. Smolka, P. C. Attie, and E. L. Sonderegger. Turing machines, transition systems, and interaction. *Information and Computation*, 194(2):101–128, Nov. 2004.
13. D. Harel. Statecharts: A visual formalism for complex systems. *Science of Computer Programming*, 8:231–274, 1987.
14. G. Kahn. The semantics of a simple language for parallel programming. In J. Rosenfeld, editor, *Information Processing 74*, pages 471–475. North–Holland, 1974.
15. G. Kahn and D. B. MacQueen. Coroutines and networks of parallel processes. In B. Gilchrist, editor, *Information Processing 77*, pages 993–998. North–Holland, 1977.
16. N. A. Lynch and E. W. Stark. A proof of the Kahn principle for input/output automata. *Information and Computation*, 82:81–92, 1989.
17. S. J. Magnussen. *Mechanizing the Transformation of Higher-Order Algebraic Specifications for the Development of Software Systems*. Logos Verlag Berlin, 2003.
18. B. Möller. Ideal stream algebra. In B. Möller and J. Tucker, editors, *Prospects for Hardware Foundations*, number 1546 in Lecture Notes in Computer Science, pages 69–116. Springer, 1998.
19. L. Motus, M. Meriste, and W. Dosch. Time-awareness and proactivity in models of interactive computation. ETAPS-Workshop on the Foundations of Interactive Computation (FInCo 2005). *Electronic Notes in Theoretical Computer Science*, 2005. (to appear).
20. Object Management Group (OMG). *OMG Unified Modeling Language Specification, 3. UML Notation Guide, Part 9: Statechart Diagrams*, Mar. 2003.
21. J. Rumbaugh, I. Jacobson, and G. Booch. *The Unified Modeling Language Reference Manual*. Addison-Wesley Object Technology Series. Addison-Wesley, 1998.
22. P. Scholz. Design of reactive systems and their distributed implementation with statecharts. PhD Thesis, TUM-I9821, Technische Universität München, Aug. 1998.
23. G. Ştefănescu. *Network Algebra*. Discrete Mathematics and Theoretical Computer Science. Springer, 2000.
24. R. Stephens. A survey of stream processing. *Acta Informatica*, 34(7):491–541, 1997.
25. A. Stümpel. *Stream Based Design of Distributed Systems through Refinement*. Logos Verlag Berlin, 2003.
26. P. Wegner. Why interaction is more powerful than algorithms. *Communications of the ACM*, 40(5):80–91, May 1997.
27. G. Winskel and M. Nielsen. Models for concurrency. In S. Abramsky, D. Gabbay, and T. Maibaum, editors, *Semantic Modelling*, volume 4 of *Handbook of Logic in Computer Science*, pages 1–148. Oxford University Press, 1995.

NuEditor - A Tool Suite for Specification and Verification of NuSCR

Jaemyung Cho, Junbeom Yoo, and Sungdeok Cha

Department of Electrical Engineering and Computer Science,
Korea Advanced Institute of Science and Technology (KAIST),
373-1, Guseong-dong, Yuseong-gu, Daejon, Republic of Korea
{jmcho, jbyoo, cha}@dependable.kaist.ac.kr

Abstract. NuEditor is a tool suite supporting specification and verification of software requirements written in NuSCR. NuSCR extends SCR (Software Cost Reduction) notation that has been used in specifying requirements for embedded safety critical systems such as a shutdown system for nuclear power plant. SCR almost exclusively depended on fine-grained tabular notations to represent not only computation-intensive functions but also time- or state-dependent operations. As a consequence, requirements became excessively complex and difficult to understand. NuSCR supports intuitive and concise notations. For example, automata is used to capture time or state-dependent operations, and concise tabular notations are made possible by allowing complex but proven-correct equations be used without having to decompose them into a sequence of primitive operations. NuEditor provides graphical editing environment and supports static analysis to detect errors such as missing or conflicting requirements. To provide high-assurance safety analysis, NuEditor can automatically translate NuSCR specification into SMV input so that satisfaction of certain properties can be automatically determined based on exhaustive examination of all possible behavior. NuEditor has been programmed to generate requirements as an XML document so that other verification tools such as PVS can also be used if needed. We have used NuEditor to specify a trip logic of RPS(Reactor Protection System) BP(Bistable Processor) and verify its correctness. It is a part of software-implemented nuclear power plant shutdown system. Domain experts found NuSCR and NuEditor to be useful and qualified for industrial use in nuclear engineering.

1 Introduction

Many validation and verification techniques (e.g. inspection, fault tree analysis, simulation, model checking, etc) have been proposed to ensure safety. In nuclear power plant control systems, software safety became a critical issue as traditional RLL (Relay Ladder Logic)-based analog systems are replaced by digital controllers [1]. KNICS project [2] in Korea is developing DPPS (Digital Plant Protection System) RPS (Reactor Protection System) which is classified as being safety-critical by government regulation authority. To maximize safety of RPS software, proven-effective formal methods are being used. For example, SCR-style notation was previously used to specify software requirements for Wolnsung SDS2, a shutdown system currently in service at a different plant in Korea.

W. Dosch, R.Y. Lee, and C. Wu (Eds.): SERA 2004, LNCS 3647, pp. 19–28, 2005.

Experts who performed critical analysis on SCR and other formal specification languages came to the conclusion that SCR-like notation is well-suited for specifying and verifying requirements for RPS but that the notation in its current form is too verbose to be effectively used. Furthermore, availability of SCR* toolset was unsatisfactory from the viewpoint of KNICS project management office. Therefore, an effort was initiated to (1) customize SCR so that characteristics unique to nuclear engineering domain are best reflected in the design of a specification language; and (2) develop a tool suite, NuEditor, to integrate graphical editing capability and formal verification environment. In addition to performing built-in completeness and consistency analysis on NuSCR specification, NuEditor can generate SMV [3] input program automatically so that one can perform model checking with minimal intervention. It also generates XML output that is used as input to PVS for deductive verification of structural and functional properties [4].

To find out if NuSCR and NuEditor are useful enough to nuclear engineers, we conducted a joint study with a group of domain experts in which trip logic of RPS BP (Bistable Processor) was specified and verified. This paper introduces key features of NuEditor and reports our experience from the case study. Section 2 briefly introduces NuSCR, and section 3 provides an overview of NuEditor features. After reporting our experience with NuEditor from the case study in section 4, we conclude the paper and discuss planned extensions to NuEditor.

2   NuSCR

NuSCR [5] is a formal requirement specification language designed for nuclear domain. It was developed with active participation of and consultation by nuclear engineers who are familiar with software engineering knowledge in general and formal methods in particular. It uses three kinds of variables to capture the behavior of software system efficiently. Readability of the specification to domain experts was a key concern when deciding which notation to use to capture various aspects of requirements.

The software system is specified within a function overview diagram (FOD) in a notation similar to data flow diagrams. An FOD illustrates hierarchical organization of variable nodes. A node has its inputs and outputs, and nodes are connected in an acyclic graph. A node is specified by structured decision table (SDT), finite state machine (FSM), and timed transition system (TTS) by the variable categorization for function variable node, history variable node, and timed history variable node, respectively. These three representations are used for specifying different characteristics of behaviors of nodes. A function variable node specifies mathematical function in a table representation called an SDT. A history variable node specifies variable's states and transition relationships between the states in an FSM. A timed history variable node specifies an FSM with timing constraints in a TTS.

We extracted an example system from APR-1400 RPS which is currently being developed by KNICS consortium. This example is based the prototype version of the system, and we did not have access to later versions. ⟨Fig.1 (a)⟩ shows an FOD for the fixed set-point rising trip logic[1], which is the basic reactor shutdown logic. The

---

[1] It denotes the logic named *g_Fixed_Set_Point_Rising_Trip_With_OB*, a part of bistable process(BP). We simplified the variable names to facilitate understanding.

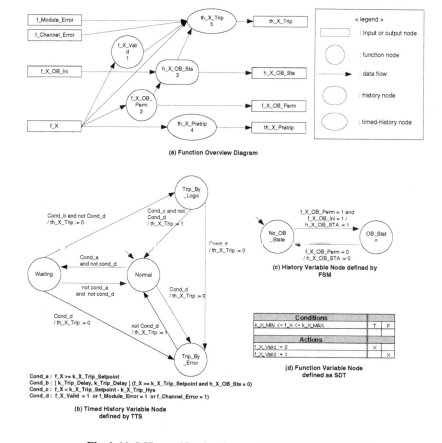

(a) Function Overview Diagram

Cond_a : f_X >= k_X_Trip_Setpoint
Cond_b : [k_Trip_Delay, k_Trip_Delay] (f_X >= k_X_Trip_Setpoint and h_X_OB_Sta = 0)
Cond_c : f_X < k_X_Trip_Setpoint - k_X_Trip_Hys
Cond_d : f_X_Valid = 1 or f_Module_Error = 1 or f_Channel_Error = 1)

(b) Timed History Variable Node
defined by TTS

(c) History Variable Node defined by
FSM

(d) Function Variable Node
defined as SDT

Fig. 1. NuSCR specification for a part of APR-1400 RPS BP

rectangles are inputs and outputs of the node, and it is composed of three types of nodes and their data-flow relationships.

⟨Fig.1 (b)⟩ represents the timed history variable node names th_X_Trip defined in TTS. The behavior is followings. Condition $f\_X = k\_X\_Trip\_Setpoint$ with a previous state *Normal* make the TTS entering *Waiting* state. And then, the system produces output $th\_X\_Trip = 1$ (not to generate a trip signal) during it stays *Waiting* states. If time duration k_Trip_Delay elapsed with satisfying condition $(f\_X >= k\_X\_Trip\_Setpoint$ and $h\_X\_OB\_Sta=0)$ (satisfying *Cond_b* and *Waiting* state), the system moves to *Trip_By_Logic* state and produces $th\_X\_Trip=0$ (generate a trip signal). Other parts can be interpreted in the similar way. ⟨Fig.1 (c)⟩ is an FSM definition for the history variable node named $h\_X\_OB\_Sta$. The behavior of an FSM is similar to TTS without considering timing constraints. An SDT in ⟨Fig.1 (d)⟩ shows the definition of function variable node named f_X_Valid. The behavior of f_X_Valid is as follows: If the value of f_X_Valid is between k_X_MIN and k_X_MAX, output f_X_Valid is 0. Otherwise, the output is 1.

NuSCR supports designers three different kinds of variables to express various aspects of requirements according to their unique characteristics. NuSCR has been evaluated as being easy to specify and understand by domain engineers [6].

3   NuEditor Features and Capabilities

Main functionalities of NuEditor are shown in ⟨Fig.2⟩. NuEditor, developed in Java, is platform independent. All constructs in NuSCR (e.g., FOD, SDT, FSM, and TTS) can be graphically edited using NuEditor. Various nodes are colored differently so that they roles are visually apparent. NuEditor stores models in hierarchically organized folders, as shown on the left side of the tool window, so that requirements for large and complex industrial systems can be conveniently organized. Users can add annotations and comments as needed.

In addition to a specification editor, consistency and completeness checker was included. ⟨Fig.3 (a)⟩ shows FOD and FSM editing windows, and ⟨Fig.3 (b)⟩ shows SDT window and XML generator window. As shown in ⟨Fig.4⟩, analysis on structural correctness is automated. That is, when a group node is expanded in a separate page, inputs and outputs declared at a higher-level node are shown. If detailed specification of inputs and outputs on that page neglects to use them all, error message pops up to warn users that usage of variables is inconsistent. Variables can also be dragged so that users need not explicitly type variable names repeatedly.

To support formal verification, NuEditor includes a XML (Extensible Markup Language) generator and a SMV input generator. The XML generator is used to prove the structural and functional properties of NuSCR specification using PVS [7]. Theorem proving is a deductive verification method. While powerful, proof sessions are often lengthy and tedious in practice. Fortunately, modern theorem provers like PVS provide excellent support in proof automation and development of proof strategies. To best utilize capabilities of tools like PVS, NuEditor generates XML documents which can then be used as input to other applications. XML documents, for example, can be used in developing design specification written in FBD(Function Block Diagram) notations [8] as is the case in the KNICS project [2].

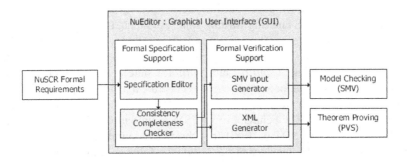

Fig. 2. Functionalities of NuEditor

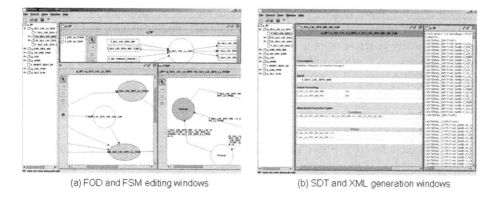

(a) FOD and FSM editing windows (b) SDT and XML generation windows

Fig. 3. Screen shots of NuEditor

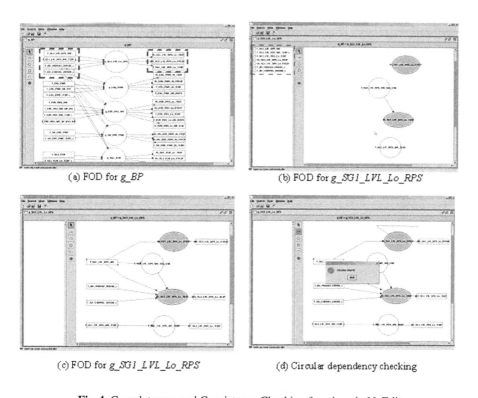

(a) FOD for g_BP (b) FOD for g_SG1_LVL_Lo_RPS

(c) FOD for g_SG1_LVL_Lo_RPS (d) Circular dependency checking

Fig. 4. Completeness and Consistency Checking functions in NuEditor

The SMV input generator is used to check if specification satisfies certain properties written in temporal logic. Model checking [9] is a technique enabling "push-button" verification based on exhaustive search of possible behavior. Model checking is becoming popular in industry because (1) it is automated; and (2) a counterexample is generated if the property does not hold in the specification. Counterexample can reveal the presence of subtle flaws in the specification or can be used to automatically construct test cases. SMV is arguable the most widely used model checker to date, and NuEditor can automatically generate input to SMV model checker. User simply needs to execute SMV software (e.g., Cardence SMV), load the specification file and property file, and select verify all menus in the option.

4   Case Study

KNICS RPS includes RPS, ESF-CCS (Engineering Safety Features - Component Control System), and ATIP (Automatic test and Interface Processor) as major components. RPS is designed to protect the reactor, while ESF-CCS is intended to reduce the influence of other accidents including loss of coolant. ATIP tests RPS and ESF-CCS automatically. In this section, we present how NuEditor was used in specifying requirements for BP (Bistable Logic) logic. We performed model checking of BP specification. RPS BP periodically accepts inputs from 18 different safety sensors installed in the system and performs necessary comparison against predefined trip logics and threshold values.

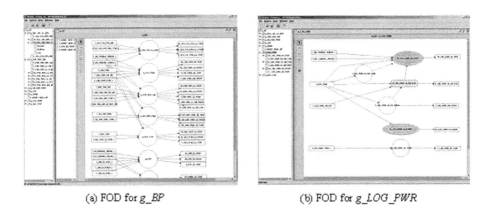

(a) FOD for g_BP   (b) FOD for g_LOG_PWR

Fig. 5. FODs for g_BP in KNICS RPS

For example, ⟨Fig.5⟩ is a part of NuSCR specification for RPS BP. In ⟨Fig.5 (a)⟩, g_BP, a group node, is decomposed as shown in ⟨Fig.5 (b)⟩. NuSCR software requirements specification for KNICS BP is about 400 pages, and it took 5 months by a number of domain experts. We present the results of model checking fixed set-point rising trip logic with operating bypass. The logic description written in natural language took about four pages. Translation rules used in NuEditor are similar to those proposed in [10,11,12,13]. [10] translates SCR specification into SMV input language, whereas [11] translates SCR specification into language accepted by SPIN [12]. Since NuSCR, due to inclusion of FSM and TTS in its notation, is more analogous to RSML than SCR, our rule were mainly based on translation rules for RSML [13]. More detailed translation methods are described in [14].

```
-- Generated by NuEditor 1.1 , SMV Input for Nu-SCR , SE Lab. KAIST --

01 : MODULE main
02 : VAR
03 : th_X_Trip : boolean;
04 : f_X_Valid : boolean;
05 : f_Module_Error : boolean;
06 : h_X_OB_Sta : boolean;
07 : f_Channel_Error : boolean;
08 : f_X : 0..1000;
09 : time_1 : 0..4;
10 : STATE_th_X_Trip : {NORMAL, WAITING, TRIP_BY_LOGIC, TRIP_BY_ERROR};
11 :
12 : ASSIGN
13 : init(STATE_th_X_Trip) := TRIP_BY_ERROR ;
14 : next(STATE_th_X_Trip) := case
15 : FROM-WAITING-TO-NORMAL-taken : NORMAL;
16 : FROM-TRIP_BY_LOGIC-TO-NORMAL-taken : NORMAL;
17 : FROM-TRIP_BY_ERROR-TO-NORMAL-taken : NORMAL;
18 : FROM-NORMAL-TO-WAITING-taken : WAITING;
19 : FROM-WAITING-TO-TRIP_BY_LOGIC-taken : TRIP_BY_LOGIC;
20 : FROM-NORMAL-TO-TRIP_BY_ERROR-taken : TRIP_BY_ERROR;
21 : FROM-WAITING-TO-TRIP_BY_ERROR-taken : TRIP_BY_ERROR;
22 : FROM-TRIP_BY_LOGIC-TO-TRIP_BY_ERROR-taken : TRIP_BY_ERROR;
23 : 1 : STATE_th_X_Trip;
24 : esac;
25 : init(th_X_Trip) := 0;
26 : next(th_X_Trip) := case
27 : FROM-WAITING-TO-TRIP_BY_LOGIC-taken : 0;
28 : FROM-TRIP_BY_LOGIC-TO-TRIP_BY_ERROR-taken : 0;
29 : FROM-WAITING-TO-TRIP_BY_ERROR-taken : 0;
30 : FROM-NORMAL-TO-TRIP_BY_ERROR-taken : 0;
31 : FROM-TRIP_BY_LOGIC-TO-NORMAL-taken : 1;
32 : FROM-TRIP_BY_ERROR-TO-NORMAL-taken:1;
33 : 1 : th_X_Trip;
34 : esac;
35 : init(time_1) := 0;
36 : next(time_1) := case
37 : in-WAITING & time_1 < k_Trip_Delay & (f_X>=k_X_Trip_Setpoint & h_X_OB_Sta = 0)&!(f_X_Valid =1 | f_Module_Error = 1 | f_Channel_Error = 1) : time_1 + 1;
38 : 1:0;
39 : esac;
40 :

41 : DEFINE
42 : k_Trip_Delay := 4;
43 : k_X_Trip_Setpoint := 700;
44 : k_X_Trip_Hys := 1;
45 : in-NORMAL := STATE_th_X_Trip = NORMAL;
46 : in-WAITING := STATE_th_X_Trip = WAITING;
47 : in-TRIP_BY_LOGIC := STATE_th_X_Trip = TRIP_BY_LOGIC;
48 : in-TRIP_BY_ERROR := STATE_th_X_Trip = TRIP_BY_ERROR;
49 : FROM-NORMAL-TO-WAITING-enabled := in-NORMAL & ((f_X<k_X_Trip_Setpoint) & !(f_X_Valid =1 | f_Module_Error = 1 | f_Channel_Error = 1));
50 : FROM-NORMAL-TO-TRIP_BY_ERROR-enabled := in-NORMAL & ((f_X_Valid =1 | f_Module_Error = 1 | f_Channel_Error = 1));
51 : FROM-WAITING-TO-TRIP_BY_LOGIC-enabled := in-WAITING & ((time_1 = k_Trip_Delay) & (f_X>=k_X_Trip_Setpoint & h_X_OB_Sta = 0)&!(f_X_Valid =1 | f_Module_Error = 1 | f_Channel_Error = 1));
52 : FROM-WAITING-TO-NORMAL-enabled := in-WAITING & (!(f_X>=k_X_Trip_Setpoint) & !(f_X_Valid =1 | f_Module_Error = 1 | f_Channel_Error = 1));
53 : FROM-WAITING-TO-TRIP_BY_ERROR-enabled := in-WAITING & ((f_X_Valid =1 | f_Module_Error = 1 | f_Channel_Error = 1));
54 : FROM-TRIP_BY_LOGIC-TO-NORMAL-enabled := in-TRIP_BY_LOGIC & (f_X<k_X_Trip_Setpoint + k_X_Trip_Hys& !(f_X_Valid =1 | f_Module_Error =
55 : FROM-TRIP_BY_LOGIC-TO-TRIP_BY_ERROR-enabled := in-TRIP_BY_LOGIC & ((f_X_Valid =1 | f_Module_Error = 1 | f_Channel_Error = 1));
56 : FROM-TRIP_BY_ERROR-TO-NORMAL-enabled := in-TRIP_BY_ERROR & (!(f_X_Valid =1 | f_Module_Error = 1 | f_Channel_Error = 1));
57 : FROM-NORMAL-TO-WAITING-taken := FROM-NORMAL-TO-WAITING-enabled;
58 : FROM-NORMAL-TO-TRIP_BY_ERROR-taken := FROM-NORMAL-TO-TRIP_BY_ERROR-enabled;
59 : FROM-WAITING-TO-TRIP_BY_LOGIC-taken := FROM-WAITING-TO-TRIP_BY_LOGIC-enabled;
60 : FROM-WAITING-TO-NORMAL-taken := FROM-WAITING-TO-NORMAL-enabled;
61 : FROM-WAITING-TO-TRIP_BY_ERROR-taken := FROM-WAITING-TO-TRIP_BY_ERROR-enabled;
62 : FROM-TRIP_BY_LOGIC-TO-NORMAL-taken := FROM-TRIP_BY_LOGIC-TO-NORMAL-enabled;
63 : FROM-TRIP_BY_LOGIC-TO-TRIP_BY_ERROR-taken := FROM-TRIP_BY_LOGIC-TO-TRIP_BY_ERROR-enabled;
64 : FROM-TRIP_BY_ERROR-TO-NORMAL-taken := FROM-TRIP_BY_ERROR-TO-NORMAL-enabled;
```

Fig. 6. Generated SMV input program from *th_X_Trip* in Fig.1 (b)

⟨Fig.6⟩ shows SMV input program for *th_X_Trip* shown earlier in ⟨Fig.?? (b)⟩. Since variables in SMV must have finite discrete values, user must abstract infinite values (e.g. f_X at line 8) as integer although f_X actually returns a real number as its result. Constants defined in the systems (lines 42 through 44) are separately managed by NuEditor. Lines 35 through 39 and 51 reflect TTS specification including timer variables, i.e. *time_1* is a clock variable in TTS and line 51 is an action triggered by the variable.

The following properties were verified using SMV:

1. System is free from deadlock.
2. Conflicting transitions are never enabled simultaneously.
3. If module error, channel error, or input value error occur, trip signal is generated immediately.
4. Trip signal is generated if the processing value rises above the predefined set-point, and the condition lasts for some predefined time.
5. If trip conditions aren't satisfied, then trip signal shall never be fired.
6. Trip signal is never fired during operating bypass.

Properties, written in CTL formula, are as follows. It must be noted that there are no automated support built in NuEditor in specifying properties. Users are expected to be familiar with basics of temporal logic and its operators.

⟨Fig.7⟩ shows how SMV-based model checking results look like. Results marked TRUE indicate that the property is satisfied in all possible system spaces. In this case study, all properties are proved to be true using SMV model checker, so we can confirm that RPS model satisfies properties (1) through (6).

1. **Deadlock-freeness**
   SPEC AGEX 1

2. **Non-determinism**
   SPEC AG ! (FROM-WAITING-TO-TRIP_BY_LOGIC-taken & FROM-WAITING-TO-NORMAL-taken)
   SPEC AG ! (FROM-WAITING-TO-TRIP_BY_LOGIC-taken & FROM-WAITING-TO-TRIP_BY_ERROR-taken)
   SPEC AG ! (FROM-WAITING-TO-NORMAL-taken & FROM-WAITING-TO-TRIP_BY_ERROR-taken)
   SPEC AG ! (FROM-WAITING-TO-NORMAL-taken & FROM-WAITING-TO-TRIP_BY_ERROR-taken)
   SPEC AG ! (FROM-TRIP_BY_LOGIC-TO-TRIP_BY_ERROR-taken & FROM-TRIP_BY_LOGIC-TO-NORMAL-taken)
   SPEC AG ! (FROM-NORMAL-TO-TRIP_BY_ERROR-taken & FROM-NORMAL-TO-WAITING-taken)

3. **Trip occurred by error**
   SPEC AG ((f_Channel_Error = 1 | f_Module_Error = 1) $\longrightarrow$ AF th_X_Trip = 0)

4. **Trip occurred by logic**
   SPEC AG(((f_X > k_X_Trip_Setpoint) & (time_1 > 4)) $\longrightarrow$ AF th_X_Trip = 0)

5. **Normal status**
   SPEC AG ((!(f_Channel_Error = 1 | f_Module_Error = 1 | f_X_Valid = 1) & (f_X <= k_X_Trip_Setpoint)) $\longrightarrow$ AF th_X_trip = 1)

6. **Trip in operating bypass**
   SPEC AG((h_X_OB_Sta = 1 & ! (f_Channel_Error = 1 | f_Module_Error = 1 | f_X_Valid = 1) & AF AX th_X_Trip = 1) $\longrightarrow$ AF AX th_X_Trip = 1)

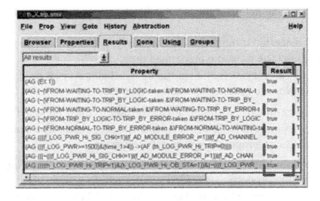

Fig. 7. Verification result of *th_XTrip*

5   Conclusion and Future Work

In this paper, we presented key features of NuEditor, an integrated tool suite to perform both specification and verification of requirements specification written in NuSCR. The NuEditor includes a graphical editor, consistency and completeness checker, XML output generator, and SMV input generator. NuEditor provides graphical and user-friendly interface and relieves engineers from tedious and uninteresting work. It allows them to work on more creative tasks. Automated consistency checks save considerable time of developers and reviewers. It also increases confidence that specification is correct by allowing engineers to enjoy benefit of formal methods. NuEditor tool was well liked by nuclear engineers, and addition of simulation and backward analysis capabilities would further improve its usefulness in real applications like KNICS.

Acknowledgements. This research was partially supported by Advanced Information Technology Research Center(AITrc), Software Process Improvement Center(SPIC), and Internet Intrusion Response Technology Research Center(IIRTRC) in Korea.

References

1. NRC, U.: Digital Instrumentation and Control Systems in Nuclear Power Plants: safety and reliability issues. National Academy Press (1997)
2. KNICS: Korea nuclear instrumentation and control system research and development center. (http://www.knics.re.kr/english/eindex.html)
3. McMillan, K.L.: Symbolic Model Checking. Kluwer Academic Publishers (1993)
4. Kim, T., Cha, S.: Automated structural analysis of scr-style software requirements specifications using pvs. Journal of Software Testing, Verification, and Reliability **11** (2001) 143–163
5. Yoo, J., Kim, T., Cha, S., Lee, J.S., Son, H.S.: A formal software requirements specification method for digital nuclear plants protection systems. Journal of Systems and Software **74** (2005) 73–833
6. Yoo, J., Cha, S., Oh, Y., Kim, C.: Formal software requirements specification for digital reactor protection systems. Journal of Korea Information and Science Society **31** (2004) 750–759
7. Owre, S., Rajan, S., Rushby, J.M., Shankar, N., Srivas, M.K.: PVS: Combining specification, proof checking, and model checking. In: Proceedings of the Eighth International Conference on Computer Aided Verification CAV. Volume 1102., New Brunswick, NJ, USA, Springer Verlag (1996) 411–414
8. Commission), I.E.: International standard for programmable controllers: Programming languages (1993) part 3.
9. Clarke, E.M., Emerson, E.A., Sistla, A.P.: Automatic verification of finite-state concurrent systems using temporal logic specifications. ACM Trans. Programming Languages and Sysems **8** (1986) 244–263
10. Atlee, J.M., Buckley, M.A.: A logic-model semantics for scr software requirements. In: International Symposium on Software Testing and Analysis. (1996) 280–292
11. Ramesh, B., Heitmeyer, C.L.: Model checking complete requirements specifications using abstraction. Automated Software Engineering **6** (1999) 37–68

12. Holzmann, G.J., Godefroid, P., Pirottin, D.: Coverage preserving reduction strategies for reachabily analysis. In: IFIP/WG6.1 Symposium, Protocol Specification, Testing, and Verification(PSTV92). (1992) 349–364
13. Chan, W., Anderson, R.J., Beame, P., Burns, S., Modugno, F., Notkin, D., Reese, J.D.: checking large software specification. Transaction on Software Engineering **24** (1998) 498–520
14. Cho, J.: Nueditor : An environment for nuscr specification and verification. Master's thesis, Korea Advanced Institute of Science and Technology (KAIST) (2002)

A UML Profile for Goal-Oriented and Use Case-Driven Representation of NFRs and FRs

Sam Supakkul[1] and Lawrence Chung[2]

[1] Titat Software LLC
ssupakkul@ieee.org
[2] The University of Texas at Dallas
chung@utdallas.edu

Abstract. In order for a software system to be of value, it should meet both functional requirements (FRs) and non-functional requirements (NFRs). Concerning FRs, UML has been used as the de facto object-oriented analysis and design notation. Concerning NFRs, the NFR Framework extends, and complements, UML, by treating NFRs as potentially conflicting or synergistic softgoals to be achieved, thereby allowing for the consideration of alternatives and analysis of trade-offs among the alternatives. Albeit the complementary nature of the two, UML and the NFR Framework offer two different notations - syntactically, semantically and visually, which makes it difficult to produce requirements models that integrate both FRs and NFRs. In this paper, we propose an integrated modeling language by extending UML with the NFR framework using the standard UML extension mechanism called UML profile where we define a metamodel to represent the concepts in the NFR Framework and identify the extension points for integrating the two notations. We also show how CASE tools may use this profile in building an integrated requirements model based on a model of the well known London ambulance case study.

1 Introduction

In order for a software system to be of value, it should meet both functional requirements (FRs) and non-functional requirements (NFRs). Concerning FRs, UML [1][16] has been used as the de facto object-oriented analysis and design notation. Concerning NFRs, previous works have dealt with NFRs quantitatively and qualitatively. Quantitative approaches support time- and resource-critical applications with concrete specification of NFRs. For instance, KAOS [5][22] is a goal-oriented framework for addressing FRs with a formal temporal logic that requirements engineer can use to precisely specify NFRs, such as performance, as part of attribute specification of FRs. The performance engineering [6] annotates quantitative performance constraints to UML diagrams such as actor-usecase communicatation, message in the sequence diagram, and state in the state machine diagram. A number of UML profiles [17][18][7] provide extensive taxonomy of NFR related concepts in UML for quantitative specification and modeling of NFRs. In qualitative approaches, the goal-driven approach [11] identifies initial set of use cases based on functional goals. Additional use cases are then created to represent non-functional goals and associated with FRs use cases through use case "extend" rela-

W. Dosch, R.Y. Lee, and C. Wu (Eds.): SERA 2004, LNCS 3647, pp. 29–41, 2005.

tionship. The NFR Framework [13][2] treats NFRs as potentially conflicting or synergistic softgoals to be achieved, thereby allowing for the consideration of alternatives and analysis of trade-offs among the alternatives. The NFR Framework has been adopted by several proposals for integrating NFRs with UML. Among them, the Language Extended Lexicon (LEL) driven approach [4] first describes application domain in LEL to provide context for both FRs and NFRs, which are then separately analyzed and later integrated by associating use cases representing FRs with use cases representing NFR operationalizations (solutions for achieving NFRs) using use case "include" relationship. The cross-cutting quality attributes approach [12] adopts the NFR Framework's goal analysis framework, without the visual notations and diagram, to textually analyze NFRs for "cross-cutting" relevance to one or more use cases. The NFRs are then represented by unnamed use cases with stereotype indicating the type of NFR such as security. These use cases are included by the use cases representing FRs found relevant during the analysis process. We have previously presented a use case driven approach [21] that also adopts the NFR Framework. This approach complements the KAOS approach [5] with a goal-oriented analysis framework for NFRs and the representation of NFRs as first-class modeling elements using the notations and diagram from the NFR Framework. It is similar to the LEL driven approach [4] except it does not adopt the use of LEL and integrates with FRs use cases sooner at the NFR softgoal level.

Albeit the complementary nature of the two, UML and the NFR Framework offer two different notations - syntactically, semantically and visually, which makes it difficult to determine what are and are not valid in the integrated models. The ability to determine as such is important for CASE tools to support the integrated requirement modeling we proposed [21]. In this paper, we present a UML profile to formally integrated the two notations. In the proposed UML profile, we define a metamodel that represents the concepts in the NFR framework and identify the extension points in the UML metamodel where the concepts from the two notations are integrated. We show how CASE tools may use this profile in building an integrated requirements model based on a simplified model of the well known London ambulance case study, and how the metamodel helps prevent modeling detects.

This paper is organized as follows. Section 2 provides an overview of UML profile, the NFR Framework, and the integrated goal-oriented and use case driven approach. Section 3 describe the proposed UML profile. Section 4 shows how the UML profile may be used by CASE tools. We offer some discussions regarding related work in Sec. 5, and conclusion remarks in Sec. 6.

2   An Overview of UML Profile and the Goal-Oriented and Use Case Driven Approach

We use UML profile [16] as the mechanism for integrating notations from the NFR Framework to UML, specifically the use case diagram.

2.1   UML Profile

OMG has defined four-layer metamodel hierarchy: M0, M1, M2, and M3 layers with the concept that what is a metamodel in one case can be a model in another case [15].

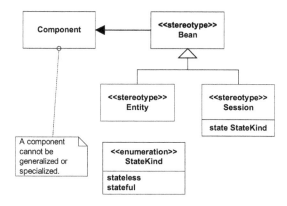

Fig. 1. Part of EJB profile adapted from [16]

M0 layer model runtime systems that consist of instances of M1 layer model elements. M2 layer models the modeling languages used to build M1 layer models. It defines the syntax and semantics of the modeling languages. The last layer, M3, specifies facilities for constructing metamodels in M2 layer. UML, as a modeling language, is defined by a metamodel in M2 layer using Meta Object Facility (MOF) [14], an M3 layer model. It is often desirable to tailor popular modeling languages to more specific domains and environments to provide built-in subject matter knowledge from within the modeling language. To allow such tailoring, UML provides a lightweight extension mechanism called UML profile [16]. Each extension, also called a UML profile, is a specification that defines the syntax and semantics of concepts in a particular domain [8]. It identifies a subset of the UML metamodel that are applicable for the intended purpose and "well-formedness rules" to describe a set of constraints that governs the validity of the resulting model when the UML profile is used. The concepts in the new domain are represented using existing UML notations with unique designators defined in the profile called stereotypes. Like a class, a stereotype may have properties, which may be referred to as tag definitions. When a stereotype is applied to a model element, the values of the properties may be referred to as tagged values [16]. Figure 1 shows a portion of UML profile for EJB [16]. In this profile, UML Component is extended (denoted by solid arrow) and used to represent the Bean concept in EJB domain using "Bean" stereotype.

2.2   The NFR Framework

The NFR Framework [13][2] is a goal-oriented approach for addressing NFRs. In this framework, we represent NFRs as *NFR softgoals* to be *satisficed*. NFR softgoals are satisficed when there is sufficient positive and little negative evidence, and they are unsatisficed otherwise. NFR softgoals are identified by nomenclature "**Type[Topic]**", where Type represents a non-functional aspect and Topic represents the context for the Type. Criticality of NFR softgoals is either neutral, critical (!) or very critical (!!). Softgoals may be refined into offspring softgoals with more specific Type or Topic using

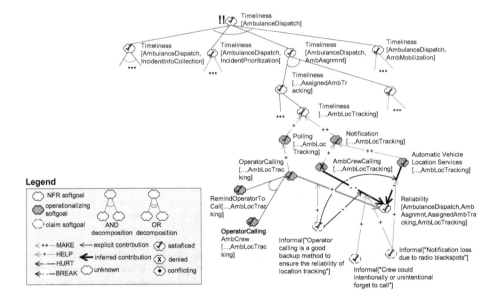

Fig. 2. An SIG for timeliness of ambulance dispatch services

AND- or OR-decompositions. When Topic is refined, the Topic of parent softgoal is inherited by offspring softgoals. To determine satisficeability, we identify one or more operationalizing softgoals (solutions for achieving NFRs) and their corresponding degree of contribution indicating how well they achieve NFR softgoals (MAKE (++), HELP (+), HURT (−), or BREAK (−−)). We then label the desirable leaf-node solutions with $\sqrt{}$ and label the undesirable ones with ×. We may manually or automatically, via a CASE tool, propagate these leaf-node labels upstream the goal hierarchy using the label evaluation procedure defined by the NFR Framework [2]. Rationale for the decisions made during the process can be recorded by associating a claim softgoal to any nodes (softgoals) or links (contributions). All of these modeling activities are recorded in a diagram call Softgoal Interdependency Graph (SIG). Figure 2 shows an SIG for representing and analyzing timeliness NFR of ambulance dispatch service based on the well-known London ambulance dispatch system [19]. We could refine and operationalize softgoals manually; however, it is often time consuming especially when the domain knowledge or system knowledge (e.g. for exploring alternatives) are not readily available. Even if they are available, they may not be in the form that are easily shared and reused [2]. To alleviate these difficulties, the NFR Framework provides *method* and *correlation rule* concepts for cataloguing and reusing the captured subject matter and modeling knowledge.

2.3   The Goal-Oriented and Use Case Driven NFRs and FRs Modeling

Using this approach, we represent NFRs as softgoals and associate them with appropriate use case model elements, as shown in Fig. 3, that provide the most relevant context.

Figure 4 show an example of integrated FRs and NFRs models for the London ambulance dispatch application. To analyze NFRs for satisficeability, an SIG is created with top NFR softgoals derived from the NFRs identified in the use case model. The Type of the NFR softgoals are derived from the textual description and the Topic derived from the associated use case element. For example, the timeliness NFR associated with "Review and prioritize new tickets" use case is represented by "Timeliness[Review and prioritize new tickets]" softgoal on the SIG. To eliminate the need for redundant NFRs specification, we proposed the NFR propagation rules [3] where equally or more strict form of NFRs may be propagated along use case relationships, including specialization, extend, and include relationships.

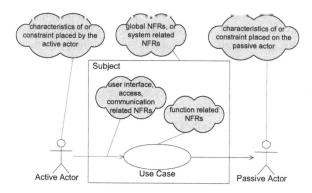

Fig. 3. NFR association points in use case model for different types of NFRs

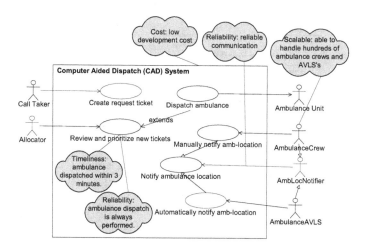

Fig. 4. An example of NFRs associated with use case model elements

3   A UML Profile for the Goal-Oriented and Use Case-Driven Approach

This section presents a UML profile, which we call Softgoal profile, that consists of two subprofiles: SIG and Procedure subprofiles. The SIG subprofile represents the concepts in the NFR Framework used in SIG, while Procedure subprofile represents the concepts related to method, correlation rule, and evaluation procedure. The Procedure subprofile imports the SIG subprofile to access the contained stereotypes. The namespaces for the two subprofiles are Softgoal::SIG and Softgoal::Procedure respectively. The subprofiles are created based on the description and formalization of the NFR Framework [13][2]. Any extensions will be clearly stated.

3.1   SIG Subprofile

Figure 5 shows the SIG subprofile. Here, SIG extends UML Artifact to represent a goal model that may contain one or more Propositions. Proposition is either a Softgoal or Contribution. This specialization is complete and disjoint [16], that is, there are no other specializations possible for Proposition. The *name* attribute of Proposition can be derived from the associated Type and Topic using "Type[Topic]" nomenclature. Type extends UML Class so any NFR aspects may be represented . Topic extends UML El-ement, an abstract metaclass that generalizes all other UML metaclasses. This allows NFRSoftgoal to be defined in the context of any model elements. Enumerations in the subprofile list all possible values of the tagged definitions. It is interesting to note that

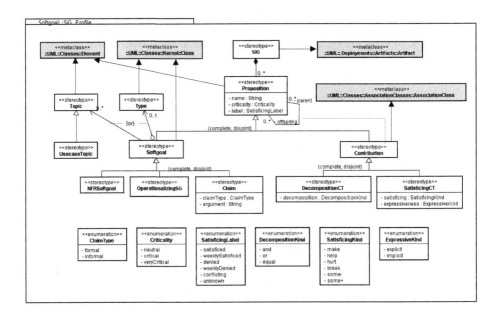

Fig. 5. SIG subprofile

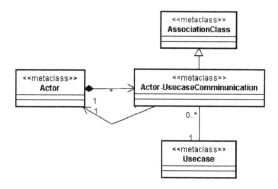

Fig. 6. ActorUsecaseCommunication metaclass proposed to support NFR association

Contribution extends UML AssociationClass that itself can be both Class and Association. This is to support an interesting feature of the NFR Framework that is less often used. We usually see softgoal refinement in the literature, but according to the formalization for the framework [13], refinement of Contribution is also allowed, which is correctly supported by the SIG subprofile.

The well-formedness rules for this subprofile are defined in UML OCL. The complete rules are available in [20]. An example is shown in the excerpt below, which states that Proposition must be parent or offspring of at most one DecompositionCT.

```
context Proposition
  inv: self.decompositionCT[offspring]
          ->size() <= 1
  inv: self.decompositionCT[parent]
          ->size() <= 1
```

To support the association between NFRSoftgoal and use case elements (see Fig. 2.3), we define UsecaseTopic stereotype to restrict NFRSoftgoal to be associateable only to subject, actor, use case, and actor-usecase-communication in use case model. However, UML metamodel does not define a metaclass for the association between actor and use case, making it not associateable to any modeling elements, including NFRSoftgoal. To solve this problem, we propose that a new UML metaclass called ActorUsecaseCommanication be included as part of the UML reference metamodel. Figure 6 shows the proposed metaclass and its relationships with actor and usecase. We feel this new metaclass is appropriate and beneficial to UML as a whole. For instance, it can serve as an traceability source for architectural components and design such as user interface and system-to-system interface.

3.2 Procedure Subprofile

Figure 7 shows the Procedure subprofile for the concepts related to method, correlation rule, and evaluation procedure. This subprofile introduces Procedure and Procedure

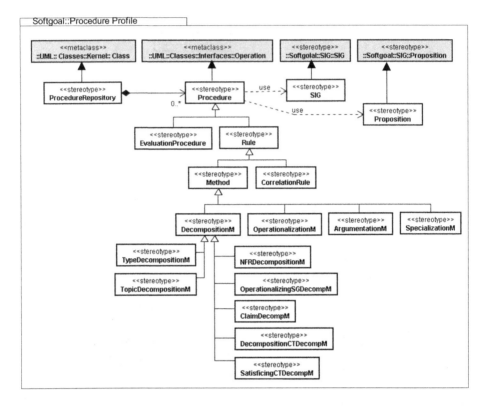

Fig. 7. Procedure subprofile

Repository as extensions to Operation and Class so that we can define well-formedness rules using pre- and post-conditions as they are more appropriate than using OCL invariance because method, correlation rule, and evaluation procedure do not have internal states to be enforced by invariance, but they rather only create or update Propositions in SIG. Specific constraints for the subprofile are defined as UML OCL in [20]. An example is shown in the excerpt below, which states that Correlation Rule, as a UML operation, expects *sig* (stereotype SIG - an extension of Artifact) and *source* (stereotype Proposition - an extension Element) as input parameters and produces zero or more Propositions as output. Pre-condition of Correlation Rule ensures that source Proposition is an OperationalizingSG and the post-condition guarantees that only one new SatisficingCT is produced and the parent of the SatisficingCT is an NFRSoftgoal and the offspring is the *source* OperationalizingSG and the tagged value of *expressiveness* is "inferred".

```
context ProcedureRepository::CorrelationRule
  (sig: Artifact, source: Element:
   Element[0..*]
pre: source.stereotypes->
           includes(OperationalizingSG)
```

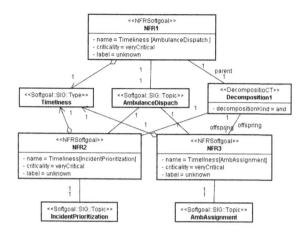

Fig. 8. An M1 model for NFR Timeliness[AmbulanceDispatch] refinement

```
post: result->notEmpty() implies
  result->size() = 1 and
  result->forAll (
    oclIsNew() and
    stereotypes->includes(SatisficingCT)
    and parent.stereotypes->
      includes(NFRSoftgoal)
    and offspring->includes(source)
    and expressiveness =
      ExpressiveKind::inferred
  )
```

The NFR Framework defines three kinds of methods: decomposition, operationalization, and argumentation methods. In our use case driven approach, an equal or more strick form of NFRs may be propagated along use case model relationships. This is analogous to inheritance in object-orientated paradigm, which is a different concept from decomposition [9]. To support this concept, we introduce specialization method (SpecializationM) as shown in Fig. 7.

4   Softgoal Profile Application

This section shows how CASE tools may use the Softgoal profile in modeling FRs and NFRs. CASE tools could support the profile in two modes: UML mode and SIG mode. In UML mode, CASE tools would allow user to model using standard UML notations such as Class coupled with stereotype to represent the concepts in the profile. For example, user could model the SIG on Fig. 2 as class diagram, whose portions are depicted on Fig. 8 and Fig. 9. In Fig. 8, NFR1 is a system-generated class name with NFRSoftgoal stereotype to represent the root NFRSoftgoal "Timeliness[AmbulanceDispatch]", which is AND-decomposed (decomposition relationship represented by Decomposition1) to

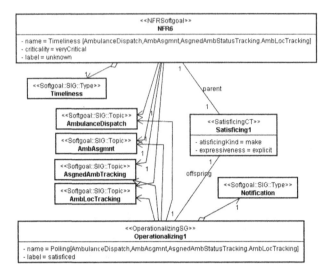

Fig. 9. An M1 model for Notification operationalization of NFR Timeliness[...,AmbLocTracking]

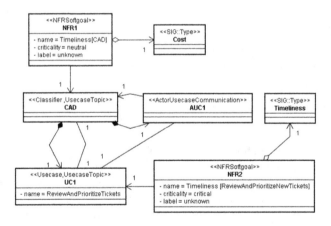

Fig. 10. An M1 model for NFRs association with usecase model elements

four offsprings, two of them are represented by NFR2 and NFR3. In Fig.9, NFRSoftgoal NFR6 represents NFRSoftgoal "Timeliness[...,AmbLocTracking]" is linked via Satisficingict "Satisficing1" to operationalizing softgoal "Operationalization1". When modeling NFR softgoals in use case diagram, user could model using class diagram as shown in Fig. 10 if allowed by the tool, but this is a less intuitive diagram than use case diagram. Optionally, the Softgoal profile can provide the cloud icons as used in Fig. 2 and 4 as part of profile configuration used by the CASE tools, which would replace some class icons with the cloud icons depending on the type of softgoal. However, this simple icon substitution is not possible for Contributions as it is more complex to hide the

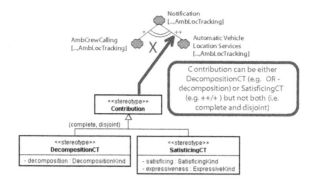

Fig. 11. An example of modeling defects preventable by the Softgoal profile

icon representing DecompositionCT and SatisficingCT, and replace them with single arc, double arcs, and directed lines. In the SIG mode, the tools should be customized to support these native notations as shown in 2 and 4. Internally, the CASE tools would maintain the same M1 models in the memory as shown in Fig. 8, 9 and 10. Supporting the SIG mode may require customization to the CASE tools but it would make the requirements modeling more intuitive and productive. In either mode, using the Softgoal profile, the CASE tools that support OCL well-formedness rules should be able to prevent modeling defects such as the one shown in Fig. 11.

5 Related Work

We have mentioned some previous work that are related to goal-orientation (e.g. KAOS) and the integration of NFRs with UML in Sec. 1. This section will discuss mainly UML profile related work in the context of goal-orientation and NFRs integration with UML. A UML profile has been defined for KAOS [10]. At a glance, the NFR Framework being also a goal-oriented method, we might be able to adopt and extend this KAOS profile. However, we found there are some fundamental differences that may require a different UML profile at the foundation. For example, in KAOS, goal refinement is a lightweight model entity that itself may not be further refined or related to other model elements. Consequently, the KAOS profile represents this relationship with UML Dependency. On the contrary, the refinement in the NFR Framework (represented by DecompositionCT in the Softgoal profile) are first class model elements that can be further refined/decomposed and associated with other model elements such as claim softgoal. Therefore, we need to represent them with AssociationClass in our Softgoal profile. Regarding the OMG adopted UML profiles for modeling NFRs [17][18], we feel our Softgoal profile is more general and complementary to the UML profiles. It is possible to integrate these UML profiles by having the Softgoal profile serve as the base profile to be imported by those specific profiles. The resulting integrated profiles could provide extensive ready-to-use NFR taxonomy as well as a framework for goal-oriented analysis.

6 Conclusions

The utility of a software system is determined not only by its functional requirements (FRs) but also its non-functional requirements (NFRs). In this paper, we have presented the Softgoal UML profile for seamlessly representing NFRs and FRs using the goal-oriented NFR Framework and the use case-driven UML. This profile precisely defines the visual syntax and semantics of the modeling concepts, relationships between such concepts, and constraints on the individual concepts and their relationships. Using the well-known London ambulance dispatch system case study, we have also shown how CASE tool may use the Softgoal profile in both standard UML notation mode and the native Softgoal Interdependency Graphs (SIG) mode. The well-formedness rules of the profile helps CASE tools ensure that the resulting NFRs and FRs models are valid, while avoiding model defects. Future work includes experimentation and customization of existing Commercial and open-source CASE tools to evaluate this UML profile. We also aim to develop a framework for mapping an integrated FRs and NFRs model into software architectural design.

References

[1] G. Booch, J. Rumbaugh, and I. Jacobson. *The Unified Modeling Language User Guide.* Addison-Wesley, 1999.

[2] L. Chung, B. A. Nixon, E. Yu, and J. Mylopoulos. *Non-Functional Requirements in Software Engineering.* Kluwer Academic Publishers, 2000.

[3] L. Chung and S. Supakkul. Representing NFRs and FRs: A goal-oriented and use case driven approach. *Lecture Notes in Computer Science*, 2005.

[4] L. Cysneiros and J. do Prado Leite. Nonfunctional requirements: from elicitation to conceptual models. *IEEE Transactions on Software Engineering*, 30:328–350, May 2004.

[5] A. Dardenne, A. van Lamsweerde, and S. Fickas. Goal-directed requirements acquisition. *Science of Computer Programming*, 20(1-2):3–50, 1993.

[6] E. Dimitrov and A. Schmietendorf. UML-based performance engineering possibilities and techniques. *IEEE Software*, pages 74–83, January/February 2002.

[7] S. Flake and W. Mueller. A uml profile for real-time constraints with the ocl. In *Proceedings of UML 2002 - The Unified Modeling Language : 5th International Conference*, pages 179–195, Sep. 30-Oct. 4 2002.

[8] L. Fuentes, J. M. Troya, and A. Vallecillo. Using uml profiles for documenting web-based application frameworks. *Annals of Software Engineering*, 13:249264, 2002.

[9] S. Greenspan, A. Borgida, and J. Mylopoulos. *A Requirements Modeling Language and Its Logic.* Elsevier Science Ltd., 1986.

[10] W. Heaven and A. Finkelstein. a UML profile to support requirements engineering with kaos. *IEE Proceedings - Software*, 151:10–27, 2004.

[11] J. Lee and N. Xue. Analyzing user requirements by use cases: A goal-driven approach. *IEEE Software*, pages 92–100, July/August 1999.

[12] A. Moreira, I. Brito, and J. Arajo. Crosscutting quality attributes for requirements engineering. *The fourteenth International Conference on Software Engineering and Knowledge Engineering (SEKE'02)*, pages 167–174, July 15-19, 2002.

[13] J. Mylopoulos, L. Chung, and B. A. Nixon. Representing and using nonfunctional requirements: A process-oriented approach. *IEEE Transactions on Software Engineering*, 18(6):483–497, 1992.

[14] Object Management Group.   Meta object facility (MOF) 2.0 core specification. http://www.omg.org/cgi-bin/apps/doc?ptc/03-10-04.pdf, Oct. 2003.

[15] Object   Management   Group.   UML   2.0   infrastructure   specification. http://www.omg.org/cgi-bin/apps/doc?ptc/ptc/03-09-15.zip, Apr. 2004.

[16] Object   Management   Group.   UML   2.0   superstructure   specification. http://www.omg.org/cgi-bin/apps/doc?ptc/04-10-02.zip, Oct. 2004.

[17] Object Management Group. UML profile for modeling quality of service and fault tolerance characteristics mechanisms. http://www.omg.org/cgi-bin/apps/doc?ptc/04-09-01.pdf, Sep. 2004.

[18] Object Management Group. UML profile for for schedulability, performance, and time specification. http://www.omg.org/cgi-bin/apps/doc?formal/05-01-02.pdf, Jan. 2005.

[19] South West Thames Regional Health Authority. Report of the inquiry into the london ambulance service. http://www.cs.ucl.ac.uk/staff/ A.Finkelstein/las/lascase0.9.pdf, 1993.

[20] S. Supakkul and L. Chung. A UML profile for goal-oriented and use case-driven requirements modeling notations. *Working Memo*, 2005.

[21] S. Supakkul and L. Chung. Integrating FRs and NFRs: A use case and goal driven approach In *Proc., 2nd International Conference on Software Engineering Research, Management & Applications (SERA04)*, pages 30–37, May 2004.

[22] A. van Lamsweerde. Goal-oriented requirements engineering: A guided tour. In *Proc. Fifth Intl'l Symp. Requirements Eng.*, pages 249–262, 2001.

MARMI-RE: A Method and Tools for Legacy System Modernization

Eun Sook Cho[1], Jung Eun Cha[2], and Young Jong Yang[2]

[1] Div. Of Computer & Information Science,
Dongduk Women's University,
23-1 Wolgok-dong, Sungbuk-gu, Seoul 136-714, Korea
escho@dongduk.ac.kr
[2] Software Engineering Department,
Electronics and Telecommunications Research Institute,
161 Gajeong-dong, Yuseong-gu, Daejeon 305-350, Korea
{mary2743@, yangyj}@etri.re.kr

Abstract. Software evolution is the process of adapting an existing software system to conform to an enhanced set of requirements. Software reengineering is software evolution performed in systematic way. Especially software system is fundamentally different from developing one from scratch. Consequently, tools to support evolution must go beyond forward engineering tools. This paper presents a reengineering method and tools for software evolution or modernization. The paper briefly describes MARMI-RE methodology before presenting the individual tools and how they interoperate to support legacy system modernization. We expect that our proposed methodology can be used flexibly because it presents various scenarios of migration process.

1 Introduction

Legacy software systems may be defined informally as "large software systems that we do not know how to cope with but that are vital to our organization" [1]. Many legacy systems are performing crucial work for their organizations, and usually they represent years of accumulated experience and knowledge. We must trade-off the cost of continuing to cope with the legacy system against the investment needed to improve it and the benefit of easier subsequent maintenance [1,2].

System evolution is a broad term that covers a continuum from adding a field in a database to completely re-implementing a system. These system evolution activities can be divided into three categories [3]: maintenance, modernization, and replacement. Fig. 1 illustrates how different evolution activities are applied at different phases of the system life cycle. The dotted line represents growing business needs while the solid line represents the functionality provided by the information system. Repeated system maintenance supports the business needs sufficiently for a time, but as the system becomes increasingly outdated, maintenance falls behind the business needs. A modernization effort is then required that represents a greater effort, both in time and functionality, than the maintenance activity. Finally, when the old system can no longer be evolved, it must be replaced[4].

W. Dosch, R.Y. Lee, and C. Wu (Eds.): SERA 2004, LNCS 3647, pp. 42–57, 2005.

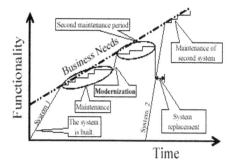

Fig. 1. Information System Life Cycle

Until now, many researches for reengineering legacy system have been progressed. However, most approaches focuses on only reverse engineering or some of reengineering process. For example, there is only program analysis, design recovery, restructuring programs, and so on. Especially researches for reengineering approaches for component-based system are few conducted[5]. In this paper, we propose a reengineering methodology to transform legacy system into component-based system.

This paper is organized as follows. Section 2 describes the related works of reengineering methodology. Section 3 presents the process architecture of our methodology and activities of each phase. Section 4 describes case study applied proposed methodology into lease business management system. Section 5 presents tools developed in order to support techniques of our methodology. Section 6 summarizes the work, concluding with future works.

2 Related Works

In this section, we describe several reengineering methodologies such as MORALE, RENAISSANCE, and Butterfly methodology. Also, we suggest the limitations of existing methodologies and reengineering techniques.

2.1 MORALE Methodology

The MORALE project addresses the problem of designing and evolving complex software systems. The MORALE acronym summarizes the its goals[6]. **Mission ORiented:** They want the legacy system enhancement process to be driven by the mission to be accomplished rather than by purely technical criteria. **Architectural:** The most time consuming and costly alternations to software are those that distort architecture, by which they mean its structure and behavior. **Legacy Evolution:** They want to provide a cost effective way of analyzing existing software, and once analyzed, extracting those parts of it that can be used in the new version.

2.2 RENAISSANCE

The Renaissance₁ method was developed to support the reengineering of legacy software systems [7]. The method is structured into two main phases. The first one, or *what to do*, aims to assess the organization and the legacy system and identify both the need and urgency of reengineering and the best candidate strategy to adopt for renewing the system: continue with the current maintenance approach; reengineer the system from user-interface, structure, architecture, and/or design point of views; replace the existing system with a new developed one. The second phase, or *how to do*, supports the implementation of the planned transformation, and drives the overall process of migrating the legacy system to its immortal dimension.

2.3 Butterfly Methodology

The objective of the Butterfly Methodology is to guide the *migration* of a mission-critical legacy system to a target system[8,9]. The Butterfly Methodology is based on the assumption that the data of a legacy system is logically the most important part of the system and that, from the viewpoint of the target system development it is not the ever-changing legacy data that is crucial, but rather its semantics or schema(s). Thus, the Butterfly Methodology separates the target system development and data migration phases, thereby eliminating the need for gateways.

2.4 Limitations of Existing Researches

There are several solutions; wrapping, screen scrapping, and transformation to migrate legacy system into modern system. First of all, wrapping involves surrounding existing data, individual programs, application systems, and interfaces to give a legacy system a 'new and improved' look or improve operations[10,11]. However, this technique does not solve the problem of inertia of the legacy system, which will remain unchanged. The most popular implementation is "Screen Scrapping". It reduces training costs for new employees and allows an interface to the legacy system be placed on the desktop. Thus the problems legacy systems pose can only be overcome using a comprehensive migration strategy[9]. The MORALE methodology focuses on "screen scrapping". Therefore the methodology cannot overcome the problems legacy systems pose.

Renaissance methodology deals with overall scope of reengineering. Therefore, its activity is broad. Also it focuses on architecture migration. Therefore mechanical or specific mechanisms or activities are not defined clearly. Butterfly methodology focuses on data migration strategies and techniques. Because it deals only with data migration problems, more systematic and stepwise activities are defined.

3 Our Approach

Until now, there has been few systematic way to identify components for reuse and to understand the types of changes required to insert legacy system components into a software product line or a new software architecture [12,13]. In this paper, we suggest a new architecture-centric reengineering approach, which can reduce potential risks and improve new system's quality. Fig. 2 illustrates the overall reengineering process architecture supported by the MARMI-RE methodology.

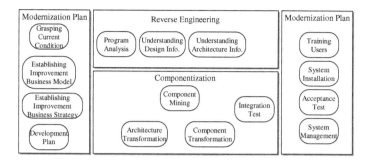

Fig. 2. Overview of MARMI-RE

3.1 Modernization Plan Phase (Phase 0)

Reengineering begins with an assessment of the current system. Prior to reengineering current legacy system, modernization plan phase is executed. Modernization plan phase is designed to understand and estimate current system's organization, current system's status, reengineering costs, future complementary components, and so on. We outline main activities of plan phase in the following. First of all, activity of grasping the present situation is carried out. This activity includes business environment analysis, legacy system analysis, and maintenance task analysis. The main activities within this phase are listed in Fig. 3.

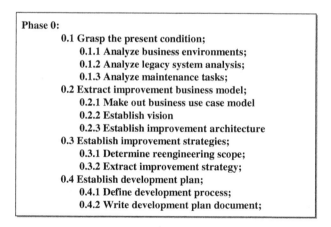

Fig. 3. Migration Activities in Phase 0

In activity 0.1.1, organization structure, business workflow, and internal issues are identified. In activity 0.1.2, the functionalities of business tasks, application system analysis, and system environments analysis are done. System environment means operational environment, development environment, and test environment.

In activity 0.2.2, requirements are identified and project scope and objectives are defined. Activity 0.2.3 establishes improvement architecture. Improvement architecture is divided into system architecture and software architecture.

Table 1. A Sample of Reengineering Object Selection

Element BT		Bn			Sn			Sum	Priority
		V	R	E	Q	MC	TD		
		30%	10%	10%	20%	20%	10%	100%	
A	AV	+2	-1	+2	+1	-1	-3		2
	EV	60%	-10%	20%	20%	-20%	-30%	40%	
B	AV	5	-3	3	4	-1	-4		1
	EV	150%	-30%	30%	80%	-20%	-40%	170%	

* Bn:Business Element, Sn:Systematic Element, V: Value, R:Risk, E:Extensibility, Q:Quality, MC:Maintenance Cost, TD:Technical Difficulty, AV: Assigned Value, EV:Estimated Value

In activity 0.3.1, reengineering scope is determined. In order to determine reengineering scope, we decide business elements and systematic elements. Furthermore, relative weight for each element is given. After reviewing these weights, we select reengineering objects. A sample of reengineering selection is depicted in Table 1. The 'BT' means business task.

In the Table 1, A or B means business task, AV means the assigned value of each business task, and EV means the estimated value of each business task. We divide assessment element into business element and systematic element. We define the value of business as 30%, the risk as 10%, and the extensibility as 10%. We regard these values as weight value(W) of each element. AV means thing appropriate the degree of importance for business elements and systematic elements of each business task. The range of assigned value is from –5 to 5.

We compute EV based on weight value of each element and AV. EV is computed the following equation;

$$EV = W * AV$$

The sum means the assessment value of each business task. After computing the value of sum for all business tasks, we compute average value by dividing the total sum of all business tasks into the number of total business tasks.

For each business task, if assessment value of each business task larger than the average value, we select the business task to modernize.

There are various scenarios to apply phases and activities into migration process according to migration strategies in activity 0.4.1. These scenarios are shown in Fig. 4.

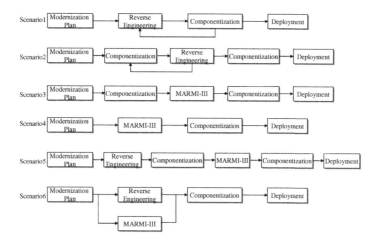

Fig. 4. Possible Scenarios of MARMI-RE Process

For example, scenario 1 can be applied in case of following:

- In case that the legacy system's documents are enough;
- In case that the legacy system's worker(developer, operator, or maintainer) is exist;
- In case that the quality of legacy program's code is high or too is supported;
- In case that the legacy source codes can be separated into modules according to each business task;
- In case that legacy code's reuse is needed strategically;

In case that migration strategy is not disuse or transformation plan is incomplete;

3.2 Reverse Engineering Phase (Phase 1)

The objectives of this phase are extraction of current system's core functionalities and core elements, understand static and behavioral aspect of current system, and support easily transforming current system into modern system. The activities identified within this phase are listed in Fig. 5.

Activity 1.1.1 restructures program's logics by identifying codes to restructure, eliminating redundant or dead codes with structured, and reformatting identified codes into structured codes. This activity is supported itself with restructuring tool. Program's syntactic analysis, variable reference information, and semantic information analysis for each program are achieved through activity 1.1.2. Activity 1.1.3 catches data information, system resource information, call relations among programs, and screen flow information.

Activity 1.2.1 and 1.2.2 can be done with parallel. Activity 1.2.1 recovers entity relationship information from database information. Activity 1.2.2 recovers functional information from main screen units, which are core business work's executions. We represent functional information as use case model.

Phase 1:
    1.1 Analyze program;
        1.1.1 Restructure program's code;
        1.1.2 Analyze program's semantic information;
        1.1.3 Analyze system's semantic information;
    1.2 Understand design information;
        1.2.1 Understand data information;
        1.2.2 Understand functional information;
    1.3 Understand architecture;
        1.3.1 Understand structural architecture;
        1.3.2 Understand behavioral architecture;
        1.3.3 Understand technical architecture;

Fig. 5. Migration Activities in Phase 1

After activity 1.2 is done, activity 1.3, architecture understanding, is executed. Activity 1.3.1 recovers structural aspect of architecture. It abstracts subsystem units from modules of legacy system and understands how to organize relations among these subsystems. Activity 1.3.2 understands and recovers how call relations among subsystems are achieved based on structural architecture information.

3.3 Componentization Phase(Phase 2)

All the components of legacy system are migrated to the target system during this phase. In this phase, "Forward" engineering principles and methods will be one of the guidelines for migration. Fig. 6 lists activities in this phase.

Activity 2.1 is very important to migrate legacy system into component-based system. We adopt use case driven approach to mine reusable components from legacy system. In order to mine reusable components, first of all, activity 2.1.1 should be done. Activity 2.1.1 is done with identifying system elements related with use case. Identifying system elements uses program analysis information, obtained from activity 1.1, and design information, obtained from activity 1.2, of reverse engineering phase. Especially system elements are identified for each use case extracted from activity 1.2. For example, paragraph, program statement, global variable, program, map file, transaction, database, and library can be system elements in case of COBOL legacy system.

And then, use cases are analyzed and candidate components are identified. Use cases are analyzed with respect to boundary, control, and entity. The reason is to identify use cases carrying out similar business functions or responsibilities, to integrate identified use cases, and to recognize coarse-grained components. Use case analysis process is depicted in Fig. 7. Circle means each use case, arrow means the control flow between use cases. Thick arrow means reference relation between use case and map file(screen file). And then, candidate components are identified with identifying and grouping use cases with similar business function or responsibility and grouping.

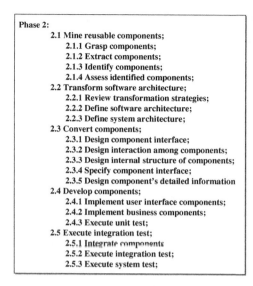

Phase 2:
    2.1 Mine reusable components;
        2.1.1 Grasp components;
        2.1.2 Extract components;
        2.1.3 Identify components;
        2.1.4 Assess identified components;
    2.2 Transform software architecture;
        2.2.1 Review transformation strategies;
        2.2.2 Define software architecture;
        2.2.3 Define system architecture;
    2.3 Convert components;
        2.3.1 Design component interface;
        2.3.2 Design interaction among components;
        2.3.3 Design internal structure of components;
        2.3.4 Specify component interface;
        2.3.5 Design component's detailed information
    2.4 Develop components;
        2.4.1 Implement user interface components;
        2.4.2 Implement business components;
        2.4.3 Execute unit test;
    2.5 Execute integration test;
        2.5.1 Integrate components
        2.5.2 Execute integration test;
        2.5.3 Execute system test;

Fig. 6. Migration Activities in Phase 2

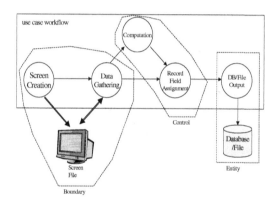

Fig. 7. Use Cases Analysis Process

Activity 2.1.2 includes understanding common elements, component identification, association and interaction among components. The objective of understanding common elements is to construct separate components with high reusability from other components. Basically components with high reusability can be shared among several functions in a system. A method to identify common elements uses association table shown in Table 2.

As shown in Table 2, use case UC1 and UC2 share P11, P12, P13, and P14. However, UC3, UC4, and UC5 share only both P12 and P13. Therefore, common elements between two candidate components, Comp1 and Comp2, are P12 and P13.

Table 2. Association Table

		UC1		UC2		UC3		UC4	UC5
		Pg1	Pg2	Pg3	Pg4	Pg6	Pg7	Pg8	Pg9
S u b P r o g r a m	P11	✓	✓	✓	✓				
	P12	✓		✓	✓	✓	✓		✓
	P13	✓	✓	✓	✓	✓		✓	✓
	P14	✓	✓		✓				
	...								
	Pn	✓			✓				

3.4 Deployment Phase (Phase 3)

During the delivery phase, the users take final delivery of the system, while operating under realistic conditions. Under the supervision of the users, the actual enterprise data managed by the legacy system is migrated to the new system.

The first task of deployment is to install the new system on site-On the actual hardware upon which it will operate, with the actual software packages, etc. This is done together with the onsite operational personnel. Also training system users are executed with parallel. Main activities of this phase are listed in Fig. 8.

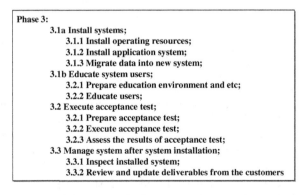

Fig. 8. Migration Activities in Phase 3

4   Case Study

In this section, we present a case study of applying MARMI-RE in modernizing legacy COBOL system; capital business management system. This system is a COBOL-based system which being operated in IBM AS/400 Machine. This system has 124 programs containing 30thousands line of code. A capital company merges three companies and operates heterogeneous three lease management systems. This company tries to transform heterogeneous systems into unified and modernized systems in order to reduce maintenance costs and operate systems effectively.

4.1   Phase 0

In order to understand existing tasks and present information effectively and systematically, we established examination. We produced organization chart, task workflow diagram, and analysis report of existing condition. Fig. 9 shows an example of task workflow diagrams. Fig. 9 describes total workflows of lease task.

Also we produced analysis report for legacy system. Total businesses to migrate consist of 5 systems and 36 sub systems. We only focused on business management system of total business tasks.

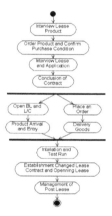

Fig. 9. An Example of Task Workflow Diagram

Table 3 shows program lists contained in legacy lease management system. For each program, program name, program's lines and program description are depicted.

Table 3. Program Lists of Legacy System

No	Program	Lines	Description
1	Lp1000.mbr	233	Total business
2	Lp1010.mbr	231	Lease business
3	Lp1020.mbr	222	Lease Post Management
4	Lp1030.mbr	222	Funds Management
5	Lp1040.mbr	230	Account Management
...	...	...	...

Second activity of Phase 0 is to extract improvement business model. We produced a use case diagram to extract improvement business model. Fig. 10 depicts of use case diagram for lease management.

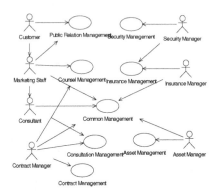

Fig. 10. Use Case Diagram for Lease Management

4.2   Phase 1

In reverse engineering phase(phase 1), we recovered design and program information through activity 1.1, 1.2, and 1.3.

Fig. 11 shows an example of subroutine call graph for lease business tasks. A blue box means a program, and red box means subroutine.

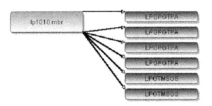

Fig. 11. An Example of Subroutine Call Graph

Fig. 12 shows an example of subroutine control flow for lease business management.

Fig. 12. Subroutine Control Flow Graph

Fig. 13 shows an example of application use case diagram. While business use case diagram is extracted from business tasks, application use case diagram is extracted from existing legacy system.

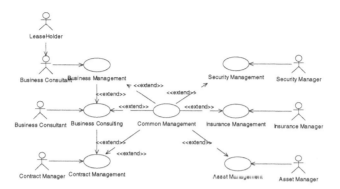

Fig. 13. An Example of Application Use Case Diagram

Table 4 shows mapping table between business use cases and application use cases.

Table 4. Use Case Mapping Table

No of BU	BU's name	AU's NO	AU's name
BU-1	Public Relation		
BU-2	Counsel Management	AU-1	Business Management
BU-3	Consultation Management	AU-2	Business Management
BU-4	Contract Management	AU-3	Contract Management
BU-5	Security Management	AU-4	Security Management
BU-6	Insurance Management	AU-5	Insurance Management
BU-7	Asset Management	AU-6	Asset Management
BU-8	Common Management	AU-7	Common Management

4.3 Phase 2

In this phase, we first produced association table to identify shared elements. Table 5 shows some parts of association table extracted from legacy system.

Table 6 shows a component specification for business consultation component. Identified components should be mapped into application use cases and business use cases. The reason is that we confirm whether functional requirements of existing and future system are reflected into components appropriately or not.

Also we should establish modernization strategies for identified components; wrapping, transformation, screen scrapping, and replacement.

Component architecture for component-based modern system is depicted in Fig. 14.

Table 5. Association Table

Task		Sub-Prog/File Program	Code Check	Message Edit	Date Verify	Lease No	Screen
			LPGT CODE	LPGT MSGS	LPGTI LCK	LMG YCMF	SKREE N
Business Counsel	1101	Input Business Info.	√	√	√	√	√
	7107	Change Business Info.		√			
	1201	Input Customer Info	√	√	√	√	√
	1205	Input Lease Condition	√	√		√	√
	1104	Write Counsel Report	√	√	√	√	√
	1102	Receipt Counsel		√	√		√
	1103	Counsel Company Spec.	√	√	√		√
	1105	Contract Estimation					

Table 6. Component Specification for Business Consultation Component

Component's Name	Business Consultation
Containing Program	Input Business Info
	Changing Business Info
	Input Customer Info
	Input Lease Condition
	Write Counsel Report
	Receipt Counsel
	Counsel Company Spec
	Contract Estimation
Composition DB	Customer DB,Lease Info
Composition Map	SCREEN
Association	

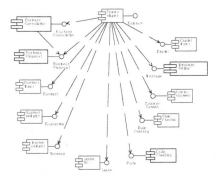

Fig. 14. Component Architecture for Lease Business Management System

5 Tool Support

Proposed MARMI-RE methodology is supported by reengineering tool, called REFLECT(REengineering tool For LEgacy Cobol Transfomation). Fig. 15 shows the framework of REFLECT tool. The REFLECT is a supporting tool that creates wrapper components based on COBOL legacy system and connect with EJB component system. COBOL analyzer creates defined syntax file by using JavaCC. It produces abstract syntax tree (AST) through lexical analysis and syntax analysis process by regard COBOL program as input, and saves AST and symbol table into information repository. Understanding tool supports users to understand analysis information easily for legacy program's analysis information. Therefore it provides convenience of maintenance.

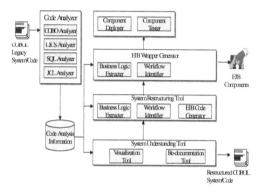

Fig. 15. Framework of REFLECT Tool

Understanding tool is divided into two types: visualization tool and re-documentation tool. Visualization tool is shown in Fig. 16.

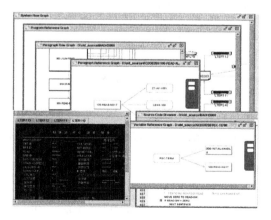

Fig. 16. Visualization Tool

System restructuring tool is a tool that restructure unstructured source program into commonly recognizable and easily understandable program for system migration or maintenance. Especially EJB code generator creates EJB wrapper component automatically to connect COBOL system with EJB-based component system.

6 Conclusion

In this paper a new approach to the problem of legacy system migration has been presented. The existing migration processes have dealt broadly or limitedly. Especially the migration process as a whole is a very complex procedure encompassing many different cases. The proposed MARMI-RE methodology is applied into the whole process of legacy system migration with the main focus specifically on the migration of legacy business logic, which is high reusable part in the modernization strategies. In the future work, we integrates proposed MARMI-RE methodology with forward engineering methodology; MARMI. Also, we identify and develop necessary tools to support legacy modernization or migration workflows.

References

1. SEI(1996), "Assessing the Evolability of a Legacy System", Software Engineering Institute, Carnegie Mellon University.
2. William Ulrich, Legacy Systems : "Transformation Strategies", Prentice Hall, 2002.
3. Weiderman, Nelson H.; Bergey, John K.; Smith, Dennis B.; & Tilley, Scott R. Approaches to Legacy System Evolution(CMU/SEI-97-TR-014). Pittsburgh, Pa.: Software Engineering Institute, Carnegie Mellon University. Available WWW <URL:http://www.sei.cmu.edu/publications/documents/97.reports/97tr014/97tr014abstract.html> (1997).
4. Rick Kazman, Steven G. Woods, S. Jeromy Carriere, "Requirements for Integrating Software Architecture and Reengineering Models: CORUM II", Fifth Working Conference on Reverse Engineering, Honolulu, Hawaii, Oct, pp. 154-163, 1998.
5. Ransom, J.; Sommerville, I.; & Warren, I. "A Method for Assessing Legacy Systems for Evolution," Proceedings of the Second Euromicro Conference on Software Maintenance and Reengineering (CSMR98), Florence, Italy, March 8-11, 1998.
6. Gregory A., et. al., "MORALE: Mission Oriented Architectural Legacy Evolution", Proceedings of International Conference on Software Maintenance'97, Bari, Italy, September 29-October 3, pp.150-159, 1997.
7. Nelson Weiderman, Dennis Smith, Scott Tilley, "Approaches to Legacy System Evolution", *CMU/SEI-97-TR-014.*
8. Bing Wu, et. al., "The Butterfly Methodology: A Gateway-free Approach for Migrating Legacy Information Systems" Proceedings of the 3rd IEEE Conference on Engineering of Complex Computer Systems(ICECCS97), Villa Olmo, Como, Italy, September 8-12, pp.200-205, 1997.
9. Bing Wu, et. al., "Legacy Systems Migration – A Method and its Tool-kit Framework", Proceedings of the APSEC'97/ICSC'97:Joint 1997 Asia Pacific Software Engineering Conference and International Computer Science Conference, Hong Kong, China, 2-5 December, pp.312-320, 1997.

10. Systems Techniques Inc., "Wrapping Legacy Systems for Reuse: Repackaging vs. Rebuilding", http://www.systecinic.com/white/splist.html.
11. Sneed, H.M, "Encapsulating Legacy Software for Use in Client/Server System", Proceedings of Working Conference on Reverse Engineering(WCRE'96), Moterey, Calif., Nov.8-10, pp.104-119, 1996.
12. Clements, P. & Northrop, L. *Software Product Lines: Practice and Patterns*, Boston, MA:Addison Wesley Longman, Inc., 2001.
13. Muller, H.; Jahnke, J.; Smith, D.; Storey, M.; Tilley, S. & Wong, K., "Reverse Engineering: A Roadmap", 47-60, The Future of Software Engineering, New York, NY:ACM, 2000.

A Study on Frameworks of Component Integration for Web Applications*

Haeng-Kon Kim[1], Hae-Sool Yang[2], and Roger Y. Lee[3]

[1] Department of Computer Information & Communication Engineering,
Catholic University of Daegu
hangkon@cu.ac.kr
[2] Graduate School of Venture, HoSeo Univ. Bae-Bang myon, A-San,
Chung-Nam, 336-795, South Korea
hsyang@office.hoseo.ac.kr
[3] Dept. of Computer Science, Central Michigan Univ. Mt.Pleasant,
MI 48859,U.S.A
lee@cps.cmich.edu

Abstract. As web application systems become increasingly complex to build developers are turning more and more to integrating pre-built components from third party developers into their systems. This use of Commercial Off-The-Shelf (COTS) software components in system construction presents new challenges to web system architects and designers. Web applications are seldom developed in isolation. Frequently there are many projects building, maintaining and evolving the applications, each with its own life cycle of requirements, design and implementation. To gain improvements in productivity and quality across these applications, it is necessary to consider the main element of theses solutions, to abstract them from the individual solutions, and to manage them as a core asset of the organization. The continuing increase of interest in Component Based Development (CBD) signifies the emergence of a new development trend within the Web application industry. This paper describes issues raised when integrating COTS components for web application, outlines strategies for integration, and presents some informal rules we have developed that ease the development and maintenance of such systems.

Keywords: CBD, Web Application, Component Modeling, Component Architecture, Repository

1 Introduction

Modern web application systems are becoming increasingly expensive to build and maintain and users are becoming more sophisticated in terms of the capability they expect. To build such systems, developers must use a large number of standards, protocols, technologies, and tool kits, each one of which is complex and involves a steep learning curve. Development organizations have met this challenge by using

---

* This research was supported by University IT Research Center Project.

W. Dosch, R.Y. Lee, and C. Wu (Eds.): SERA 2004, LNCS 3647, pp. 58–70, 2005.

off-the-shelf software components that have been developed outside their organization and which provide much of the functionality and capability required, rather than building their own components. Components that are bought from a third-party vendor and integrated into a system are defined as *Commercial Off-The-Shelf* (COTS) software components. Building a system from a set of COTS components introduces a different set of problems than building a system from scratch or building a system by re-using components that have been previously constructed internally in the development organization [1,2]. Many of these problems are introduced because of the nature of COTS components: they are truly black-box and the developers have no method of looking inside the box; developers have little or no influence over the maintenance. Evolution of the components and the behavior of the component may be inadequately specified to understand its behavior in a multi-component system. Often the COTS component is meant to run as a standalone application and has no mechanism for interacting with other programs. In order to address these problems we have been experimenting with building systems by integrating COTS components. Among the objectives of these experiments is to look at: technologies that support component integration such as CORBA or ActiveX; languages that are useful for gluing components together [3,4,5] and system architectures for using COTS components [6,7,8,9].

In Web application development projects on a commercial scale, view support is highly desirable for a number of reasons. *First*, the Web development projects are multi-user environment in most cases. Accordingly, many users who have different perceptions on a Web system exist and what they want from the system is different for each user. *Second*, as Web grows to incorporate new kinds of information, the definition of the Web system must also extend consequently. Without the effective solution for expansion, the ever-growing network of information becomes hard to maintain and finally will be a chaos. *Third*, it might become necessary to restructure the Web system although the content of overall information remains the same. Web applications are seldom developed in isolation. Frequently there are many projects building, maintaining and evolving applications, each with its own life-cycle of requirements, design and implementation. To gain improvements in productivity and quality across these applications it is necessary to consider the main element of theses solutions, to abstract them from the individual solutions, and to manage them as a core asset of the organization. These key assets consists of two things: The components which form the building blocks of an application; The patterns describing how these component can be used in combination to satisfy some higher level business need.

In this paper, we try to find a component based Web design methodology by optimizing various objectives of users, designers and developers. We propose the component based Web design methodology. It considers the pre-mentioned aspects of design and maintenance for Web application using component. This paper also describes issues raised when integrating COTS components, outlines software architecture for integration, and presents some informal rules.

2 Related Works

2.1 Domain Analysis

Component-based Software development process presented in this study is as in Fig. 1.Our process model for component-based software development explicitly considers reuse-specific activities, such as componential design, component identification, and component adaptation. It is comprised of seven major activities, starting with context comprehension and requirement analysis, continuing with the combination of componential design and component identification, component creation, component adaptation, and finally ending with component assembly. Throughout the process, explicitly stated domain artifacts- domain Specifications, domain model, and domain architecture - are produced. Component-based Domain Engineering depends on the component-based software development process.

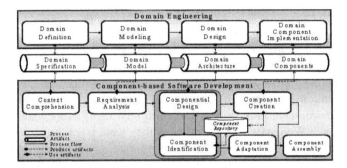

Fig. 1. Domain based CBD process

2.2 Repository

Component repository as in figure 1 is a library system that supports finding, providing and managing components for building a business application. So it is a kind of tool to store, register manage all of the artifacts produced in the component life cycle based on component architecture, and support a Reuse with component in the CBD process through performing advanced retrieval and browsing of information. Most of all, component repository is a central mediator for component generation and utilization. So, analyzing and applying consistent meta and user feedback information can establish the CBD process including creation, verification, configuration management and circulation of component[3,4].

2.3 CBD Process

CBD promises cost-effective productivity assuring a high flexibility and maintenance by assembling the components as independent business processing. The parts. The CBD environment is divided into two aspects according to process evolution level. That is, we consider the CBD process as a supply process producing and providing the commercial components into a repository, and consume process supporting component utilization for constructing business solutions in figure 1 [6,7]. The big picture represents essential works for realizing the CBD process, subjecting the basic principles for component reuse that is acquisition understanding applying as shown in figure 1.

2.4 Component Interfaces

In an ideal situation, component interfaces would be formally specified, and a CBWDM would perform formal reasoning to ensure the semantic compatibility of component implementations with their interfaces. However, such reasoning tools are still not widely available or widely used by practitioners, and most commercial components do not have formally specified interfaces. A global namespace of interfaces partly solves the problem of how a CBWDM will ensure consistency between the semantics of a provided component and the semantics required of the component [10,11]. While there may be different interfaces providing the same functionality in a global namespace of interfaces, two interfaces with the same name are intended to be functionally equivalent. On a fundamental level, this greatly simplifies the problem of matching provided components to required semantics, since the problem is reduced to name equality. Only when components do not match at the interface level is human intervention required: Either they are truly incompatible (i.e., incompatible on a semantic level), or the incompatibility is only syntactic, so that they can be matched by simple manual adaptation (for example by wrapping one of them). Of course, mechanisms are still needed to ensure that a component correctly implements the semantics promised by its interfaces, but this problem already existed along-side the component matching problem.

2.5 Component Composition and Adaptation Process

A component based development process looks different from a traditional one. The process is bipartite: The development of components, and the composition of an application from the components, is separated. Typically, different organizations, the component manufacturer and the organization that wants to license and reuse the manufactured components will execute the two process parts. We refer to these organizations as the *component developer* and the *application composer,* respectively. Component development is a traditional development process since all the usual lifecycle phases are traversed. The main difference is that the end product is not a complete application. This means that the product is comparatively small, which may make development processes suited to small projects preferable. A CBWDM(Component Based Web Design Methodology) in this paper can support traditional component development and be composed those component based on ABCD architectures as in figure 2.

In the ideal extreme, all components can be *bought* or otherwise obtained, since the goal of component reuse is to minimize the implementation phase of an application. The application composer must select the right components, connect and adapt them, and identify and build components that might be missing. In the near future, it will not be possible to completely eliminate the implementation phase except for trivial projects, but it can be minimized and simplified using appropriate components and environment capabilities. Finding components that match arbitrary requirements will be difficult or impossible; instead one is forced to select from prepackaged components with given architectural assumptions. The cost savings gained by component reuse will often make it feasible to adapt requirements and design to the components that are available. Thus, the availability of components must be considered during the whole process [12]. Once the decision to reuse a certain component is made, it will have to be configured within a CBWDM. Component configuration consists of connection and adaptation. Components have to be connected to each other so that they can cooperate. In the simplest case, the connector is just a link between a given required service and a given provided service. In other words, a connector establishes how a requirement is fulfilled. But connectors can be more complex; it is useful to have them encapsulate functionality that logically belongs within a shared infrastructure (for example, communication protocols in a distributed system) rather than to either of the two components that are being connected [13]. Adaptation increases the value of components. The more flexible and adaptable a component is, the more often it will be reused. Ideally, a component will provide ways for application composers to adapt it. However, a component manufacturer will not be able to foresee all adaptations that might be necessary. For this reason, there should be means to adapt a component externally without having to interact with it, for example wrapping.

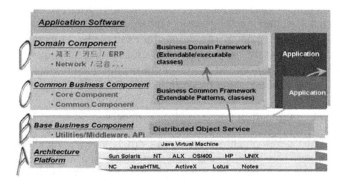

Fig. 2. Component Composition on Architecture

2.6 Other Approaches for Web Applications

2.6.1 Enhanced O-R Model (EORM)

Object-oriented ideas have been used in the hypermedia field for several years. EORM[6] was the first object-oriented design methodology. EORM consists of 3 frameworks including class framework, composition framework and GUI framework as shown in figure 3. The main concepts of EORM in Figure4 are explained as follows.

•Class framework

Two activities are related to this framework: class identification and class refinement. The first step is to identify relevant classes from the problem domain. Class refinement is about detailing the information of each classes by defining its attributes, operations, and inheritance relationships.

•**Composition framework**

The composition framework consists of reusable library of link class definitions. Two activities related to this framework are defined: composition identification and composition refinement.

•**GUI framework**

The GUI framework includes two activities: presentation and window identification and mapping of classes and compositions to presentations.

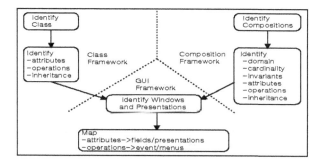

Fig. 3. Overview of EORM

2.6.2 O-O Hypermedia Design Method

In OOHDM[7], a hypermedia application is built in a four-step process supporting an incremental or prototype process model. Each step focuses on a particular design concern, and an object-oriented model is built. Figure 4 illustrates products and mechanisms of each step in OOHDM. Detailed explanation is as follows.

•**Domain Analysis**

In this step a conceptual model of the application domain is built using well-known object-oriented principled, augmented with some primitives such as of users and tasks.

•**Navigational Design**

Here, OOHDM describes the navigational structure of hypermedia application in terms of navigational contexts, which are induced from navigation classes such as nodes, links, indices, and guided tours. Navigational contexts and classes take into account the types of intended users and their tasks.

•**Abstract Interface Design**

The abstract interface model is built by defining perceptible objects in terms of interface classes. Interface classes are defined as aggregations of primitive classes and recursively of interface classes. Interface objects map to navigational objects, providing a perceptible appearance. Interface behavior is declared by specifying how to handle external and user-generated events and how communication takes place between interface and navigational objects.

•**Implementation**

Implementation maps interface object to implementation objects and may involve elaborated architectures (e. g., client-server), in which applications are clients to a shared database server containing the conceptual objects.

3   A Component Based Web Application Development

3.1   Web Design Process

A Web application consists of pieces of information in the form of text, images, sound, video and other programs. Each piece of information is called node. Nodes are connected to each other by links. Links are associated with a small part of the node called the anchor. When the user wants some information he/she activates the anchor and the system follows the associated link to access and display the target node. To design a Web application, we need to decide hoe to divide the information domain into pieces, how the resulting pieces are to be linked, and how the user is to interact with the system.   Web application design process must include additional design steps on the traditional approach. Navigational design is a typical design step used in Web design process. Splitting process can be coordinated mainly in two ways, top-down approach and bottom-up approach.   It is important to differentiate a Web system from a Web application. The former is an environment that facilitates the creation of the latter. A data model for a Web system details its internal architecture but is of little value in modeling Web applications. This is because describing the layout of a general-purpose engine is quite different from modeling an application domain; a different kind data model is needed for this purpose. In our case, CBWDM (Component Based Web Design Methodology) provides a language for describing the information objects and the navigation mechanisms in Web applications.

Web application design model is a set of logical objects used to provide an abstraction of a part of the real world for the Web applications and Internet. Data models are necessary to express an application's design. Many models are presented targeting Web applications and Web system. In this process, Web design methodologies should consider the needs of user, designer and developer in the design phases from informal user requirement to formal Web systems. The first stage of Web application design process is about capturing navigational user requirement, which is the origin of the various Web design models. The result of user requirements analysis must be conceptualized and instantiated. Conceptualizing process is a bottom-up approach for producing a generic structure from a set of examples. Conceptualizing is necessary to bridge bottom-up and top-down approaches. Given a structure resulting from conceptualizing, the design environment should help repopulate it with existing information or instantiate it with new information. CBWDM architecture is divided two main process as for component and with component based on a bottom-up approach. CBWDM with component spans fundamental stages of SDLC, which range over domain analysis, component engineering (Component Searching, Selection, Development and execution) and navigational mapping of a domain and mapping the result into target Web application system. The first Web design process on CBD step is to identify the domain components and to develop the domain architecture as in figure 4. The domain component, which is different from the physical component that can be deployed immediately during software development, is defined as a service central unit package of platform independent logical level. ABCD CBD architecture is represented out of the identified domain components in a concrete and analyzable format.

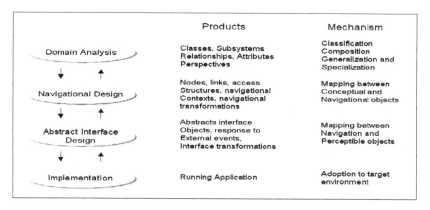

Fig. 4. Summary of OOHDM Methodology

3.1.1 Identify Web Domain Component

The most important process of component-based software development is that of extracting the component. Therefore, this process is also important for component-based domain design. When creating web applications, it is possible to allocate different granularity, which can be extracted from the requirement of the system. Variable granularity of these components can be supplied through the web Component that was extracted based on the service. So the web domain component is extracted based on domain use case as in figure 5.

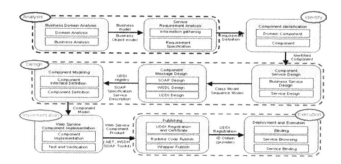

Fig. 5. Web Design Process on CBD

The usecase is a description of set of sequences of actions that a system performs that yield an observable result of value to an actor. We have identified web components and layered on ABCD architecture as shown figure 7. These components such as can be used for and with direction on CBD process.

3.1.2 Searching for Components

Typically, the application composer will start with a broad search using natural-language keywords. The composer enters the search terms into the CBWDM, which in turn sends a search command to all the repository servers it knows about. Search commands are implemented as pieces of mobile code. A repository server executes the mobile Code and allows it to search through all its stored components. The mobile code then queries the self-description of the identified components in order to check them against some associated search criteria. The default search command just checks the search terms against a list of keywords provided by the semantic self-description of a component. However, the repository architecture leaves the decision of how to search to the client CBWDMs. A CBWDM could easily replace this basic search strategy with a more complex one, for example one that makes use of natural language processing features. All the management of meta-information, dependencies, and so on that is typically done by a reuse repository is delegated to the components themselves, or rather their self-description. When a component is found that matches the search criteria, a part of the component is transferred to the client. CBWDM adds the component to its set of available components, and uses the component self-description to present information about the component to the composer.

3.1.3 Web Components Extraction

Often, the set of available components will be very large, since it is difficult to specify search criteria in a sufficiently precise way. The application Composer uses the Available Components View to browse through the available components, to look at their properties, and to select the ones that are needed as in figure 8. CBWDM has a window that displays a selection of relevant properties of the available components for easy comparison. Among them are name, manufacturer, size, price, and number of *provides* and *requires* ports. The numbers of ports allow an easy estimation of the architectural complexity of the component.

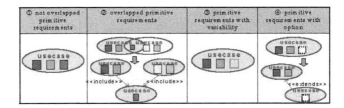

Fig. 6. Identifying Web Component with UML

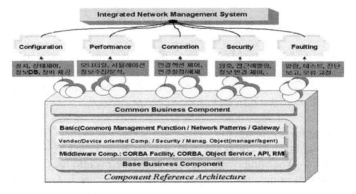

Fig. 7. Identified Web Component

For example, a component that has zero *requires* ports will be at the bottom of the architecture because it does not depend on any other components. An alternate view of the available components is sorted by the interfaces that the components implement, making it easy to compare all components that are possible suppliers for a given data type. However, since a component usually implements more than one interface, this view is less compact.

3.1.4 Component Configuration
CBWDM has a design editor that allows the composer to connect components. Components selected from a repository are represented in these diagrams by icons provided in the self-description of the components. When the diagram is opened, all selected components are displayed with their respective *requires* and *provides* ports. *Requires* ports are depicted as hollow circles, *provides* ports as filled circles. Each port is labeled with the name of the interface for which an implementation is required or pro vided. The composer can drag the components and create directed connections in the form of UML dependencies from *requires* ports to matching *provides* ports. Each *provides* port can be used by any number of *requires* ports, but a *requires* port cannot be connected to more than one *provides* port. A component Diagram gives an overview of the architecture that is being built and makes it easy to see which requirements are not yet fulfilled.

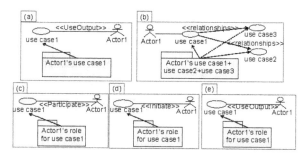

Fig. 8. Extracted Web Component

Each unfulfilled requirement corresponds to a *requires* port that is not connected to any *provides* port. To conclude type configuration, the composer must specify the main method of the application, i.e. the method with which execution is started. The environment presents a list of all public methods that could be used as main methods, and the composer chooses one of them.

3.1.5 Component Integration and Development
In an ideal situation, component interfaces would be formally specified, and a CBWDM would perform formal reasoning to ensure the semantic compatibility of component integration with their interfaces. However, such reasoning tools are still not widely available or widely used by practitioners, and most commercial components do not have formally specified interfaces. A global namespace of interfaces partly solves the problem of how a CBWDM will ensure consistency between the semantics of a

provided component and the semantics required of the component. After the components are extracted and configured, those web components are should be integrated through anyhow. The figure 9 shows an example of components integration that simply gets a web services from primitive web components such as user authentication, DB connection and e-applications. CBWDM uses Visual Café for instance-oriented configuration. Visual Café is a commercial Java development environment that sup-ports visual connection and adaptation of Java Beans on an in-stance basis. CBWDM uses Remote Method Invocation (RMI) to communicate with a Visual Café plug-in, which automatically loads the components into the component library of Visual Café, from where they can be dragged into Visual Cafés visual editor.

3.2 Execution

After the application has been configured, it can be executed. For testing, it can be executed in the CBWDM environment; this allows an iterative build process of alternating phases of configuring and executing as in figure 9. To make it possible to run the application outside of CBWDM, the environment can generate a configuration file that stores the names and URLs of the components that participate in this application, and how they are configured.

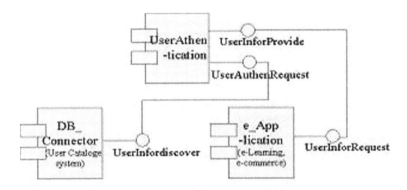

Fig. 9. Web Component Integration

When an application is being executed and a component implementation needs to instantiate a data type that is specified by one of its requires ports, it will query the runtime environment for a new instance of that data type as in figure 10. After instantiation, the component uses regular method calls to communicate with the other one; the polymorphism of the programming language makes it possible for one object to use another object without knowing the latter's precise type. The connection is explicit, because no component ever knows which of the other components provides the data type that it is using. At the same time it avoids most of the runtime overhead of message assing or similar de-coupling strategies. An overhead occurs only when a data type is being instantiated, not each time its instances are used.

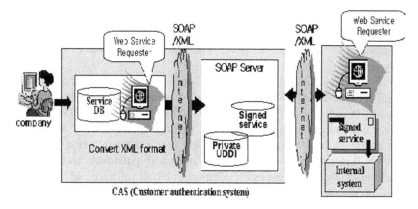

Fig. 10. Web Component Execution Environment

3.3 Component Evolution

When a component is marked as selected, the downloaded self-description can be implemented in one of two ways to provide access to the implementation of the component. In the usual case, it downloads a copy of the implementation and caches it locally. Then, it subscribes with the repository for update notifications. When an updated version of the component is published at the repository, the component is notified and can update itself. The other possible strategy is service reuse. Analogous to client-server application architecture, the downloaded part of the component for-wards requests to the master copy of the component that is located at the repository. Since the component is encapsulated, the difference between the two strategies is transparent to the user of the component, and thus to CBWDM. This means that the component can decide at runtime which strategy to use. For example, when the network transfer rate is high enough, the most current data can be directly accessed on the remote server. At times when the network is overloaded, the component can decide to use the locally cached version. Both these strategies realize reuse by reference. In both cases, a logical connection between the application using a component and the original copy of the component is created in order to prevent the maintenance problems associated with reuse.

4 Conclusion

Designing, developing and maintaining components for reuse is a very complex process, which require not only for the component functionality and flexibility, but also for matured development organization. In this paper, we focus on suggesting practices for component development processes. This includes the model management strategy and development and delivery of web component, adopted by an organization. In this paper, we have motivated the need for a new generation of CBD environments to support the web application. We identified important components for CBWDMs, and we described a prototype environment called CBWDM that we are building to implement these requirements and to provide a basis for further evaluation and study of the role of environment technology based on component-based development. There are several issues that remain to be resolved. Type-based adaptation does not exist yet in our prototype.

We expect that the same methods of internal and external adaptation can be used in varied forms for type-based adaptation. Integration with development environments is another issue. It remains to be seen if tight integration of the CBWDM with a commercial development environment is the optimal solution, or if an alternative solution is needed. Updating of components still requires manual effort. For further research we will put more effort to create an open and extendable architecture. We also will address the standard issues for component based software and CBD process, which covers component requirement analysis, component development, and component certification.

Acknowledgments

This research was supported by the MIC(Ministry of Information and Communication), Korea, under the ITRC(Information Technology Research Center) support program supervised by the IITA(Institute of Information Technology Assessment)

References

1. George T. Heineman and William T. Councill, Component Based Software Engineering, Addison Wesley Publication Company, June, 2001.
2. Clemens Szyperski, *Component Software: Beyond Object-Oriented Programming*, January 2001, Addison-wesley.
3. Harvey M. Deitel, Paul J.Deitel, TemNieto and T.R.Nieto, e-Business & e-Commerce, Prentice Hall, 2001.
4. Reash Trivedi, "Web Service Architecture Models," RCG IT, 2002. 4.
5. Michael Champion, "Web Services Architecture," at URL :
   http://dev.w3.org/cvsweb/~checkout~/2002/ws/arch/ wsa/wd-wsa-arch.html ,
6. John D. Poole, "Model Driven Architecture: Vision, Standards and Emerging Technologies," European Conference on Object-Oriented Programming,
   URL: http://www.omg.org/mda/mda_files/Model-Driven_Architecture.pdf
7. Kruchten, P.B., Rational Unified Process, The: An Introduction , Second Edition, Addison-Wesley,2000 http://www.rational.com
8. Cheesman, J. and Daniels, J., UML Components: A Simple Process for Specifying Component-Based Software, Addison-Wesley,2000
9. Atkinson, C., et al., "Component-Based Product Line Engineering with UML", Addison-Wesley, 2001 http://www.iese.fhg.de/KobrA/book/
10. I. Jacobson, G. Booch, and J. Rumbaugh, The Unified Software Development Process, Addison-Wesley, 1999.
11. D. D'sousz and A. Wills, Objects, Components, and Frameworks with UML: The Catalysis Approach, Addison-Wesley, 1998.
12. "Select Perspective," White Paper, Princeton Softech, Jan., 10, 2000,
    http://www.pricetonsoftech.com/index.asp .

A Study on Metrics for Supporting the Software Process Improvement Based on SPICE

Sun-Myung Hwang[1] and Hye-Mee Kim[2]

[1] Department of Computer Engineering Daejeon University, 96-3 Yongun-dong,
Dong-gu, Daejon 300-716, South Korea
sunhwang@dju.ac.kr
[2] Department of Computer Engineering, Jeonju Technical College, 1070 Hyoja-dong 2-ga,
Wansan-gu, Jeonju 560-760, South Korea
hmkim@jtc.ac.kr

Abstract. Software Process Improvement (SPI) is the set of activities with which an organization attempts to reach better performances on product cost, time-to-market and product quality, by improving the software development process. Changes are made to the process based on 'best practices': experiences of other, not necessarily similar organizations. Within SPI methodologies there is a focus on the software development process, because it is based on the as-sumption that an improved development process positively impacts product quality, productivity, product cost and time-to-market. This paper defines stan-dard metrics for quantitative measurement of quality indicators of processes through Software Process Assessment (SPA) based on SPICE. Through accom-plishment of this, we are able to control and to measure SPI activity, and pro-vide for a basis of quantitative S/W process management. The results of our re-search will represent a circulatory architecture for SPI and support of the risk management through the improvement activities and the Process Asset Library with collected and measured data.

1 Introduction

Recently, there are various efforts to improve the quality of software, the development capability, and of the organization through the Software Process Improvement (SPI)[1]. That is, it is realize that fundamental problem of S/W industry is absence of the capability of S/W process management and intend to maximize the quality and productivity of software through the SPI[2][3]. SPI is the set of activities with which an organization attempts to reach better performances on product cost, time-to-market and Process based on 'best practices': experiences of other, not necessarily similar organizations. Within SPI methodologies there is a focus on the software development process, because it is based on the assumption that an improved development process positively impacts product quality, productivity, product cost and time-to-market.

To be able to improve software practices /products, organizations make their implicit knowledge explicit according to models.

W. Dosch, R.Y. Lee, and C. Wu (Eds.): SERA 2004, LNCS 3647, pp. 71–80, 2005.

This information will be useful for planning and projecting future behavior and actions. Process models were created during 1989s to deal with these needs and crystallized in international initiatives like SPICE(ISO/IEC 15504) or CMM. There are some models of SPI/SPA that are: CMM, Canada BNR's Trillium, Europe's Bootstrap, ISO 9000 and SPICE[4,5,9]. But, these models are not describe a concrete assessment procedure and improvement one. ISO/IEC 15504 is the same, which has only the definition of general standards and it's guidance [6,8]. Therefore, it has been met with many problems that for finding the solution of the organization itself that finding the solution of the organization itself that has a plan of S/W process assessment and improvement.

This paper defines standard metrics for quantitative measurement of quality indicators of processes based on SPICE. Through accomplishment of this, we are able to control and to measure SPI activity, and provide for a basis of quantitative S/W prc-ess management.

2 Software Process Improvement Methodologies

The four SPI methodologies that are most referred to in literature are: CMM, ISO 9000-3, SPICE and BOOTSTRAP. Those methodologies will be described in more detail.

2.1 CMM

Based on best practices from industry, the Software Engineering Institute (SEI) devel-oped the Capability Maturity Model (CMM). The model was originally developed to assess the software development process of third party suppliers, of the US Depart-ment of Defence; however, this model also helped those suppliers to improve their software process through an evolutionary path, of five maturity levels <Table1>, from 'ad hoc and chaotic' to 'mature and disciplined' management. As organizations be-come more 'mature', risks are expected to decrease and productivity and quality are expected to increase.

Each CMM maturity level contains a set of Key Process Areas (KPA's) which de-scribe the main capabilities for that level.

2.2 ISO 9000

An other well-known methodology for SPI is the ISO 9000 approach. The assumption behind the ISO 9000 standards is that a well-managed organisation with a defined engineering process is more likely to produce products that consistently meet the purchaser's requirements, within schedule and budget, than a poorly managed organisation that lacks an engineering process. ISO 9001 describes 'Quality systems-model for quality assurance in design/development, production, installation and servicing'.

ISO 9001 is a set of quality system requirement that consistes of twenty clauses that represent requirements for quality assurance in design, development, production, installation and serving, the defines which aspects of a quality system have to be available within an organisation. Details on how these aspects should be implemented and institutionalized are not provided by ISO 9001. As ISO 9001 was added specifically for software-development: 'Guidelines for the application of ISO 9001 to the development, supply and maintenance of software'. ISO 9000-3 provides guidelines for applying ISO 9001 to the specification, development, supply and maintenance of software [ISO 9000-3]. The requirements for ISO 9000-3 certification are divided over twenty requirements classes <Table 2>.

Receiving ISO 9000-3 certification assures customers that in an audited company all its processes and work instructions documented conform the ISO requirements, and that these processes and work instructions are being followed on a continuous basis. ISO certification does not give any guarantee for quality, it only indicates that the procedures are used to a certain extent.

Table 1. The five levels and KPA's of the CMM [4]

Level	Key Process (KPA)
1.Initial The software process is characterized as ad hoc, occasionally or chaotic. Few proc-esses are defined, and success depends on individual effort and heroics	
2. Repeatable Basis project-management processes are established to track cost, schedule and functionality. The necessary process disci-pline is in place to repeat earlier successes on projects with similar applications.	•Requirements management (RM) •Software project planning (SPP) •Software project tracking & oversight (SPTO) •Software subcontract management (SSM) •Software quality assurance (SQA) •Software configuration management (SCM)
3. Defined The software process for both manage-ment and engineering activities is docu-mented, standardized, and integrated into a standard software process for the organisa-tion. All projects use an approved, tailored version of the organization's standard software process for developing and main-taining software.	•Organisation process focus (OPF) •Organisation process definition (OPD) •Training program (TP) •Integrated software management (ISM) •Software product engineering (SPE) •Inter-group co-ordination (IC) •Peer reviews
4. Managed Detailed measurements of the software process and product quality are quantita-tively understood and controlled.	•Quantitative process management (QPM) •Software quality management (SQM)
5. Optimising Continuous process improvement is en-abled by quantitative feedback from the process and from piloting innovative ideas and technologies.	•Defect prevention (DP) •Technology change management (TQM) •Process change management (PCM)

Table 2. ISO 9000-3 Guideline classes [10]

Nr	Guideline Classes
4.1	Management responsibilities
4.2	Quality system requirements
4.3	Contract review requirements
4.4	Product design requirements
4.5	Document and data control
4.6	Purchasing requirements
4.7	Customer-supplied products
4.8	Product identification and tracing
4.9	Process control requirements
4.10	Product inspection and testing
4.11	Control of inspection equipment
4.12	Inspection and test status of products
4.13	Control of non-conforming products
4.14	Corrective and preventive action
4.15	Handling, storage and delivery
4.16	Control of quality records
4.17	Internal quality audit requirements
4.18	Training requirements
4.19	Servicing requirements
4.20	Statistical techniques

2.3 BOOTSTRAP

The BOOTSTRAP method is the result of an European project under the auspices of the European Strategic Programmer for Research in Information Technology (ESPRIT). It provides an alternative for organizations that are interested in improving their software development process and attaining ISO 9001 certification, as it combines and enhances the methods provided by the CMM and the ISO 9000 quality standard.

The basis of the BOOTSTRAP methodology is established by CMM. Like the CMM, an assessment is based on five maturity levels, but the BOOTSTRAP method uses a different scale to measure an organisations' or projects' overall strengths and weaknesses. The ISO 9000 quality standards (ISO 9001 and ISO 9000-3) are incorpo-rated in the methodology because they provide guidelines for a company-wide quality system. The CMM does not include such guidelines. Furthermore, many European companies use ISO 9000 as a primary quality standard. BOOTSTRAP can be used by organizations to determine readiness for ISO 9001 certification.

BOOTSTRAP distinguishes three areas that identify the maturity of an organisation: technology, methodology and organisation. Methodology is sub-divided into a life-cycle dependent, life-cycle independent and process related area, of which the life-cycle independent are is further divided into management, support and customer-supplier. For each are in this BOOTSTRAP tree, a number of 'processes' are defined. Each process has a number of 'key-practices' that need to be addressed for that process. Furthermore, each process has a 'capability dimension', which identifies the current status of that process on a scale from 0 to 5. Unlike the CMM, quartiles between these levels are distinguished, which make it possible to assess on organisation on for example level 2.5, expressing that level 2 is established and that 50% of the level 3 capabilities are in place.

2.4 SPICE

SPICE (Software Process Improvement & Capability determination) is a major inter-national initiative to develop a Standard for Software Process Assessment. ISO 15504 <Fig. 1> is used as z-dimensional architecture for software process capability deter-mination. It is based on other popular approaches, mainly on BOOTSTRAP, CMM and ISO 9001.

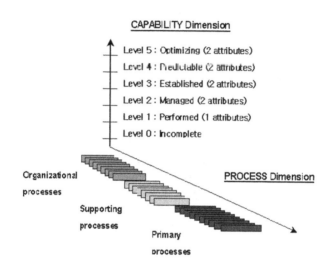

Fig. 1. ISO 15504 Architecture

Changes with respect to the CMM are [7]:

• a broader scope: processes that are indirectly related to the software development processes are also considered
• a different architecture: levels are distinguished in all Key Process Areas, whereas specific Key Process Areas within the CMM are only of importance within a certain level
• an integration of other SPI-models, such as ISO 9000. TicklT and Trillium

3   Design of S/W Process Metric

3.1 Definition of Basic Quality Metric

In order to maximize effect of QMS (Quality Management System), it is needed to support that metrics for quantitative measurement of practice activities. Actually, in order to have level4 or more process level of SPICE or CMM, it should be constituted quantitative process management and measured all practice activities.

We researched and analyzed case studies of metrics that manage a project and s/w process at KOREA SI enterprises.

They have a little difference in terminology. But, if they are classified in semantic side, there are S/W product size, development schedule and cost, MM(Man Month), computer resource, change, risk, defect and so on. Through analyzing for these results, we define basic quality metrics as <Table 3>.

Table 3. Basic quailty metrics

Metrics Name	Formulas
Observation Ratio of planned process	(# of process / planned process) * 100
Observation Ratio of process	(Actual progress / planned progress) * 100
Observation Ratio of planned MM	(# of Actual MM / planned MM) * 100
Observation Ratio of planned budget	(Fulfilled budget/ planned budget) * 100(%)
Productivity per process	Analysis: requirement / Fulfilled MM Design : # of design / Fulfilled MM Implementation : output size (FP/LOC)/ Fulfilled MM Testing : # of test suit/ Fulfilled MM
Observation Ratio of size	(Actual size / planned size) * 100(%)
Observation Ratio of computer resources	(Actual computer resource / esthmated computer resource) * 100(%)
Changed Ratio of Requirements	(# of changed req. / #of planned req.) * 100(%)
Ratio of Risk occurrence	(# of Actual Risk / # of planned req.) * 100(%)
Ratio deleted defect	(# of deleted defect / # of fined defect) * 100(%)

3.2 Definition of Standard Metrics

In this paper, being based on BPs of 40 sub- processes in 5 categories on SPICE, referencing from related metrics that are analyzed through mapping relation of CMM's KPAs with SPICE's processes and above basic metrics, we define standard metrics of SPICE's processes as <Table 4>.

Also, we introduce concrete definition document about standard metric as <Table 5>. The structure items of it are metric name, metric ID(SM-[process name]+[serial number(two-digit serial number)]), criteria of the metric, which is semantic same type with the basic metric, the SPICE process, reporting time of measured metric, lower bound and upper bound of the measured values, which is permissible scope for meaningful them, formulas for the metric, unit of the value, information of measured value, appli-cation guidance of the metric, which is compose with analysis method and explanation of the result.

Table 4. Standard metrics of SPICE's processes

Process			Metrics	Formulas
CUS.1		.2	Ratio of required supply days	(Actual supply days / estimated supply days) *100(%)
			Ratio of Actual required cost	(Actual supply cost / estimated supply cost) *100(%)
		.3	Ratio of Actual Auditing MM for supplier	(Actual Auditing MM / estimated Auditing MM)*100(%)
		.4	Changed Ratio of customer request	(# of Actual changed request / # of customer request)*100(%)
			Evaluating MM of delivered product	(Average evaluation hour)*(# of evaluating man) *(evaluated item)
CUS.2			Observation Ratio of Acceptance criterion	(Satisfied A.C / contracted A.C)*100(%)
CUS.3			Correction Ratio for requirement	(Corrected requirements / acquired requirement)*100(%)
			MM for requirement correction	(Actual MM / estrmated MM)*100(%)
CUS.4		.1	Ratio of operational risk	(# of Actual Risk / # of estimated Risk)*100(%)
			MM for operational testing	(Actual MM / estimated MM)*100(%)
			Handling Ratio of user request	(# of handled function / user requests)*100(%)
ENG.1		.2	System design productivity	# of system design item / MM
			Accord Ratio of sys.reg. analysis	(# of S/W requirement /# of S/W req. in system require)*100(%)
			Correction Ratio of customent reg	# of corrected reg. / # of customer reg.
		.3	S/W requirement analysis productivity	# of S/W R.A / MM
			S/W design productivity	# of S/W design / MM
			Accord Ratio of S/W reg. Analysis	(# of S/Wdesign / # of S/W reg.)*100(%)
		.4	S/W implementation productivity	S/W (product size (FP/LOC) / MM)
		.6	S/W testing productivity	# of S/W test / MM
		.7	Sys testing productivity	# of sys. Testing / MM
ENG.2			implementation productivity for changed Items	(Changed size (FP/LOC) / MM)
			Testing productivity for changed Items	(chnanged Testing Items / MM)
SUP.1			Ratio for documentation	(# of changed doc. / # of estimated doc.)*100(%)
SUP.2			# of changed request	# of changed request record
			Observation Ratio of C.M	(# of Actual QA Review / # of estimated QA Review)*100(%)
			MM Ratio of Actual C.M	(Actual MM for C.M / estimated MM for C.M)*100(%)
			Ratio of Actual Q.A Review	(# of Actual QA Review / # of estimated QA Review) *100(%)

		MM Ratio of Review meeting	Actual MM of QA Review Meeting / estimated MM of QA R.M) *100(%)
SUP.4		Edtermination Actual Ratio for verification results	(# of determination actors for V.R / # of finded total problems in V.R)*100(%)
SUP.5		Observation Ratio for validation results	(# of determination actions for V.R / # of finded total problem in V.R) *100(%)
SUP.6		Observation Ratio for joint Review results	(# of determination actions for J.R / # of finded total problem in J.R) *100(%)
SUP.7		Progress ratio Ratio for Audit process	(Actual Audit progress / estimated Audit progress)*100(%)
SUP.8		Observation Ratio for problem resolution results	(# of determination actions / # of problem resolution) *100(%)

Table 5. Standard Metrics Definition –Example

Metrics Name		Ratio of actual required supply days			
Metric ID	SM-CUS1201	Domain	Schedule	SPICE Process	CUS.1
Reporting Time	Plan - close	Lower bound	N/A	Upper bound	N/A
Formulas	A/B*100			Unit	%
Information of measured value					
A	Actual supply days				
B	Estimated supply days				
Guidance for application					
Analysis Method	(Actual supply days / Estimated supply days)*100(%) - This is measured for actual days to acquire by supplier against estimated supply days. - Whenever it re-estimated, this analysis a trend of increase or decrease.				
Chart	A graph of broken line				
Explanation of the result	- 90 <= result <=110 : suitable estimation - result > 110 : underestimation for the schedule. It is possible for cost to increase, so through re-planning, it is needed demand of changing budget or additional fulfilling of MM - result < 90 : overestimation for the schedule. It is possible for cost to waste, so through re-planning, it is needed demand of changing of superfluous budget or manpower.				

4   Experiment

We analysis the degree of organization's process improvement through the field experiment using proposed process metrics. First, we selected measured values that was obtained through real project and applied on proposed standard metrics and then analyzed the degree of the process improvement using SPICE assessment method. Referencing from the results of first assessment, we consulted to the organization about SPICE assessment process, application guidance of our standard metrics for the process improvement. Since then, through results of the second assessment, we wished to comprehend whether it improve or not and the degree of the effect.

4.1 Background

For the adequacy of proposed metrics, we wished to get the example of real project data that was comprehended all SPICE processes. It is impossible. And so, we referenced with analysis results of real KSPICE(Korea SPICE) assessment[9], which was assessment results of 19 OU's 189 processes : ENG.(89), SUP.(62), MAN.(29) and CUS.(9)

4.2 The Result of First Assessment

It makes the first assessment on the excluded state of our standard metric. That result is SPICE level 1. The process profile is as <Table 6>.

Table 6. Process profile of the first assessment

Process	PA1.1	PA2.1	PA2.2	PA3.1	PA3.2	PA4.1	PA4.2	PA5.1	PA5.2
ENG.1.2	F	F	L	P	N				
ENG.1.3	F	L	L	P	P				
MAN.2	F	L	L	P	N	Not Rated			
SUP.2	F	L	L	P	P				
SUP.3	F	L	L	L	N				

4.3 The Result of Second Assessment

After the 1st assessment, we supplied the education and consulting for understanding of proposed metrics and concepts of SPICE's SPI. About six month later, second assessment was operated in same OU and selected similar project to 1st in application domain and scope. That result is SPICE level 2 except MAN.2 process. The process profile of 2nd assessment is as <Table 7>

Table 7. Process profile of the second assessment

Process	PA1.1	PA2.1	PA2.2	PA3.1	PA3.2	PA4.1	PA4.2	PA5.1	PA5.2
ENG.1.2	F	F	F	L	P				
ENG.1.3	F	F	F	L	P				
MAN.2	F	F	L	P	N	Not Rated			
SUP.2	F	F	F	L	P				
SUP.3	F	F	F	L	P				

For 1st and 2nd assessment, applying our metrics for one of collected project's value, that result shows as <Table 8> at only the ENG.1.2 process.

Through the result of <Table 8>, we could be acquainted with increase of a little process improvement and process capability applying our proposed metrics.

Table 8. Applied results at ENG.1.2(%)

Metrics / Classification	Accord ratio of system analysis	Correction ratio for customer req.	S/W requirement analysis productivity
1st assessment	85.3	71.3	83
2nd assessment	92.3	85.8	89

5 Conclusions

This paper defines standard metrics for quantitative measurement of quality indicators of processes based on SPICE and then we show the effect of process improvement through 1st and 2nd assessment that are applied with real data of the project. For the purpose of obtaining of these result, we researched and analyzed case studies of related metrics that manage a project and S/W processes at Korea SI enterprises and also mapping relations between CMM that has been offered improvement roadmap and already has been applied management metrics in the filed and SPICE. By means of these, we could define a basic quality metrics and standard ones for each process based on SPICE.

The results of our research in this paper will represent a circulatory architecture for SPI and a support of the risk management through the improvement activities and the Process Asset Library with collected and measured data.

References

[1] G .J. Kim, "Internal and external trends of SPI technology", Software Engineering Review, Vol.11, No.3, pp.61-73, 1998. 9
[2] ESI, "SPICE(ISO15504) Training", V.2.0, ESI, 1996
[3] Hwasik Kim, "Beyond ISO9000 : the movement for process improvement of Software", Software Engineering Review, Vol.11, No.3, 1998
[4] M.C Paulk, B. Cutis, and M.B. Chrissis, "Capability Maturity Model for Software", Version 1.1, CMU/SEI-93-TR-24, 1993
[5] Bell Canada, "Trillium-Model for Telecom product Development & Support Process Capa-bility", Internet Edition, Release 3.0, 1994
[6] Part 3 : ISO/IEC TR 15504, "Part 3 : Performing an assessment", ISO/IEC JTC1/SC7 1998
[7] Sassenburg,H., Matser, G., Kazil, P., 'Software Process Improvement: Why and when?' (In Dutch), Informatie, 38, July/August, 1996
[8] Part 7 : ISO/IEC TR 15504. "Part 7 : Guide for use in process improvement", ISO/IEC JTC/SC7 1998
[9] C.Y Yoon, "Relation Analysis of Software Processes using SPICE Level", M.Eng. thesis, Daejeon University, 2003. 2
[10] Part 3 : ISO 9000-3, "Part 3: Quality Management and Quality Standards", ISO 9001 1997

Uniformly Handling Metadata Registries

Dongwon Jeong[1,*], Young-Gab Kim[2], Soo-Hyun Park[3], and Doo-Kwon Baik[2,*]

[1] Dept. of Informatics & Statistics, Kunsan National University,
San 68, Miryong-dong, Gunsan, Jeollabuk-do, 573-701, Korea
djeong@kunsan.ac.kr
[2] Dept. of Computer Science & Engineering, Korea University,
1, 5-ka, Anam-dong, Sungbuk-gu, Seoul, 136-701, Korea
ygkim@software.korea.ac.kr
[3] School of IT Business, Kookmin University,
861-1, Chongnung-dong, Sungbuk-ku, Seoul, 136-702, Korea
shpark21@kookmin.ac.kr

Abstract. This paper proposes a query language to consistently access metadata registries. In current, many metadata registries have been built in various fields. Unfortunately, there is no access method to access the metadata registries in a standard manner. Thus many management systems have been developed in various and different access methods to build and manage their metadata registry. In this paper, we propose a metadata registry query language that allows us to access consistently all metadata registries in a standardized manner. The query language is an extension of the standard query language for the relational databases SQL which is familiar to existing database managers. Consequently, the proposed metadata registry query language reduces the development cost of a metadata registry management system. And it also enables all metadata registries to be accessed in a consistent manner.

1 Introduction

ISO/IEC JTC 1 developed ISO/IEC 11179 to enhance interoperability of databases. The main concept of this standard is the data element which is a set of attributes such as identification, representation, and allowable value of data and is a minimal unit to specify data. A metadata registry is the set of data elements and is one of the key elements of ISO/IEC 11179: [1] [15]

Because of its advantages such interoperability and dynamic metadata management, until now, many metadata registries in various fields have been built to efficiently manage data. The representative examples of the metadata registries are as follows:

- KISTI (Bibliographic metadata registry): [2]
- EPA (Environmental Data Registry): [4], [10]
- NHIK (Australian National Health Information Knowledgebase): [5], [11]
- U.S. ITS (U.S. Intelligent Transportation System): [6], [12]

---

[*] The Corresponding Author.

W. Dosch, R.Y. Lee, and C. Wu (Eds.): SERA 2004, LNCS 3647, pp. 81–91, 2005.
© Springer-Verlag Berlin Heidelberg 2005

The built metadata registries are based on the standard, ISO/IEC 11179. Thus, there are similar access patterns to handle the metadata registries. ISO/IEC 11179 provides no standard metadata registry access method. Until now, no research on the standard access method has been made. It causes several problems such as duplicate developments of the access method, metadata registry access in different manners, etc. Most of all, even though metadata registries are created according to the standard, there is no standard access method to consistently access them.

This paper proposes a metadata registry query languages as the standard access method to solve the issues aforementioned. The metadata query language is an extension of SQL, the international standard query language.

To achieve this goal, we first analyzed and defined query patterns. The metadata registry query language is designed based on the query patterns and extended from SQL: [13], [14]. The query language is the metadata registry query language to access the metadata registries in a standardized manner. Therefore, it reduces time and effort for developing systems. It enables all metadata registries to be accessed consistently, thus we can increase interoperability between metadata registry systems.

2   System Structure for Uniformly Handling MDRs

This section shows a system structure to uniformly handle various metadata registries. The main goal of this paper is to define a SQL-like protocol for realizing interoperability between metadata registries. To do this, we first analyzed query patterns that are used to handle metadata registries. These patterns are defined as metadata registry query operators.

2.1   Overall System Structure

Fig. 1 shows the overall system structure for implementing and supporting the uniform handling method. The system simply consists of three layers. The first layer is UI Manager processing user interfacing. The UI Manager is composed of Result Manager and Query Manger. The Query Manager provides the graphic user interface or text-based interface to users. General users can use the graphic interface and obtain results of their request. Sophisticated users such as database administrator and database designers can use the text-based interface.

The second layer is MDR Query Processor which is the core component of the system. The MDR Query Processor is almost similar to the query processor of the traditional relation database management systems. The MDR Query Processor has an additional function to process the metadata registry query operators. Therefore, as shown in Fig. 1, it consists of Non-MDR query processing module and MDR query processor module. There are two alternatives to realize the MDR Query Processor. The first is to perfectly integrate the metadata registry query operators into the existing query processor. The other alternative is to use the wrapping approach like the Object-relational database model. This choice is better than the first in the implementation view. However, its processing performance is less than the first. This issue is out of bound of this paper scope. So we leave it as a further study.

The final layer includes many metadata registries. The metadata registry query operators in the MDR Query Processor are used as an interface for the various metadata registries.

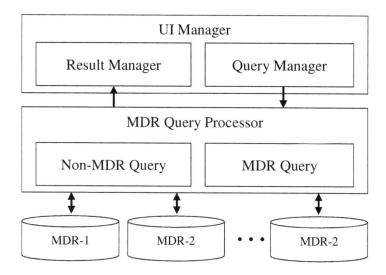

Fig. 1. Overall system structure. The system architecture for the metadata registry query processing is similar to the traditional relational database management system. But this system additionally includes operators and corresponding operations to process the requests to search information of the metadata registries.

2.2 Common Operations for Metadata Registry Querying

The basic operations for managing metadata registry are classified into data element search, grouping element search, data element registration, registration status management, version management of data element, and so on. Metadata registries are managed and extended by these operations.

The data element search is a function to retrieve a proper data element. A data element has many attributes, so we can retrieve proper data elements using the attributes. When we retrieve a data element, we use various search options for exact searching. Therefore, various search operations can be used to find a data element. ISO/IEC 11179 has several logical group elements that can group data elements. It includes data element concept, object class, concept domain, etc. This paper defined them as group elements. The group element search is to retrieve them with a given search condition.

The goal of the data element registration is to extend a metadata registry. In other words, in case that there are no data elements, a new data element can be proposed by users. After confirmation, the proposed data element can be registered into the metadata registry. The proposed data element must be filled in with the mandatory attributes according to ISO/IEC 11179. Hence, Data element registration has many detailed operations.

The registration status management of data elements is an operation to change their standardization level. There are six standardization levels: Submitted, Registered, Qualified, Standard, Preferred standard, and Retired. Therefore, we must provide operations for these access patterns.

There are many access patterns to create and manage the metadata registries. We can define standardized access interfaces for consistent handling the metadata registries through analysis on the operation patterns. This paper showed the basic operations that are required managing the metadata registries.

This paper focuses the search operations. In the metadata registry management systems, the result of searching is mainly a set of data elements. As aforementioned, a data element has many attributes to depict data. Hence, data elements can be retrieved using the values of the attributes. All of the metadata registries are built according to the standard specification, ISO/IEC 11179. Therefore, they have the same mandatory attributes.

As a result, we can define search operation patterns for retrieving proper data elements. In general, most retrieval systems provide additional search options to retrieve exact results. Thus, the search options can be added the search operations.

The analyzed operation patterns of the metadata registry are summarized as follows: Search operation of data elements by the mandatory attributes (Definition, name, context, etc.); Data element search operation by data element's registration status (Submitted, recorded, qualified, standard, preferred standard, and retired); Group element search operations (Data element concept, object class, conceptual domain, etc.); Data element search operations using group elements (This group elements are used as qualifiers to retrieve data elements. The final target of these operations is a set of data elements); Data element search options (Exact matching, partial matching, starting with. These options can be expressed using the original SQL. However, we added these options into the metadata registry operators to be used explicitly).

The group element search operations retrieve data element concepts or object classes. In other hands, the data element search operations using the group elements are to retrieve data elements.

Generally, most operations produce a set of data elements as the result of search because the most important object is the data element in the metadata registries. If anonymous metadata registry is built according to the standard specification, the operations above are available to the management systems managing the metadata registries. In other words, all of the standard-based metadata registries produce correct results of the search operation patterns. If we cannot get a result from a metadata registry using the operations, it means that the metadata registry has no instance or has not been built according to the standard. In case of the latter, the metadata registry must be reconstructed or updated to follow the international standard.

2.3 Metadata Registry Query Operators

This paper first defines several conceptual operators for detailed query operators based on the analysis results. The conceptual operator is named as abstract query operator and includes DE_mandatory_attribute_name(), DE_registration_status(), DE_group_element(), and group_element().

The abstract operators are conceptual operators that generalize concrete query operators. Thus, they can be materialized into concrete query operators. For example, DE_mandatory_attribute_name() is the conceptual operator for concrete query operators that retrieve data elements using their mandatory attributes. Thus, this abstract operator is materialized into concrete query operators such as DE_name(), DE_definition(), DE_context(), and so on. The details of the abstract operators are given in the next section.

These abstract operators are defined to conceptually cluster operations from the analysis of metadata registry access patterns. In other words, they are not actual query operators to be integrated into SQL3. Therefore, they must be detailed and defined as concrete metadata registry query operators. This paper describes it in the next section.

A part of the defined concrete operators is shown in Table 1. Because the MDR operators are extracted and defined based on the query operations provided from the standard specification of ISO/IEC 11179, these operators can be used as the standard query interface for handling metadata registries.

In Table 1, KW means keywords given by users and OPT means search options such as partial matching, exact matching, starting with matching, and so on. RA and DA respectively mean registration attribute and mandatory attributes of data elements such as name, definition, context, etc.

Table 1. Metadata registry query operators. The operators in this table are used for writing queries.

Metadata registry query operators	Descriptions
DE_name(KW, OPT) , DE_definition((KW, OPT) , DE_context(KW, OPT) , . . . , DE_reg_orgnization(KW, OPT)	Operators to search data elements using the attributes that are corresponding to mandatory fields of every data element. KW: Keyword given by an user; OPT: Searching options such as partial matching, exact matching, etc.
DE_status(RA, DA, KW, OPT) , DE_status(RA) , DE_status_submitted(DA, KW, OPT) , . . . ,DE_status_retired(DA, KW, OPT)	Operators to find data elements using the statuses of data elements. RA: Registration attributes; DA: Mandatory attribute of data elements.
DE_object_class(KW, OPT) , DE_conceptual_domain(KW, OPT) , . . . , DE_concept(KW, OPT)	Operators to find data element using the key components such as Object Class, Conceptual Domain, Element Concept, etc.
object_class(KW, OPT) , conceptual_domain(KW, OPT) , . . . , element_concept(KW, OPT)	Operators to search key components. The search target is not a data element set.

3   Metadata Registry Query Language and Evaluation

This section describes a part of the defined metadata registry query language. Then some evaluation results are shown.

3.1 MDR Query Language

Now SQL has been using as a standard query language for relational databases and so it is familiar to many database users. Therefore, existing database users can easily use the metadata registry query language because our approach is to extend and integrated the metadata registry query operators into SQL. The following BNF description shows a partial metadata registry query language.

```
<extended query specification>
::=   SELECT <extended attribute list>
FROM <extended relation list>
WHERE <extended attribute qualification>;
<extended attribute list>
::=   <attribute list>|<MDR attribute list>|<MDR opera-
tor>;
<extended relation list>
::=   [COMMA]<general relation list>|<MDR relation
list>[<extend attribute list>];
<extended attribute qualification>
::=   <general qualification>|<MDR qualification>;
<MDR qualification>
::=   [<boolean term>]<MDR operator>[<extend attribute
qualification>];
<MDR operator>
::=   <DE mandatory attribute name> | <DE registration
status> | DE_STATUS
L_PAREN<MDR param list>R_PAREN;
<DE mandatory attribute name>
::=   NAME | DEFINITION | … | ORGANIZATION;
<DE registration status>
::=   DE_STATUS_SUBMITTED | DE_STATUS_RECORDED
| DE_STATUS_QUALIFIED | DE_STATUS_STANDARD
| DE_STATUS_PREFERRED | DE_STATUS_RETIRED;
<MDR relation list>
::=   DATA_ELEMENT | DATA_ELEMENT_CONCEPT | … |
OBJECT_CLASS;
```

The metadata registry query language is an extension of SQL to provide a consistent access interface for metadata registries. Before extending SQL, we first defined a standardized interface of table names and their attribute names used in metadata registries. The interface means a set of predefined and promised table names and attribute names that can be validly used in all metadata registries according to ISO/IEC 11179. Therefore, the interface allows metadata registry query statements to be simplified.

Most of all, we can verify the built metadata registries are valid or not. In addition, it improves interoperability between metadata registries that have been built independently and remotely.

3.2 Comparative Evaluations

The defined MDR query language allows the standardized and consistent access method for the metadata registries. It is based on the standard query language SQL.

Therefore, most database users are familiar to and utilize it for access metadata registries. The mechanism for sharing and exchanging between metadata registries is simpler than other approaches because of its standardized access method.

The previous metadata registry management systems use different access methods. It causes several problems such as high cost for achieving interoperability, complicated mechanism for exchanging and sharing, and many query statements writing for one request.

Fig. 2 illustrated the processing step of the previous approaches. In Fig. 2, there are two metadata registries, and they have respectively different data schemas for maintaining the same information. In other words, MDR-1 is designed with the following structure: data_element_table includes all of the data elements; de_name is a field name of the table data_element_table; status field is also included in the same table. MDR2 has a different schema structure as follows: table1 holds name and status field, reg_status is in table2. table1 and table use name as join key (Foreign key constraint).

Therefore, the queries reflecting each MDR structure are required to process the given query because the two MDRs have different metadata registry structure and also there is no consistent access interface between them. If the number of metadata registries be N, then the previous approach requires N-query statements. Consequently, the query modeling cost, distributed query process cost, preprocessing cost, and complexity of exchanging mechanism exponentially increase.

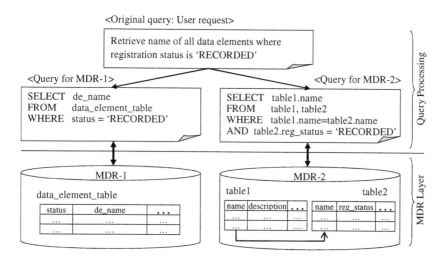

Fig. 2. Query processing steps in the existing approaches

Fig. 3 shows the MDR query language-based approach. In our approach, only one query statement is written to get the response because the defined query language provides the standard interface for accessing metadata registries. It has many advantages in against the previous access methods as follows: Ease to share and exchange metadata; Decrease of development cost; Observance of the standard specification.

In addition, the MDR query language is an extension of SQL, which is the international standard for query language of databases. Most of the database handlers are familiar to SQL. Therefore, it provides high familiarity.

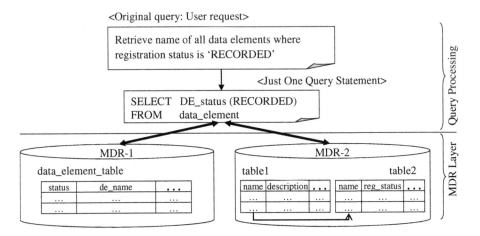

Fig. 3. The metadata registry query language-based approach. In case of our approach, the only one query statement is written to accomplish the request.

In this paper, we show simple simulation results to help users' understanding about the proposed language's advantages intuitively. According to the examples in Fig. 2 and Fig. 3, the calculation model is as follows:

Calculation model $\rho = (N_M, C_M, C_R)$,
  where
    N_M: The number of metadata registries
    C_M: Average cost for query writing according to the given metadata registries
    C_R: Time(cost) to make the final result from several query results obtained from each metadata registry.

For simulation, several factors must be defined. In this simulation model, the number of the metadata registries is the most important factor. Also, the sub-query writing time depend on each metadata registry schema structure. However, in this paper, we assume the writing time is uniform. The time to generate the final result with several sub-query results is one of the key factors. We assume that one temp final result generating time from two sub-query results is uniform.

With the calculation model, we can get the simulation result in Fig. 4. The variable factor is the number of metadata registries and we use a value set {2, 6, 10} for the simulation. The simulation result value is presented by the unit of relative cost value. In this figure, let the results of previous approach and proposed approach are respectively R_{pre} and R_{pro}. The performance ratio between them is R_{pre} and R_{pro} = 1: 1.83.

In the calculation model has some assumptions. For example, we assumed the final result generating time is uniform. Actually, the generating cost of the previous approach is higher than the proposed approach, because the previous approach must match the corresponding fields to the final field. Therefore, the previous approach's generating time is higher. That is, if the generating time of the proposed approach is c, then the generating time of the previous approach is c or more.

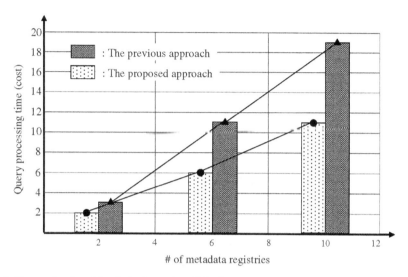

Fig. 4. The evaluation (simulation) results. This figure respectively illustrates the simulation results of the proposed approach and the previous approach. As the query processing time (cost), a relative cost value is used.

4 Conclusion

The international standard ISO/IEC 11179 provides many advantages such as the interoperability of data, dynamic metadata management, standardized metadata management process supporting, etc. Its key components include the data element and the metadata registry which is the set of data elements. Owing to its merits, there are many metadata registries which have been built for various application fields.

The application field contains the environmental information field, bibliographic information field, e-business application, etc. To handle the metadata registries for these application fields, the institutes and organizations has made the management system respectively. However, the management systems provide different metadata registry structures each other in the database level and unique access methods for their registry. The ISO/IEC 11179 standard is the international standard and so the metadata registry structures described in its specifications. It means it is possible the same operations to access them. However, there is no standard method to uniformly handle the metadata registries. It causes the heterogeneity between the access methods of the existing metadata registry management systems. Also, the interoperability between them, i.e., the exchanging and sharing of metadata has difficulties.

The metadata registry is a kind of database instances and it has the standardized structures. This is a clue to resolve the issues. In this paper, we supposed a metadata registry query language to uniformly handle and manage every metadata registry in a standard manner like SQL. The metadata registry query language is an extension of the international standard query language, SQL. To achieve this goal, we analyzed basic operations that are required to access the metadata registries. Then we defined the metadata registry operators based on the analysis result. Finally, these metadata registry query operators were integrated into SQL.

The metadata registry query language proposed in this paper is the SQL-like query language, i.e., an extension of SQL. Thus, exiting database (especially, relational database) users can easily accept and use this metadata registry query language. It can be used as the standard protocol for all metadata registry management systems. It means that the metadata registry query language can be used as a protocol to exchange and share data elements between distributed metadata registries built independently.

The metadata registry query language provides the standard names for essential composing elements that should be defined to create a metadata registry. In other words, we can identify and check whether any metadata registry follows ISO/IEC 11179 specifications or not. Therefore, it encourages all metadata registries to be created following the standard specifications.

In further study, this paper focused on defining only metadata registry query language for searching. Therefore, various query operators for creation, delete, and update should be defined and integrated into the proposed query language. Also, its preference must be shown through experiments considering human factors.

References

1. ISO/IEC JTC 1/SC 32, ISO/IEC 11179: Specification and standardization of data elements Part 1~6. ISO/IEC JTC 1 (2003)
2. Korea Institute of Science and Technology Information, A study on the development of standardization and management model for science and technology information. Research Report (2002)
3. Electronics and Telecommunication Research Institute, Research on the Registration and Search System of Component, Research Report (2000)
4. Environmental Protection Agency, Environmental Data Registry, http://www.epa.gov/edr/. (2004)
5. Australian Institute of Health and Welfare, Australian National Health Information Knowledgebase, http://www.aihw.gov.au/ (2003)
6. U.S. Transportation System, http://www.dot.gov/. U.S. Department of Transportation (2003)
7. Egenhofer, M., Spatial SQL: A query and presentation language. IEEE Transactions on Knowledge and Data Engineering (1994)
8. Pissinou, N., Snodgrass, R., et al., Towards an infrastructure for temporal databases: Report of an invitational arpa/nsf workshop. In SIGMOD Record (1994)
9. ISO/IEC JTC 1/SC 32, ISO/IEC 13249: Information technology - Database languages - SQL Multimedia and Application Packages, ISO/IEC JTC 1 (2003)
10. Environmental Protection Agency, Data Standards Publications and Guidances (2003)

11. Australian National Health Data Committee, National Health Data Dictionary (2003)
12. ITS Architecture Development Team, ITS Logical Architecture- Volume I, Volume II: Process Specifications. Volume III: Data Dictionary (2003)
13. ISO/IEC JTC 1/SC 32, ISO/IEC 9075: Database Language SQL3 Part 1~10. ISO/IEC JTC 1 (1999)
14. Lee, J.-Y., Integrating Spatial and Temporal Relationship Operators into SQL3 for Historical Data Management. Journal of Electronics and Telecommunication Research Institute, Vol. 24, No. 3. Electronics and Tele-communications Research Institute (2002) 226-238
15. Jeong, D., Park, S.-Y., Baik, D.-K, A Practical Approach: Localization-based Global Metadata Registry for Progressive Data Integration. Journal of Information & Knowledge Management, Vol. 2, No. 4. World Scientific (2003) 391-402

Network Layer XML Routing Using Lazy DFA

Jie Dai, Kexiao Liao, and Gongzhu Hu

Department of Computer Science,
Central Michigan University,
Mount Pleasant, MI 48859, USA
{dai1j, liao1k, hu1g}@cmich.edu

Abstract. XML routers are devices that deliver the requested data from XML data streams to the destinations. Several XML stream process methodologies have been proposed and developed in recent years, but there are still many issues on XML routing at the network layer remain to be studied. In this paper we present a design of such a XML router at the network layer. An implementation of a prototype of the XML Router is also described that uses lazy Deterministic Finite Automata (DFA) to process XML streams from the network in real time. Preliminary experiments showed that our XML router has the potential of delivering requested data efficiently both in time and space.

1   Introduction

A new class of data-intensive applications has become widely recognized in recent years: applications in which the data is modeled best not as persistent relations but rather as transient data streams [4]. In the data stream model, individual data items arrive continuously in multiple, rapid, time-varying, possibly unpredictable and unbounded streams. It is not feasible to simply load the arriving data into a traditional database management system (DBMS) and operate on it there. Traditional DBMS's are not designed for rapid and continuous loading of individual data items, and they do not directly support the continuous queries [14] that are typical for data stream applications. New Data streams differ from the conventional stored relation model in several ways:

- The data elements in the stream arrive online.
- The system has no control over the order in which data elements arrive to be processed.
- Data streams are potentially unbounded in size.
- Once an element from a data stream has been processed, it is discarded or archived - it cannot be retrieved easily unless it is explicitly stored in memory, which typically is small relative to the size of the data streams.

Queries over continuous data streams have much in common with queries in a traditional database management system. However, there are several important distinctions peculiar to the XML data stream model. One important distinction is between one-time queries and continuous queries. One-time queries (including

W. Dosch, R.Y. Lee, and C. Wu (Eds.): SERA 2004, LNCS 3647, pp. 92–107, 2005.

traditional DBMS queries) are queries that are evaluated once over a point-in-time snapshot of the data set, with the answer returned to the user. Continuous queries, on the other hand, are evaluated continuously as data streams continue to arrive. Answers to a continuous query may be stored and updated as new data arrives, or they may be produced as data streams themselves.

Research has been conducted and reported in the literature on stream processing and XML routing. Most XML routers use Deterministic Finite Automata (DFA), which is the most efficient means to process XPath expressions. But DFAs were considered impossible to use when the number of XPath expressions is large, because the size of the DFA in the memory grows exponentially with that number, if all the states in the DFA are constructed before processing the XML stream (called eager DFA) [11]. On the contrary, lazy DFA is constructed on demand at run-time, starting with a single initial state. It was approved that with lazy DFA there is an upper bound on their size that is independent of the number and shape of XPath expressions [10]. This upper bound only depends on certain characteristics of the XML stream, such as the data guide [9] or the graph schema [1], [5], they are usually small in many applications.

The XML Toolkit (XMLTK) [3] developed by a research team at the University of Washington is a toolkit for highly scalable XML data processing. It employs the lazy DFA approach and their experiments showed the performance of lazy DFA achieving constant throughput independent of the number of XPath expressions. All the tools and libraries provided in XMLTK, however, only support processing XML data from the local file.

In order to accomplish XML router functionalities, we have designed an XML router that extends the current XMLTK and makes it capable to handle the data from the network on the fly in real time. The distinctive features of our XML router include:

- A pipeline method to process the XML packets to speed up the overall processing time.
- Sending the XML packets to registered XML routers in parallel at the end of the pipeline. This function guarantees that the subscribed XML data can be delivered to their destinations without waiting for other XML routers to finish their job.

We tested the preliminary prototype of our router on XML data streams of about 140 MB in size. The experiments showed that the routing system correctly filtered the desired information extracted from the XML stream and delivered. It also showed that the memory usage for each router is very minimal (less than 2% of total memory available), indicating that the use of lazy DFA is very feasible for processing XPath queries to avoid exponential growth of the DFA states.

2   Related Work

There are several methods used to process XML streams. They may process large numbers of XPath expressions (e.g. 10,000 to 1,000,000) on continuous

XML streams at network speed [10]. In this section we briefly describe four of these methods that are well known in this research area.

2.1 Content-Based XML Routing

Alex Snoeren and his colleagues at MIT proposed the content-based XML routing [13], which is an approach for reliably multicasting time-critical data to heterogeneous clients over mesh-based overlay networks. The data streams are comprised of a sequence of XML packets (application packets above TCP/IP level) and forwarded by application-level XML routers. XML routers perform content-based routing of individual XML packets to other routers or clients based upon queries that describe the information needs of down-stream nodes. Their routers use the Diversity Control Protocol (DCP) for router-to-router and router-to-client communication. DCP reassembles a received stream of packets from one or more senders using the first copy of a packet to arrive from any sender. When each node is connected to n parents, the resulting network is resilient to (n-1) router or independent link failures without repair. Associated mesh algorithms permit the system to recover to (n-1) resilience after node and/or link failure. They had deployed a distributed network of XML routers that streams real-time air traffic control data. Their experimental results show multiple sender improve reliability and latency when compared to tree-based networks.

2.2 Selective Dissemination of Information (SDI)

M. Altinel & M. Franklin [2] developed several index organizations and search algorithms for performing efficient filtering of XML documents for large-scale information dissemination systems. The applications involve timely distribution of data to a large set of customers; they include stock and sports tickers, traffic information systems, electronic personalized newspapers, and entertainment delivery. The execution model for these applications is based on continuously collecting new data items from underlying data sources, filtering them against user profiles (i.e., user interests) and finally, delivering relevant data to interested users. In order to effectively target the right information to the right people, SDI systems rely upon user profiles. They developed a document filtering system, named XFilter, that provides highly efficient matching of XML documents to large numbers of user profiles. In XFilter, user interests are represented as queries using the XPath language [7]. The XFilter engine uses a sophisticated index structure and a modified Finite State Machine (FSM) approach to quickly locate and examine relevant profiles.

2.3 Continuous Queries

In this approach, J. Chen, D. DeWitt use NiagaraCQ systems [6] to handle millions of continuous queries over the Internet. NiagaraCQ addresses the scalability of such continuous queries by grouping continuous queries based on the observation that many web queries share similar structures. Grouped queries can share the common computation, tend to fit in memory and can reduce the I/O cost significantly. Furthermore, grouping on selection predicates can eliminate a large number of unnecessary query invocations. Their grouping technique is distinguished from previous group optimization approaches in the following ways. First, they use an incremental group optimization strategy with dynamic re-grouping. New queries are added to existing query groups, without having to regroup already installed queries. Second, they use a query-split scheme that requires minimal changes to general-purpose query engine. Third, NiagaraCQ groups both change-based and timer-based queries in a uniform way. To ensure that NiagaraCQ is scalable, they have also employed other techniques including incremental evaluation of continuous queries, use of both pull and push models for detecting heterogeneous data source changes, and memory caching.

2.4   Processing of Scientific Data in Large XML Files

Recent technical advances in molecular biology have allowed the generation of an enormous volume of data, which cannot be dealt with by traditional printed publications [12]. A form of electronic data publishing has been developed to make data available in a world-wide network-accessible database, while methods and conclusions continue to be published in traditional publications. Databases such as GenBank and EMBL data library serve as repositories for DNA sequence data, the first and largest component of the database is the corpus of research papers that are stored as markup text using the Standard Generalized Markup Language. Storing the text in markup form permits the system to display the paper as it would be seen in published form. This is especially important in biology where typesetting details (such as font changes) convey semantic information. The other main component of the database is the biological knowledge base. This consists of a schema, a lexicon and annotations of papers.

Although the above methods can process large numbers of XPath expressions on continuous XML streams at network speed, all of them face the same memory usage problem when the XPath expression become more and more complex.

2.5   XML Toolkit

XMLTK, a toolkit for highly scalable XML data processing, is developed by a research team at University of Washington [3]. The toolkit has two components. The first is a collection of stand-alone tools that perform simple XML transformations (sorting, aggregation, nesting, un-nesting, etc.). The second is a highly scalable XPath processor for XML streams. There are two important technical contributions in the toolkit: a highly scalable XML stream processor, and an XML stream index. The XML stream processor achieves a sustained throughput of about 5.6MB/s and scales up to large numbers of XPath expressions (up to 1,000,000 in the experiments). The processor transforms all XPath expressions into a single deterministic automaton. It was proved theoretically in [10] that the number of states in the automaton remains relatively small. As a common library for these commands, XML Toolkit has implemented two novel technologies to realize a high-throughput XML data processing:

- Lazy DFA (deterministic finite automaton that is constructed at run-time) based on XPath processor.
- SIX (streaming index for XML data) for XML parser.

Te XML Toolkit is comprised from two fundamental libraries (XML TSAX parser and XPath processor) and a collection of simple XML processing commands built upon those libraries.

3   Lazy DFA

We briefly describe Lazy DFA in this section for this paper to be self-contained. Lazy DFA was proposed in [10] and used in the XML Toolkit for processing XML queries. A collection of XPath expression queries can be converted into a query tree, for which a deterministic finite automaton (DFA) can be built.

A query tree may contain a large number of XPath expressions that can be converted into a non-deterministic finite automaton (NFA) that is then converted to a deterministic finite automaton (DFA). The basic techniques of the conversions can be found in many textbooks. One of the issues that is important to XML routing is the size of the DFA that is constructed, meaning the number of states in the DFA. If the DFA is built based on the query tree Q, the number of states in the DFA A_d is propotional to the size of Q.

If the DFA is constrcuted from the query tree in advance, it is called an *eager DFA* that in general has a large number of states when the number of XPath expressions in the query tree is large, and hance requires large amount of memory that may not be feasible. To overcome this problem, *lazy DFA* was introduced [10] that is constructed at run time, on demand. It starts with a single initial state. Whenever a transition is to be made into a missing state, the state is computed and added to the DFA, hoping that only a small portion of the DFA is ever needed to be built.

4   System Design

The goal of our work is to extend XML Toolkit with two basic routing functionalities: network interfacing and XML package forwarding. These functionalities are provided through a group of components which can be easily used by XML-based application developers to flexibly construct their own filters or routers and integrate them into their applications. With the components, developers can add and delete XPath queries, process data streams from multiple destinations. We use the the XPath processing libraries in the XMLTK to process XML stream from the network against user predefined continous queries. Fig. 1 shows the overall architecture of the XML routing system.

The system consists of seven components: *Input, Pipe In, XPath Prosessor, Pipe Out, Output, Filter* and *Query Manager*. The XML data flows like this:

XML packets from network are received by the *Input* and transferred to the *XPath Processor* through the *Pipe In*. After being processed by the *XPath Processor*, the matched data are directed to proper destinations (local or network applicaitons) through the *Pipe out* and the *Output*. The *Pipe In, XPath Processor* and *Pipe Out* are closely related and managed by a component, called *Filter*, to process XML data stream from a single data source. The *Query Manager* manages user's queries, such as adding to and removing the queries from the system. In a *Filter*, the association between *XPath Processor* and the *Pipe*

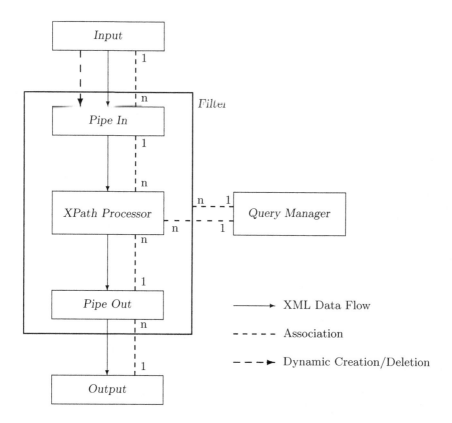

Fig. 1. Architecture of the XML Router.

In or the *Pipe Out* is n-to-1, meaning that each *Filter* may link more than one *XPath Processor* with a *Pipe In* and a *Pipe Out*. Multiple *XPath Processors* allow the *Filter* to process XML data stream against multiple XPath queries in parallel. The number of *XPath Processors* in one *Filter* is determined by the number of queries made for a single application data stream through *Query Manager*. In a router, the association between *Input* and *Filter* is 1-to-n, and so is between *Output* and *Filter*. This allows developers to flexibly construct an XML router that can handle data streams from more than one application, and forward searched results to multiple destinations. Only one *Query Manager* is needed. It maintains all queries made by a user. Its association with *Filter* is 1-to-n, as queries may be for different applicaiton data streams. At the present time, the *Query Manager* and *Output* have not been fully implemented. We used Unix pipe is out implementation.

4.1   Input

The *Input* component receives XML data streams in the form of UDP packets through sockets. Each UDP packet contains one XML packet, which is a fragment (1024 bytes) of an XML document. The 1024-byte size is an empirical value for the best transmission effect with UDP. Therefore, a data stream received by *Input* from a single application is comprised of a sequence of XML packets of sequentially sent XML documents from that applicaiton. When the *Input* receives packets from multiple applications, the data stream received is an interlaced XML packets sent from distinct applicaitons. The *Input* is able to distinguish which XML packet is from which applicaiton because each applicaiton associates a port number to each UDP packet that contains an XML packet. This association is applied by the applicaiton before transmitting the UDP packet and is taken care of by the socket communicaiton libraries provided by an operating system. The port number used by a data source to send its XML data becomes the data source identifer in our system.

The *Input* uses distinct *Filters* to separate the handling of different applicaiton data streams. After the *Input* has identified an XML packet from an applicaiton, it sends the packet to *Pipe In* of the corresponding *Filter*. If a packet was from a new applicaiton, a *Filter* is dynamically created by the *Input* before the packet can be transferred. The *Filter* then creats a *Pipe In*, a *Pipe Out* and a number of *XPath Processors* to process the received XML packet. In order to remember which applicaiton is tied to which *Filter* and send packets to the correct *Pipe In*, the *Input* maintains a table, called Input Table, shown below, to store the needed information. Each record in the table contains three field: the corresponding port number used by an applicaiton, the identifier of the *Filter* used to process the XML data, and the identifier of the *Pipe In* in the *Filter*. By checking the table, *Input* can easily find out whether an applicaiton has already registered, and where to send a packet to process. When an applicaiton has stopped communicating with the *Input*, the tied *Filter* is deleted and the corresponding record is removed from the Input Table.

Port Number	Filter ID	Pipe In ID
5204	F1	P1
...	...	...

4.2 Filter

The *Filter* component manages a *Pipe In*, one or more *XPath Processors*, and a *Pipe Out* for processing XML data stream from a single application. It performs the following tasks:

(1) Create a *Pipe In* object and a *Pipe Out* object when it is invoked by *Input*.
(2) Create one or more *XPath Processors* based on the number of predefined continuous queries made throught the *Query Manager*.
(3) Control the distribution of XML packets from *Pipe In* to the corresponding *XPath Processor*.

It is trivial to do the job (1). For the job (2), the *Filter* needs to consult a table maintained by the *Query Manager* in order to know how many *XPath Processors* need to be created. If related queries have been found in the table, the corresponding *XPath Processors* are created. Otherwise it sends a signal to the *Input* informing it to forward a packet to a default *Filter*. This default *Filter* does not contain any *XPath Processors* but a *Pipe In* and a *Pipe Out*. It is designed for forwarding any XML packets that are not specified to be checked by a router. This provides the flexibility to distribute disjoint filtering jobs to separate routers abd cascade them if needed.

While creating the *XPath Processors*, the *Filter* establishes a table, called Filter Table, which contains information about all *XPath Processors* created. Each record in the table contains a Processor ID, the associated XPath query string, and the status. The first two fields are copied from the table maintained by the *Query Manager*. The Status field indicates if the processor is doing pattern matching for a packet or for accepting a new packet, initally set to be `Free` when created. In the *Filter*, the *Pipe In* broadcasts an XML packet to all tied *XPath*

XPath Processor ID	Xpath Query String	Status
P1	....	Busy
....	....	Free

Processors. Different *XPath Processors*, however, may need different amount of time to check the same packet, we need a control to disallow the *Pipe In* to emit an XML packet until all the *XPath Processors* are free. The *Filter* achieves this by checking the Filter Table. If the status of all processors is `Free`, it sends a 'ready' signal to the *Pipe In* to let it emit a packet. It is required that each *XPath Processor* send the *Filter* a 'busy' signal when it has received an XML packet for processing and a 'ready' signal when it is done with the packet. When the *Filter* has received these signals, it sets or resets the Status field. Although the speed of a pipe may slows down a bit for synchronization, it is still much faster than sending a packet to different processors sequentially.

4.3   Pipe In

The *Pipe In* component implements a buffer used to store XML packets temporarily as they flow from *Input* to *XPath Processor*. There are three major reasons why we need it: (1) To separate data stream from different applications before they reach the processor. (2) To match the speed between the *Input* and the *XPath Processor*. (3) To speed up operations by storing received XML packet in memory rather than a file. The size of the *Pipe In* buffer has to be adequate - overflowed packets will be discarded, and this may cause problem for the linked *XPath Processor*.

Pipe In holds an XML packet from being emitted until it has received a 'ready' signal from the filter. It emits the packet to all tied processors found in the Filter Table, and sets their Status to `Busy`.

4.4   XPath Processor

This component receives XML packets from *Pipe In* and invokes the lazy DFA XML stream processing function in the XML Toolkit to analyze them. If a match is found in the packet, it will create an XML packet containing the result enclosed by two tags: `<QueryString>` and `<ApplicationID>`, to clearly identified for which application and for which user's query this result is for, as shown below. The processor then forwards the packet to *Pipe Out*. If no match is found, the packet is discarded.

```
<ApplicationID>
    <QueryString>
    <Result>

    ....
    </Result>
    </QueryString>
</ApplicationID>
```

Since the lazy DFA model requires that the XML stream be complete XML documents but in practice the first XML packet received by a *XPath Processor* may be in the middle of an XML codument, the processor will not invoke the DFA until it has detected the beginning of an XML document. All packets received before the beginning packet are discarded and all packets received after the beginning packet will be transferred to the DFA. Once the first XML document has been processed, the *XPath Processor* may continue to send the subsequent XML documents to the same DFA.

As mentioned before, the *XPath Processor* needs to generate a 'ready' signal to the *Filter* in order to get the next packet. It won't be able to get one immediately becaue it has to wait for the *Filter* to receive 'ready' signals from all other linked *XPath Processors*. This gives rise to a speed matching problem between the lazy DFA and *XPath Processor*. Fortunately, the lazy DFA functions can tolerate non-continuous XML stream by itself as long as the packets have not been damaged during network transmission, i.e. no illegal characters appear in the received packet.

4.5   Query Manager

The *Query Manager* component is used to add continuous queries into the system and delete them from the system. Each query must be made with a single XPath expression. Two methods are used in *Query Manager: addQuery* and *removeQuery*. It also maintains a table, called Query Table, containing information about all queries for the applications. Each record in the table has these fields: a Query String field that stores the XPath expression qury string provided by the user, a Data Source ID that may be the port number used by a sending applicaiton to communicate with the system, and N (say, 3) Destination IDs that may be port numbers used by the destination applications to receive matched results. The first two fields are used by the *Filter* to create *XPath Processors* and generate XML packets for the searched results. Multiple destination fields help the *Output* component to send a result to multiple destinations (limited to 3, in this case) specified by the user. The table looks like this:

Query String	Port No (Source)	Port No (Destination 1)	Port No (Destination 2)	Port No (Destination 3)
....	....	....	....	....

4.6   Pipe Out

This component implements a buffer used to temporarily store XML packets of searched results from multiple *XPath Processors* in a *Filter*. Because each packet has a `<QueryString>` header, it would be easy to distinguish which result is for which query. The *Pipe Out* component also synchronizes the speed between the *XPath Processor* and *Output* components. Again, the buffer used in *Pipe Out* should be adequate.

4.7   Output

The *Output* component sends matched XML data to one or more specified destination applicaitons in the form of UDP packets through sockets. Each UDP packet contains a search result in XML packet of up to 1024 bytes. Although these packets are from all *Filters* against various queries, the component can separate them using the `<QueryString>` and the `<ApplicaitonID>` tags in the result. After receiving this information from a packet, the *Output* object looks up the Query Table to find out where to send it. As we use socket for communicaiton, the destination applications may be local or remote.

5   Implementation

We have implemented a preliminary prototype of the XML router, mainly focused on the netwoking aspects of the components. In terms of network traffic for incoming XML stream, the combination of the *Input* and the *Pipe In* components can be viewed as a network interface. They use UDP/IP data transfer protocol to send XML packet stream from one machine to another. A 'server' program simulates the generation of XML stream that reads from a 140MB XML file and sends the data as a stream of 1024-bytes packets through Unix pipe to 'clients' upon receiving requests from the clients. The clients communicate with the server using socket and the communicaiton is synchronized as mentioned before. The *Pipe Out* and *Output* components can be implemented in a similar way. The *XPath Processor* is implemented in C++ that uses lazy DFA. The *Qury Manager* has not been fully implemented at present time.

5.1   Network Interface

The network interface represents the *Input* and *Pipe In* components and is implemented as a client-server architecture. The server program pre-forks multiple processes listening to the same port for incoming clients' requests. Each request is handled by a server process. Each client keeps track of the status of its conversation with the server. Client should also be able to resume an interrupted transfer at the point it was interrupted. The client implements the following operations:

(1) `int rropen(char *path)` – network transaction
(2) `int rclose(int filedes)` – non network transaction
(3) `int rread(int filedes, char *buffer, int nbytes)` – network transaction.
(4) `long rlseek(int filedes, long offset)` – non network transaction.
(5) `int initrcon(char *srvaddr, char *srvport)` – initializes server conversation information.
(6) `void initfiletbl()` – initialize the file table.

A data structure will be needed on client side to keep of the state of a file – a simple table (30 entries) with each entry of the format (path, read, offset). Index of the entry can be used as a file-descriptor.

Client will get file data from a server that provides UDP data transfer service. After the client gets the reply from the server, it takes the reply apartly (`bytesread` and `data`), checks if there is an error (indicated by `bytesread` being -1). If no error, it writes the data into the local file. It also checks if the number of bytes read is less than a predefined maximum transmission unit (MTU), which is the maximum packet size, in bytes, that can be tranmitted across a link. During the exchanging data with the UDP server, the client will retry the request if no reply is forthcoming from server. After no response from server for three times, client will sleep and retry the server. If no response is seen after two sleep intervals, client will declare server problem, clean up the partial transfer and terminate.

5.2 XPath Processor

Since the continuous query can be added dynamically at run-time, a special tag is nedded just before the beginning of eaxh XML document. By adding such tag, it will let *XPath Processor* know where is boundaies of XML documents in an stream. Once the *XPath Processor* detects the beginning tag, it will forward subsequent XML packets to the DFA, otherwise the XML stream will be discarded until the beginning tag is encountered. The XML stream is transferred through the pipe to multiple *XPath processors*, each of which corresponds to one application process.

The *XPath Processor* is implemented in C++ and based on XML Toolkit with some modifications to meet our situations. The class `myHandler` is used to build a lazy DFA to register XPath expressions in the DFA and to define our own XML events handlers, opens log file and gets ready for the incoming XML packets.

In our implementation, multiple UDP/IP links are added to the Linux server. These links can be added on the fly during the run-time. This mechanism can be used to add continuous queries dynamically without affecting previous ones. However, it has the side effects of increasing the network traffic, the best way to add the queries is to fork additional processes using `popen` at the end of the pipe from the network interface, as shown in Fig. 2, where `run_dblp`, `run_nasa`, and `sx_run` are specific applicaitons.

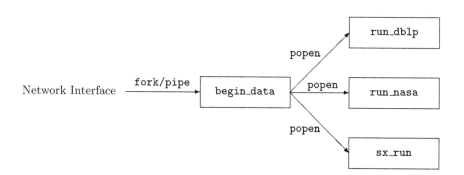

Fig. 2. Multiple forked processes for different applicaitons

Fig. 2 illustrates that multiple processes/threads are forked according the number of the user-defined continuous queries. Each query is a standalone dynamical class file that can be invoked at run-time. After all the processes/threads are generated, each packet of the XML stream is delivered to these continuous queries simultaneously with the same priority. Each continuous query corresponds to a DFA generated by query tree/query condition. Any query tree may contain tens or hundreds of thousands of XPath expressions on the XML stream. The processor converts the entire query tree into one single nondeterministic finite automaton (NFA) and then builds the corresponding deterministic finite automaton (DFA). After the DFA has been constructed, the processor simply keeps a pointer to the current state. On the `startElement` event, the processor looks up the next current state in the DFA, and pushes the old state on a stack. On an `endElement` event, the processor pops a state from the stack. Terminal states in the DFA have an associated set of variables. Whenever such state is reached, a variable match event is generated for each variable in the set. The stack gets only as deep as the maximum depth of the XML document. Since we use lazy DFA to handle the query expressions, the DFA is constructed on the fly as the XML stream packets arrive so that the number of states that ever need to be expanded is very small. Once the DFA detects the XML stream which matches the pre-defined query condition, it will save the corresponding XML stream data into a log file, these matched XML streams can also be delivered to other XML Routers for further processing. In our experiments, we just append the XML stream data into a text log file.

5.3   Query Manager

The *Query Manager* is used to add new continuous query into the system dynamically without affecting previously registered continuous queries. As discussed in the System Design section, the *Query Manager* maintains a Query Table to keep track of the users' queries from the network. Two methods that are used in the *Query Manager* are `addQuery` and `removeQuery`. The `addQuery` method adds a new continuous query to the system for processing. The `removeQuery` method removes a previously existing query from the system and stops the process against that query.

6   Experimental Benchmark Test

We have run some tests in our experiments to demonstrate the working of the XML router. Our execution environment consists of Intel Pentium based PCs running Red Hat Linux 8.0 3.2-7. The compiler is gcc version 3.2 without any optimization options.

Two benchmark XML datasets were used in our experiments. One is the NASA XML dataset [15] and the other is the DBLP Computer Science Bibliography [8] XML dataset. They are about 140 MB in size. We concatenated these two XML documents in arbitrary sequence, with the `<BeginData/>` flag inserted between the two XML documents. We tested the XML router against several queries that were registered with the Query Manager. For example, for the query that finds the references with a given reference-id

```
//reference[@referenceId='rrf19']/*
```

Fig. 3 shows the results as soon as the data in the XML stream matching the query is discovered.

The test result shows that when slowing down the reading process from one end of pipe, the writing process at another end of pipe will automatically

Fig. 3. Query process example

synchronize with the speed of reading process, so it is not possible to lose any data when using pipe in our test case. However, in our experiment, the speed for sending XML Stream from server side to client side is also controlled by the pipe, in our case only after writing current packet to the pipe successfully, then it is allowed to read new packet from the UDP socket. This means that server will wait and not send new packet to the client until client has finished processing the received packets. If the pipe itself is slowing down during the process, the transmission speed from server side to slient side is adjusted to a slow pace.

Fig. 4 is a shapshot of a monitor that shows the CMU time spent for the processes on the Linux system, including the running processes **server** and **sx_run** that had run 44 and 45 seconds respectively when the snapshot was taken a little after the result in Fig. 3 was produced. Since the pipe reads and

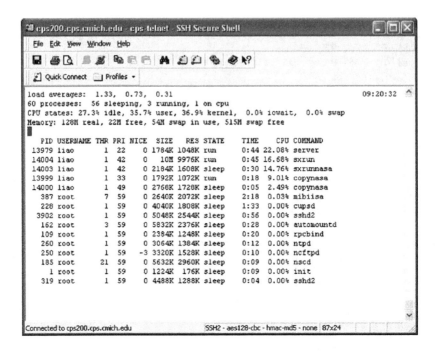

Fig. 4. Snapshot of CPU time spent on processes

writes the XML data through the memory directly without any disk I/O, the
processing speed of our router should be similar to that in [10].

Our experiment also shows that each of the **run_nasa** and **sx_run** processes
will consume a small amount of memory. The amount of memory used increases
during warm-up phase when most of the states in the lazy DFA are constructed.
The length of the warm-up phase depends on the size of the final lazy DFA
generated for the XML data. After the warm-up phase, the memory consumption
becomes stable to about 1.4 % total memory space in our experiment. The
memory space is released upon the completion of processing the query.

7   Summary and Discussion

We have presented a prototype of XML router for XML stream filtering and
delivering over the network. The main contribution of this paper is a design of
XML router that provides two basic routing functionalities: network interfacing
and XML package forwarding. It extends the current XMLTK functions so that
it can process arbitrary XML stream data from the network against user's predefined XPath queries. Our experiments show that the XML router does preform
the routing tasks correctly and is quite space efficient due to the uas of lazy
DFA. The time efficiency seems very good but we haven't done a comparitive
study.

Our implementation of the XML router is only preliminary. We have focused on the network interfacing between the XML stream source and the routing processor. We are currently working on the implementaiton of the other components in the design, particularly the *Filter* and the *Query Manager*. In additon, thorough performance analysis is to be done to determine if the router is feasible for real world applications.

References

1. S. Abiteboul, P. Buneman, and D. Suciu: Data on the Web: From Relations to Semi-structured Data and XML. Morgan Kaufmann, 1999.
2. M. Altinel and M. Franklin: Efficient filtering of XML documents for selective dissemination. In Proceedings of VLDB, pp.53-64, Cairo, Egypt, September 2000.
3. Iliana Avila-Campillo, Todd J. Green, Ashish Gupta, Mokoto Onizuka, Demina Raven, Dan Suciu: XMLTK: An XML Toolkit for Scalable XML Stream Processing, In proceedings of PLANX, October 2002.
4. Brian Babcock, Shivnath Babu, Mayur Datar, Rajeev Motwani, Jennifer Widom: Models and Issues in Data Stream Systems, Proceedings of 21st ACM Symposium on Principles of Database Systems (PODS 2002).
5. P. Buneman, S. Davidson, M. Fernandez, and D. Suciu: Adding structure to unstructured data. In Proceedings of the International Conference on Database Theory, pages 336-350, Deplhi, Greece, 1997. Springer Verlag.
6. J. Chen, D. DeWitt, F, Tian, and Y. Wang: NiagaraCQ: a scalable continuous query system for internet databases. In Proceedings of the ACM/SIGMOD Conference on Management of Data, pp. 379-390, 2002.
7. J. Clark and S. DeRose: XML Path Language (XPath) Version 1.0, W3C Recommendation. Technical Report REC-xpath-19991116, World Wide Web Consortium, November 1999.
8. DBLP Computer Science Bibliography http://dblp.uni-trier.de/xml/
9. R. Goldman and J. Widom: DataGuides: enabling query formulation and optimization in semi-structured databases. In Proceedings of Very Large Data Bases, pp. 436-445, September 1997.
10. Todd J. Green, Gerone Miklau, Makoto Onizuka, and Dan Suciu: Processing XML Streams with Deterministic Automata, In proceeding of ICDT, 2003.
11. Ashish Kumar Gupta, Dan Suciu: Stream Processing of XPath Queries with Predicates, In Proceeding of ACM SIGMOD Conference on Management of Data, 2003.
12. Processing molecular biology scientific data, European Molecular Biology Laboratory (EMBL). http://www.ccs.neu.edu/home/kenb/sdb/support/section3_2.html.
13. Alex C. Snoeren, Kenneth Conley, and David K. Gifford: Mesh-Based Content Routing using XML, 18th ACM Symposium on Operating System Principles, Banff, Canada, October 2001.
14. D. Terry, D. Goldberg, D. Nichols, and B. Oki: Continuous queries over append-only databases. In Proc. of the 1992 ACM SIGMOD Intl. Conf. on Management of Data, pp. 321-330, June 1992.
15. UW XML Repository http://www.cs.washington.edu/research/xmldatasets

Extending UML for a Context-Based Navigation Modeling Framework of Web Information Systems [*]

Jeewon Hong[1], Byungjeong Lee[1,**], Heechern Kim[2], and Chisu Wu[3]

[1] School of Computer Science, University of Seoul, Seoul, Korea
{jwhong, bjlee}@venus.uos.ac.kr
[2] Dept. of Computer Science, Korea National Open University, Seoul, Korea
hckim@knou.ac.kr
[3] School of Computer Science and Engineering, Seoul National University,
Seoul, Korea
wuchisu@selab.snu.ac.k

Abstract. Web information systems are rapidly increasing and the structure of the systems becomes more complex. When users, however, navigate such complex Web systems, they cannot often grasp the current location and get the information that they want. Therefore, a systematic approach to model the navigation of Web information systems is needed that helps users get information, purchase products, and deal with complexity. If the systems provide the information of their navigation context with useful clues for exploring, users will easily comprehend the present situation and find the information in a relatively short time. They will also travel through the systems adaptively by using the context information. In this paper, we describe extending UML for a context-based navigation modeling framework of Web information systems. An example of online bookstore is given to describe the models produced in the framework.

1 Introduction

Web-based systems are rapidly increasing and evolving from simple applications showing static information to complex ones involving dynamic contents with transaction processing. Web information systems developed to support e-commerce and online businesses contain more complex contents and are used by a diversity of users.

Web information systems are characterized by non-linear navigation because they have hypermedia documents and hyperlinks. Users can move from a level page of a contents hierarchy to lower or higher level pages or horizontally move from a branch of the hierarchy to another branch. However, when users navigate complex Web systems they cannot often grasp their current location, get the

---

[*] This work was supported by University of Seoul, Korea in 2004.
[**] Corresponding author.

W. Dosch, R.Y. Lee, and C. Wu (Eds.): SERA 2004, LNCS 3647, pp. 108–122, 2005.

information that they want, and lastly remember the important places they have already discovered. The reasonable reason for these problems is the absence of context information in Web information systems [1].

Therefore, a systematic approach to model the navigation of Web information systems is needed that helps users get information, purchase products, and deal with complexity. Constructing a navigation model is helpful for documenting the Web system structure and allows for improved navigability [2]. If Web systems also provide the information of their navigation context with useful clues for exploring, users will easily comprehend the present situation and find the information in a relatively short time [1]. They will also travel through Web systems adaptively by using the context information. Previous studies, however, describe the navigation as a part of hypermedia design [2, 5] or do not explain the navigation of Web systems including dynamic contents [3, 4].

In this paper, we describe extending UML for a context-based navigation modeling framework of Web information systems. UML provides a formal extension mechanism to allow practitioners to extend the semantics of the UML. The mechanism allows us to define stereotypes, tagged values and constraints that can be applied to model elements [13]. We adopt UML stereotypes, constraints and custom icons for the framework and explain how to model the context-based navigation using the framework. And the mappings between logical interfaces and physical elements to realize the navigation are described.

This paper is organized as follows: Section 2 presents related work. In Section 3, a framework for modeling context-based navigation is proposed. The models produced in the framework are described in Section 4. Finally, our conclusions are drawn in Section 5.

2   Related Work

Several works have studied on modeling Web applications or hypermedia applications. In [2] a design methodology for hypermedia based on UML profile has been introduced. The methodology consists of three steps that are conceptual, navigational, and presentational design. The conceptual model is constructed considering the functional requirements by using use cases. Based on this conceptual model, the navigation space model and navigation structure model are built in navigation design. The presentation model derived from the navigational design can be implemented by HTML frames. However, user activities are restricted to browsing because any frameset has two parts where the right frame contains the presentation of the navigational class or index class and the left frame represents the navigation tree. The methodology does not address the navigation of dynamic contents.

The development using OOHDM consists of a four activities including conceptual design, navigation design, abstract interface design, and implementation [3]. In OOHDM, a navigational context, the main structuring primitive of the navigational space, can be defined in six ways: simple class based, class based group, link based, link based group, enumerated, and dynamic. However, OOHDM may be not applicable to dynamic Web applications.

W2000, a framework for modeling Web applications using UML and HDM (hypermedia design model), has been introduced [4]. W2000 classifies the design activity into a number of interdependent tasks and proposes extensions to capture both operational and navigational aspects. The tasks include requirement analysis, hypermedia design, navigation design, state evolution design, and functional design activities where a few models are produced as results of the activities. However, W2000 does not address dynamic contents of Web applications and support presentation design activity.

In [5] hypermedia models based on four views of hypermedia system have been described. The models include application domain model, navigation model, presentation model, and user model, which are described using UML. The user model incorporates various characteristics of different users and supports personalization of hypermedia systems. However, since the presentation model is direct refinement of adaptive navigation model based on a state diagram, the separation between navigation and presentation is not obvious and the presentation model does not describe user interface.

UML/WAE profile has been adopted to describe Web application structures and artifacts [6]. The study represents Web-based systems at various levels of abstraction and detail such as user experience-level and design-level. However, the study only focuses on a presentation model and does not address navigation context that helps users decide the way in which they explore consistently.

In [7] statecharts have been used to model Web navigation, which is classified into intra-page, inter-page, and frame-based navigations. States in statecharts are, however, not consistent in their use since the states can represent a Web page, a position of Web page, a menu item, or a selection of script. The study describes only navigation related to pages and frames and not navigation contexts.

UWE metamodel conservatively extends the UML metamodel to provide the basis for a common metamodel for Web applications and for the CASE-tool supported design [8]. Conservative extension means that the UWE metamodel does not modify but inherits modeling elements of the UML metamodel. UWE metamodel concepts are mapped to a UML profile to be automatically checked by nearly every UML CASE tool. However, the UWE UML profile may be too complicated due to added inheritance structure, tagged values, and associations.

3   Navigation Modeling Framework

In this section we describe a framework for modeling the context-based navigation of Web applications (Figure 1). The framework defines navigation modeling phases and produces navigation models by using UML extension mechanisms. Each block in Figure 1 identifies a phase with activities. The activities are performed iteratively and incrementally while one or more models in each activity are constructed or refined. First, in navigation analysis phase domain is analyzed

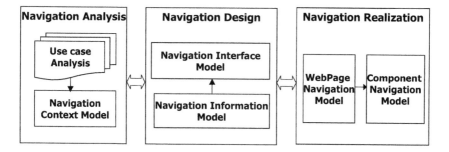

Fig. 1. A Framework for Navigation Modeling

by using use case and the analysis is described in text and represented by UML use case diagram, focusing on navigation. From this analysis a navigation context model is constructed, focusing on criteria for navigation decision frequently encountered in application modeling. The navigation context model shows the navigation associated with interacting external viewpoints.

Next, in navigation design phase we find information units and paths and produces two models: a navigation information model and a navigation interface model. The first is derived from the navigation context model and use case analysis, and defines semantic units appropriate for navigation purposes. Showing related information on one screen is not often possible since Web applications contain a lot of contents and the contents are complex. Thus we must explore a number of pages to accomplish our purpose. Since gathering related information and showing it on screens on demand help minimize cognitive overload [9], it is needed to define a navigation interface by describing how to display gathered information on screens. The navigation interface model aims at presenting information of the same semantic unit step by step and avoiding cognitive overhead, specifying which information of the unit users ask to see further. The model also identifies components playing a role of trigger in each interface for navigating Web applications. The navigation interface model is derived from the navigation information model and both of the models are designed iteratively and incrementally.

Finally, in navigation realization phase we produce a WebPage navigation model and a component navigation model based on a metamodel of Web information system. Then we associate logical navigation constituents with physical navigation elements. The logical navigation constituents include interface screens and objects derived from navigation analysis and design phases and are mapped to elements implementing Web contents.

Web traversal includes hierarchical navigation, global navigation, local navigation, and ad-hoc navigation [10]. Hierarchical navigation and local navigation are the most common because many Web sites have contents hierarchies consisting of pages with a number of links to other pages. If security is required in Web applications, navigation paths have a tunnel structure that is a linear chain of paths [11]. In Section 4 we describe access elements to support hierarchical navigation and local navigation taking into account security.

4   Framework Models

4.1   Navigation Analysis

Navigation Context Model. Domain analysis establishes goals to achieve in Web systems. The navigation context model derived from domain analysis using use case illustrates traverse of Web sites from an outside perspective, which consists of navigation contexts and their relationships. A navigation context can be defined by either describing a feature that all classes and links in the context have, or by listing its elements [3]. We define a navigation context from the viewpoint of understanding the overall navigation of Web information system, that is, a navigational use case viewpoint, while the navigation context defined in [3, 15] describes how to explore navigation elements rather than the overall navigation.

The navigation context model, adapted from the navigational use-case model in [4], shows contexts providing the information or the way about how the user should travel Web applications. The main differences between the navigation context model and the navigational use-case model are that a navigation context model shows navigation stereotypes of use case and that the navigation contexts of our model are mapped to and realized by WebPage navigation models and component navigation models. Stereotypes in the UML allow us to define new semantics for a modeling element.

Stereotyped classes can be rendered in a UML diagram with either a custom icon, or simply adorned with the stereotype name between guillemets ($\ll$ $\gg$). UML semantics can also be extended by inheriting UML metamodel and providing mapping to stereotypes [8]. For example, UML browsing semantics is extended by adding a new submetaclass for the Event metaclass in State Machines subpackage [12].

We use a $\ll$navigationContext$\gg$ stereotyped use case (see Table 1 in Appendix A.) as a use case describing the navigation of Web applications. Figure 2 represents a navigation context model of a generic online bookstore that shows not exceptional flows but basic navigation flows of the online bookstore. This model helps understand applications in abstract level. Navigating an online bookstore aims at finding and purchasing one or more books that customers want to read. Figure 2 shows that online bookstore users are initially unauthorized and are authorized if they register themselves by performing "SignIn" later. Only the authorized can update personal information of themselves and they must sign-in again to pay for books. After users browse books, they can browse their shoppingCart and pay for books.

4.2   Navigation Design

Navigation Information Model. A navigation information model identifies semantic units appropriate for each navigation context of the current Web application in particular domain. The identification and definition activities of the semantic units and their relationships perform finding classes and relationships

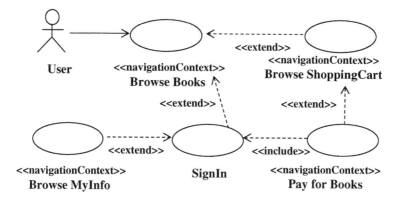

Fig. 2. A Navigation Context Model for Online BookStore

between classes and specifying attributes and operations. This model focuses on a navigation context and shows classes and their relationships in the context. This navigation information model identifies ≪navigationClass≫ stereotyped classes for semantic units and their relationships in a particular navigation context to achieve the purpose of the user. The navigation space model in [2] describes navigational classes similar to our ≪navigationClass≫ stereotyped classes, but does not focus on a navigation perspective. Thus we have extended the navigation space model to focus on a particular navigation context.

This model shows how to navigate to associated classes in a navigation context. The model is represented by UML class diagram with ≪navigationClass≫ stereo-

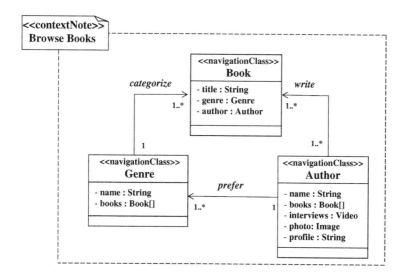

Fig. 3. A Navigation Information Model for Browse Books context

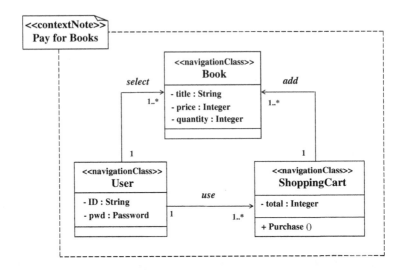

Fig. 4. A Navigation Information Model for Pay for Books context

typed classes (see Table 1 in Appendix A.) surrounding by a note with a context name and dotted lines. Figure 3 shows that "Book", "Genre", and "Author" navigation classes are explored in the "Browse Books" context from online bookstore user viewpoint. From Figure 3, we can see that this model also allows the same semantic unit to be explored in different ways and have different paths according to detailed contexts. For example, we search "J. K. Rowling", navigate to her books and then find "Harry Potter" in online bookstore. Alternatively, we can also find "Harry Potter" while exploring books about a genre of fantasy. Figure 4 shows that "User", "Book", and "ShoppingCart" navigation classes are explored in the "Pay for Books" context from the authorized user viewpoint.

Navigation Interface Model. Web pages usually have a number of links that enable us to explore other pages in the current site or other sites. We get information or purchase products, while traversing these pages and links in Web applications. Well-organized information involves a navigation context that helps choose a right path among several paths. We define a navigation interface model by applying Information on Demand pattern [9] to generic interface models. To apply Information on Demand pattern, the navigation interface model utilizes attributes of navigation classes to construct an interface providing a navigation context of well-organized information. First, we identify closely related information out of a navigation class and the information is displayed in an interface screen. Next, we make links from attributes representing the others of the information. Finally, we add the links to the interface to travel from it to the others. If each interface screen presents closely related information or cohesive information, an organization of such interfaces shows the information of a navigation context and allows users to explore efficiently. When designers also determine the

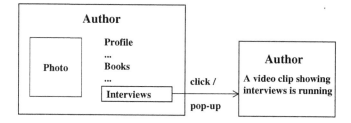

Fig. 5. How to show the information of the Author class in Fig. 3

way in which attributes and links of nodes are displayed, they should consider the cognitive capability of the user [9].

When applying Information on Demand pattern in [9], the same screen is used to show different attributes. However, our interface model shows different attributes of the same navigation class in other pop-up interface screens. We can get the feeling of seeing the same navigation class and avoid cognitive overhead naturally if the small number of pop-up interfaces show other attributes of the class on demand. Moreover, we do not have to go back to the original screen by clicking "Back" button or link in browser because we can see both of the original and pop-up screen at the same time. Things to note are that all attributes of a navigation class should be well organized so that the basic attributes of the class are displayed in the original interface screen and that the number of pop-up interface screens of a navigation class should be small.

This model also shows interface objects contained in a screen and links between the objects. The interface objects are identified when Web application architecture is designed and Web designers choose objects fit for the purpose of the user, considering cognitive overhead. Initially, Internet-based applications gained little control of a browser and the browser displayed only static page and explored the applications by clicking on hyperlinks. Now, Web applications allow dynamic contents to accept a request from users and process it. New technologies such as scripts, controls, and applets provide ways to control traveling between Web pages without activating hyperlinks. Adding or deleting links affects navigation paths and site structure in complicated Web applications and sometimes causes problems with consistency and security. Therefore interface objects should be defined and designed in detail for navigating Web applications with complex and dynamic contents. Interface objects, independent of implementation technologies, are mapped to elements of Web pages described in Subsection 4.3.

Figure 5 shows an example of how the information of the "Author" class in Figure 3 is displayed on screens. The left screen shows the information of an author except the author's interviews and includes a button or a link object to trigger a screen showing the interviews. If the user clicks the "Interviews" link, the right screen pops up, and displays the interviews of the author.

Figure 6 shows a navigation interface model corresponding to Figure 5. An AuthorScreen class has an interviews link object and two operations as an in-

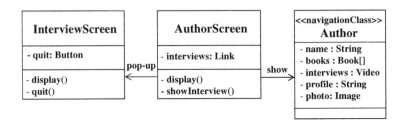

Fig. 6. A Navigation Interface Model corresponding to Fig. 5

terface screen of navigationClass Author. The AuthorScreen class shows the information of the Author class. If a user clicks the interviews link, showInterview operation is invoked. Then InterviewScreen pops up and displays a video clip showing the interviews of the author.

4.3 Navigation Realization

Figure 7 shows a metamodel of Web information systems where each leaf class is a physical element. Table 1 in Appendix A describes UML stereotypes used in this study. The stereotypes include elements of the metamodel in Figure 7. An appropriate navigation realization is done using those elements according to the characteristics of Web contents.

A window is divided into frames spatially and each frame is associated with several Web pages. Each Web page has zero or more links to other static or dynamic pages. A static page can be built from one or more dynamic pages using given parameter values. Simple or composite components contained in a static page interact with a dynamic page. Simple components are a text, a table, a list, a button, an anchor, etc. Composite components are a form, a code, a menu, a bulletin board, etc.

The navigation interface screens and objects derived from the navigation design phase are mapped to physical navigation elements to provide consistency between navigation design and navigation realization. For example, the interface screen classes in Figure 6 are mapped to WebPages in Figure 7. The interface objects in Figure 6 such as a link and a button are also mapped to an Anchor and a Button element in Figure 7.

The following well-formedness rules using OCL(Object Constraint Language) apply to the metamodel in Figure 7.

1. Two Web pages are connected by a navigation link. If a target page of the link is a dynamic page, the link may only have one or more arguments. Otherwise it may only have no arguments.

   context NavigationLink **inv**:
       self.connect->size() = 2

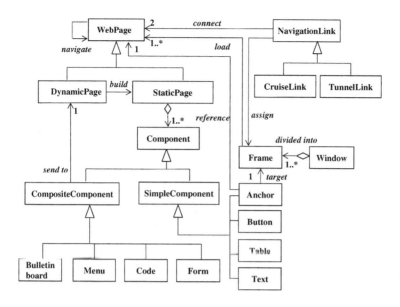

Fig. 7. Metamodel for Web Information System

if self.connect.target.oclIsTypeOf(DynamicPage) **then**
    self.connect.arguments->size() ≥ 1
else
    self.connect.arguments->size() $= 0$
endif

2. A TunnelLink may only enable us to navigate to a Web page by activating
   a link contained in the owner page of the link. The link may only invalidate
   to navigate to other pages. For example, a TunnelLink may only invalidate
   to go back to a previous visited page in a tunnel structure.

    context TunnelLink::activate(args): boolean
        pre: self.navigate.target->include(self.connect.target)

3. A composite component sends parameters to a dynamic page.

    context CompositeComponent::send(parameters): boolean
        pre: self.sendTo.oclIsTypeOf(DynamicPage)

4. More than a Web page may be loaded into a frame.

    context Frame **inv**:
        self.pages->size() ≥ 1

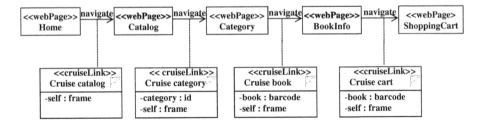

Fig. 8. A WebPage Navigation Model for Browse Books context

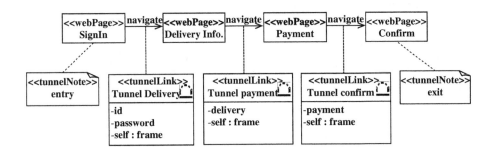

Fig. 9. A WebPage Navigation Model for Pay for Books context

5. An anchor references a Web page and specifies a frame to load the page into.

> **context** Anchor **inv**:
> self.pages->size() = 1
> self.frames->size() = 1

WebPage Navigation Model. A WebPage navigation model is expressed as a UML class diagram and a set of WebPages connected by links in the model realizes a context in the navigation context model. We define a navigation link by extending a link class used in [14], where the link class has not been specified in detail according to the structure of Web pages but represents only link parameters. If designers intend to guide normal navigation of contents hierarchy in Web applications, they use a cruise link to direct the exploration from one WebPage to other. Since a set of cruise links and WebPages implements a navigation context derived from domain analysis, the navigation can be understood easily.

In this paper we express a cruise link as a UML stereotype. Figure 8 shows that the "Browse Books" context in Figure 2 is mapped to and realized by a WebPage navigation model that describes the navigation from "Home" WebPage through "Catalog", "Category", and "BookInfo" to "Shopping Cart" WebPage to find books. In Figure 8 we can also see that stereotyped association classes with a flag

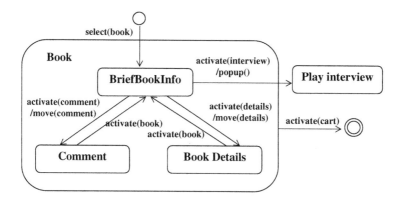

Fig. 10. A Component Navigation Model in BookInfo WebPage

icon are used to guide the traveling from the "Home" to the "Shopping Cart" Web-Page. If the link has an association class with one or more parameters except a frame parameter, it represents an exploration to a dynamic page. Otherwise, it represents an exploration to a static page. In Figure 8, The "Catalog" WebPage indicates a static page and the other WebPages indicate dynamic pages. From any WebPage of cruise navigation we can jump to global navigation by using menus or indexes, explore other WebPages, and return to the starting WebPage.

Figure 9 shows that the "Pay for Books" context in Figure 2 is mapped to and realized by a WebPage navigation model that describes the navigation from the "SignIn" to "Confirm" WebPage to purchase books. This navigation has a tunnel structure with only one entry and one exit [11]. Unlike a cruise link, if we navigate from any WebPage in a tunnel to other WebPages outside the tunnel, the tunnel link does not allow us to go back to a WebPage in the tunnel and we must again navigate from the entry WebPage. If we are presented a piece of context information about where we are in the tunnel during the time we navigate the WebPages in the tunnel, it helps us understand the tunnel and avoid traveling it in vain. The tunnel structure is best fitting for modeling the navigation of secure contents and is expressed as a stereotype with an icon and notes. From Figure 9 we can see that stereotyped association classes with a tunnel icon are used to indicate the links in a tunnel. Current Web contents introduce several navigation structures [11], and these structures can be expressed using UML stereotypes such as cruise links and tunnel links.

Component Navigation Model. Web pages contain physical navigation components that are a form, a button, a script, an applet, a control, etc. We describe component navigation by using physical elements and events triggering transition to a particular section in the same WebPage or the other WebPage. We use statechart diagrams to show navigation between components in a WebPage. Each state in this model represents a component while each state in [7] is a page, a position of page, or a menu item and each state in [12] is a Web page or an information chunk presented to a user.

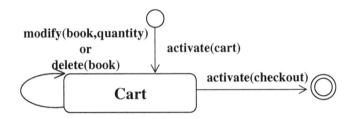

Fig. 11. A Component Navigation Model of Shopping Cart component

The component navigation model in Figure 10 shows the navigation of components in the "BookInfo" WebPage in Figure 8. This component navigation model begins with selecting a book in the "Category" WebPage. First, we see the brief information of the selected book in the WebPage. Then we may activate a comment or a book details to move to a particular section of the WebPage, or activate an interview to navigate to a pop-up WebPage showing a video clip. If we want to purchase the book, we activate a cart and navigate to the "Shopping Cart" WebPage. The component navigation model in Figure 11 shows the navigation of a cart component in the "Shopping Cart" WebPage. We may modify the quantity of the selected book in Figure 10 and delete the book. Activating checkout allows us to navigate to the entry WebPage of the "Pay for Books" context in Figure 9.

The component navigation model is also used to describe the navigation of dynamic contents because the components include code such as applets, scripts and controls that interact with each other and helps understand the behavior of components in a WebPage. Since the WebPage navigation is triggered by navigation components, a component navigation model and a WebPage navigation model complement each other.

5   Conclusion

In this paper we have described extending UML for a context-based navigation modeling framework of Web information systems. The framework has navigation models and phases such as analysis, design, and realization. One or more navigation models are constructed in each phase. We have adopted UML extension mechanisms for expressing the models and explained how to analyze and design the context-based navigation using the models. And the mappings between logical interfaces and physical elements to realize the navigation have been illustrated.

The context-based navigation assistance plays a powerful role in exploring Web information system [1]. So this framework to model the context-based navigation is expected to improve the overall navigability of Web applications. This framework also presents a consistent way to communicate about Web navigation with artistic designers and software developers. However, the modeling elements are not enough for complex navigation and this framework provides the same navigation for a diversity of users with different interests.

While the contents and the complexity of Web applications are rapidly increasing and the structure contains a wide variety, the navigation sometimes tends to have particular patterns according to the purposes of Web applications [11]. So we plan to analyze Web navigation, identify modeling elements for describing the patterns, and refine the framework by using these elements. We will provide navigation modeling of users with various interests and preferences.

References

[1] Park, J., Kim, J.: Effects of Contextual Navigation Aids on Browsing Diverse Web Systems. In Proceedings of the Conference on Human Factors in Computing Systems (2000) 257-264

[2] Hennicker, R., Koch, N.: A UML-based Methodology for Hypermedia Design. In Proceedings of the Third International Conference on UML (2000) 410-424

[3] Schwabe, D., Rossi, G.: An Object Oriented Approach to Web-based Application Design. Theory and Practice of Object Systems 4(4) (1998) 207-225

[4] Baresi, L., Garzotto, F., Paolini, P.: Extending UML for Modelling Web Applications. In Proceedings of the 34th Hawaii International Conference on System Sciences (2001)

[5] Dolog, P., Bieliková, M.: Hypermedia Modelling Using UML. In Proceedings of Information Systems Modelling (2002)

[6] Larsen, G., Conallen, J.: Engineering Web-Based Systems with UML assets. Annals of Software Engineering 13 (2002) 203-230

[7] Leung, K.R.P.H., Hui, L.C.K., Yiu, S.M., Tang, R.W.M.: Modeling Web navigation by Statechart. In Proceedings of International Computer Software and Applications Conference (2000)

[8] Kraus, A., Koch, N.: A Metamodel for UWE. Technical Report 0301, Ludwig-Maximilians-Universitat Munchen (2003)

[9] Rossi, G., Schwabe, D., Garrido, A.: Design Reuse in Hypermedia Applications Development. In Proceedings of The 8th ACM International Conference on Hypertext (1997)

[10] Rosenfeld, L., Morville, P.: Information Architecture for the World Wide Web. 2nd ed. O'Reilly (2002)

[11] Gillenson, M., Sherrell, D. L., Chen, L.: A Taxonomy of Web Site Traversal Patterns and Structures. Communications of the AIS 3 (2000)

[12] Dolog, P., Bieliková, M.: Modeling Browsing Semantics in Hypertexts Using UML. In Proceedings of Information Systems Modelling (2001)

[13] Object Management Group, Inc.: OMG Unified Modeling Language Specification, Version 2.0. OMG (2004)

[14] Conallen, J.: Building Web Applications with UML. 2nd ed. Addison Wesley (2002)

[15] Baumeister, H., Koch, N., Mandel, L.: Towards a UML Extension for Hypermedia Design: In Proceedings of UML'99 Conference. LNCS 1723 (1999) 614-629

A   Appendix

In Table 1, Base class column shows classes in UML metamodel and Parent column shows parent classes in the metamodel described in Figure 7.

Table 1. Stereotypes for Navigation Modeling of Web information systems

Stereotype	Base class	Parent	Description
NavigationContext ≪navigationContext≫	UseCase	NA	A NavigationContext describes a navigation usecase of Web systems.
NavigationClass ≪navigationClass≫	Class	NA	A NavigationClass defines a semantic unit appropriate for a navigation context.
Window ≪window≫	Class	NA	A Window is a display in browser.
Frame ≪frame≫	Class	NA	A Frame is a region of a window.
WebPage ≪webPage≫	Class	NA	A WebPage is a StaticPage or a Dynamic Page.
StaticPage ≪staticPage≫	Class	WebPage	A StaticPage is a HTML page.
DynamicPage ≪dynamicPage≫	Class	WebPage	A DynamicPage is a WebPage that contains dynamic contents on the server.
NavigationLink ≪navigationLink≫	Association	NA	A NavigationLink is a kind of association between WebPages.
CruiseLink ≪cruiseLink≫	Association	NavigationLink	A CruiseLink represents a normal link between WebPages.
TunnelLink ≪tunnelLink≫	Association	NavigationLink	A TunnelLink represents a navigation between WebPages in a tunnel structure.
Component ≪component≫	Class, State	NA	A Component is a CompositeComponent or a SimpleComponent.
CompositeComponent ≪compositeComponent≫	Class, State	Component	A CompositeComponent is a form, a code, a menu, a bulletin board, etc.
SimpleComponent ≪simpleComponent≫	Class, State	Component	A SimpleComponent is a button, an anchor, a table, a text, etc.
BulletinBoard ≪bulletinBoard≫	Class, State	CompositeComponent	A BulletinBoard is a message board to allow members to exchange their information.
Menu ≪menu≫	Class, State	CompositeComponent	A Menu is a list of various options available.
Code ≪code≫	Class, State	CompositeComponent	A Code is an applet, an ActiveX control, a script, etc.
Form ≪form≫	Class, State	CompositeComponent	A Form is a HTML form.
Anchor ≪anchor≫	Class, State	SimpleComponent	An Anchor is a HTML anchor.
Button ≪button≫	Class, State	SimpleComponent	A Button is a simple HTML button.
Table ≪table≫	Class, State	SimpleComponent	A Table is a HTML table.
Text ≪text≫	Class, State	SimpleComponent	A Text is a text string.
ContextNote ≪contextNote≫	Comment	NA	A ContextNote is a note used for describing a navigation context.
TunnelNote ≪tunnelNote≫	Comment	NA	A TunnelNote is a note used for describing a tunnel structure.

Conversion of Topic Map Metadata to RDF Metadata for Knowledge Retrieval on the Web

Shinae Shin[1], Dongwon Jeong[2], and Doo-Kwon Baik[3]

[1] Dept. of ITA/Standardization, NCA,
NCA Bldg, 77, Mugyo-dong, Chung-ku, Seoul, 100-775, Korea
sashin@nca.or.kr
[2] Dept. of Informatics & Statistics, Kunsan National University,
San 68, Miryong-dong, Gunsan, Jeollabuk-do, 573-701, Korea
djeong@kunsan.ac.kr
[3] Dept. of Computer Science & Engineering, Korea University,
1, 5-ka, Anam-dong, Sungbuk-gu, Seoul, 136-701, Korea
baik@software.korea.ac.kr

Abstract. The current Web is 'machine-readable', but not 'machine-understandable'. Therefore, new methods are required for machines to exactly understand an amount of Web information resources. A proposed solution for this issue is to use machine understandable metadata to describe information resources contained on the Web. There are two leading methods to describe metadata of Web information resources. One is Topic map, ISO/IEC JTC1's standard, and the other is RDF, W3C's standard. To implement effective semantic web (machine-understandable web), semantic web must handle all metadata of web information resources. For this, the necessity of interoperability is needed between Topic map area and RDF area. There are some previous researches on conversion method between Topic map and RDF, but these methods generate some loss of meaning or complicated result. In this paper, a new method to solve these issues is proposed. This method decreases the loss of implied semantics in comparison with the previous conversion methods and generate clear RDF graph.

1 Introduction

1.1 Motivation

The Web became a huge repository of information resources. However, the current Web is 'machine-readable' but not 'machine-understandable' [7]. Due to its huge size and high creation rate, it is impossible to manage the web information manually. It requires new methods that machines understand and handle an amount of Web information resources exactly.

A solution is to use machine-understandable metadata to describe the information resources contained in the Web [7]. Metadata is 'data describing Web resources' in the context of Web [7]. It helps structured description of resources.

There are two leading methods to describe metadata of Web information resources. One is Topic map that is ISO/IEC JTC1's standard [12] and the other is RDF that is W3C's standard [7], [8].

W. Dosch, R.Y. Lee, and C. Wu (Eds.): SERA 2004, LNCS 3647, pp. 123–137, 2005.

Topic map and RDF have a number of similarities. Both have been developed for the representation, interchange, and exploitation of semantic model-based data of information resources on the Web. Also, they describe data using a labeled graph with nodes and arcs that can be serialized in one or more XML based syntaxes [2]. Topic map was created to make high-level indexing sets of information resources. RDF was intended to support the vision of Semantic web through providing structured metadata about resources and a foundation for logical inference [1]. W3C is studying an evolution of current web to the Semantic web. The Semantic web is composed of RDF family. So the Semantic web must handle all information that is described by other methods such as Topic map. More effective Semantic web can be realized if metadata of information resources are described using both semantics of Topic map and RDF. It will help integration of various web metadata.

There are some previous researches on conversion method between Topic map and RDF. [2] proposed a conversion method emphasized on 'association' of Topic map. Therefore, an original meaning is changed after conversion. Although [3] is a more supplemented method, it makes additional edges (blank nodes). It produces a complicated RDF more than the original. [1] proposed the new conversion vocabularies by a solution about problems of [2], [3]. It has the limitation that users must understand for applying the method and add vocabularies into their original specification.

In this paper, a conversion method from Topic map into RDF is proposed. This method decreases loss of implied semantics in comparison with the previous conversion methods. In Section 2, the related researches are reviewed and analyzed. Section 3 presents our proposed method using graphs. Section 4 shows the experiment and evaluation results. Finally, Section 5 summarizes our proposal and discusses future plan.

1.2 Overview of the Topic Map and RDF

(1) Topic map
Topic map defines how to describe and handle information resources to navigate on the Web. This is the role of index. Topic map is encoded by XML. It is called XTM(XML Topic Map). Topic map captures the subjects of which information resource speaks, and the relationships between subjects [13]. Topic map is a n-ary labeled graph with prereifications [2]. Topic map graph is constructed with nodes and arcs. Fig. 1 illustrates a basic scheme of Topic map graph.

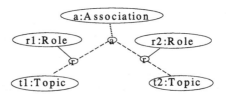

Fig. 1. Basic Topic map graph. Topic map is basically composed of two topic, an association and two role.

(2) RDF

RDF(Resource Description Framework) is a foundation for processing metadata. It provides interoperability between applications that exchange machine-understandable information on the Web [7]. RDF is a data model for *objects* (*resources*) and relations between *objects*, and provides a simple semantics for the data model. In RDF, information resources are represented by Uniform Resource Identifies(URIs) [7]. The information resources consist of any items. The information resources may be an entire Web page, a part of a Web page or a object which is not accessible via the Web [7].

RDF statement is composed of three individual parts; *subject, predicate,* and *object*. The RDF statement can be expressed by directed labeled graphs. In RDF diagrams, the nodes represent *resource*s(*subject*s, *object*s) and arcs represent *propertie*s(*predicate*s)[7]. Fig. 2 shows a basic RDF graph scheme.

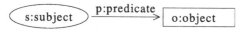

Fig. 2. Basic RDF graph. RDF is basically composed of a subject, object and predicate.

2   Related Researches on Conversion Topic Map to RDF

Several researches have been studied on mapping, integration, and conversion of Topic map and RDF [1], [2], [3], [4].

[1] uses a way in which RDF can be used to model Topic map and vice versa. For this, the author created new vocabularies to enable semantic interchange between Topic map and RDF. However, this method can not accept previous Topic map data and has difficulty on understanding and using Topic map for users.

In [2], the authors use node type. They classified nodes of Topic map as t-node(*topic* node) and a-node(*association* node). It doesn't deal *role* as a separate node. And this method converts Topic map to RDF with priority given to *association* of Topic map. It assigned *association*(a-node) of Topic map to *subject* of RDF. Therefore, it causes loss of meanings and change of original meanings after conversion.

[3] shows how the main constructions on RDF model can be expressed in Topic maps and vice versa. It has tackled the key issues of the conversion which lie around the area of *association* and *statement*. It makes additional edges(blank nodes) when conversion Topic map to RDF, thus it produces complicated RDF statements.

In [4], the XTM to RDF translator, XTM2RDF Translator has been introduced using XSLT-based technology to translate any Topic map document expressed in the XTM syntax into RDF abbreviated syntax. It generated RTM(RDF TopicMap) elements, new vocabularies, to translate XTM elements into RDF elements based on TMPM4 (Topicmap.net's Processing Model for XTM). This method also can not handle existed Topic map data and has difficulty that users must understand to using them. It also doesn't express various semantics that could be created from *topic* and *role* of Topic map. Thus, it causes loss of meanings.

3   Conversion Topic Map to RDF

3.1   Notations and Symbols

Several symbols and notations are used to describe conversion rules in this paper. Table 1 shows the defined notations and symbols.

Table 1. The defined notations and symbols for our conversion rules

Notations /Symbols	Description	Notations /Symbols	Description
TMi	instance of Topic map	p_i	i^{th} *predicate* of RDF
RDFi	instance of RDF	$_{new}p'$	new *predicate1* of RDF
t_i	i^{th} *topic* of Topic map	$_{new}p''$	new *predicate2* of RDF
r_i	i^{th} *role* of Topic map	⬭	node
a	*association* of Topic map	——	*arc* of Topic map
s_i	i^{th} *subject* of RDF	··············	*arc* of RDF
o_i	i^{th} *object* of RDF		

3.2   Concept of Proposed Method

Topic map and RDF have different schemes and syntaxes. A basic RDF graph is a binary model: one arc and two nodes. The basic Topic map graph has a much more complex model: n-ary graph. Topic map expresses more information than RDF [1]. Thus, the most important issue for conversion between them is to minimize the loss of original meanings. The proposed method will reduce the loss of meanings.

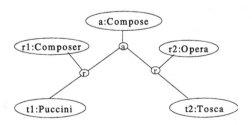

Fig. 3. Sample Topic map graph. This sample has been used often in other researches.

The six data can be extracted from Fig. 3 in view of *subject*, *predicate*, *object* as follows.

Meaning 1 (M_1) : Puccini Compose Tosca.
Meaning 2 (M_2) : Puccini's Opera is Tosca.
Meaning 3 (M_3) : Puccini is a Composer.
Meaning 4 (M_4) : Tosca is a Opera.
Meaning 5 (M_5) : Tosca's Composer is Puccini.
Meaning 6 (M_6) : Composer Compose Opera.

RDF scheme is expressed as a triple scheme that is composed of `subject`, `predicate`, and `object` as Definition 1.

Definition 1. (RDF Scheme) A RDF scheme is denoted by 3-tuple(RDF triple scheme) $R = (S, P, O)$, where:

- *S is a set of* `subject`s
- *P is a set of* `predicate`s
- *O is a set of* `object`s

The information can be expressed as RDF scheme by Definition 1 as follows:

R = {M_1, M_2, M_3, M_4, M_5, M_6}
   = {(Puccini, compose, Tosca), (Puccini, opera, Tosca),
       (Puccini, is-a, Composer), (Tosca, is-a, Opera),
       (Tosca, Composer, Puccini),(Composer, Compose, Opera)}

Our method extracts all these original meanings when convert Topic map to RDF.

3.3 Overview of Conversion Model

Our method receives a Topic map as input and extracts a RDF as output. The conversion method is composed of three parts. The first is the identifying part of `subject` and `object`. The second is the selection part of `predicate`. The last is the exception processing part to generate a complete RDF. The proposed conversion model is defined as Definition 2.

Definition 2. (*MA* : Conversion Model Topic map to RDF)
MA(I, O, Mf), where:

- $I : \sum TM_i$ (input)
- $O : \sum RDF_i$ (output)
- *Mf : (IE, SP, AE), where:*   (conversion function)
    - *IE* : a function of identifying `subject` and `object`
    - *SP* : a function to selecting `predicate`
    - *AE* : an exception processing rule

The specific rule set of conversion function *Mf is* composed of three sub-functions *IE, SP,* and *AE. IE* is a function of identifying `subject` and `object` from Topic map. This function creates pairs of `subject` and `object`: (S, O).

Definition 3. (*IE* : a function of identifying `subject` and `object`)
IE(IEi, IEo, IEr), where :

- $IEi : \sum TM_i$ (input)
- $IEo : \sum(S_i, O_i)$ (output)
- IEr : a set of rules to identify $subject$s and $object$s

SP is a function to selecting $predicate$. The $predicate$ defined between Definition 3's $subject$ and $object$ to make relations. RDF statements, (S, P, O) are created from this step. It is defined as Definition 4.

Definition 4. (SP: a function to selecting $predicate$)
$SP(SPi, SPo, SPr)$, where :

- $Spi : : \sum IE_i + : \sum IE_o$ (input)
- $Spo : : \sum (S_i, P_i, O_i)$ (output)
- SPr : a set of rules to select $predicate$s

AE is an exceptional processing rule (Definition 5) to create complete RDF

Definition 5. (AE : an exception processing rule)
$AE(AEi, AEo, AEr)$, where :   (function to process exception)

- $AEi : : \sum SP_o$ (input)
- $AEo : : \sum R_i(S_i, P_i, O_i)$ (output)
- AEr : a exception processing rule

3.4   Conversion Algorithm

(1) Step 1. Identifying subject and object
In [1], RDF and Topic map are identity-based technologies. That is, the key concept of them is "symbols" representing identifiable "things". In Topic map, the term for "thing" is $subject$(topic) and in RDF, the term for "thing" is $resource$. Therefore, $Topic$s of Topic map can be converted into $resource$s of RDF. All of $subject$, $object$ and $predicate$ in RDF can be $resource$s [7]. So $Topic$ in Topic map can be converted into $subject$ or $object$.

A $topic$ becomes a $subject$ or an $object$ in RDF according to its converting direction because Topic map is a non-direction graph but RDF is a direction graph. An $association$ or a $role$ can become a $predicate$ of RDF. The $role$s also become new $resource$s($topic$s). A $role$ becomes a $subject$ or an $object$ in $association$ relations between $role$s. And a $role$ becomes an $object$ of $Topic$. This step is presented in Rule 1.

Rule 1. (Identifying $subject$s and $object$s from $topic$s and $role$s of Topic map)

    input $TM_i (t_i, t_j, r_i, r_j, a)$
    select $topic$s and $role$s from TM_i
    convert $topic$s and $role$s to $subject$s and $object$s
       $(t_i \equiv S_i) \rightarrow (t_j \equiv O_i)$, where t_j has an $association$ relationship with t_i
       $(t_j \equiv S_j) \rightarrow (t_i \equiv O_j)$, where t_i has an $association$ relationship with t_j

$(r_i \equiv S_i) \rightarrow (r_j \equiv O_i)$, where r_i and r_j are connected with a same `association`

$(t_i \equiv S_i) \rightarrow (r_i \equiv O_i)$, where r_i is a `role` of t_i

$(t_j \equiv S_j) \rightarrow (r_j \equiv O_j)$, where r_i is a `role` of t_j

output set of (S_i, O_i)

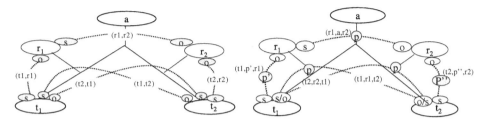

Fig. 4. Identify `subjects` and `objects`   **Fig. 5.** Selecting `predicates`

(2) Step 2. Selecting `predicate`

The `association` and the `role` are correspondent to `predicate` of RDF because they are represented as `topic` in Topic map. An `association` of Topic map can be interpreted to two types. One is a `predicate` that expresses `association` between `topics` and the other is a `predicate` between `roles`. These are correspondent to Rule 2.

When a `role` is converted to a `predicate`, the `role` is determined according to expressive direction. `Subject` corresponds to a expression target and `object` corresponds to expression target's value. For example, if *t1* is `subject` and *t2* is `object`, *r1* is selected as `predicate`.

Rule 2. (Selecting '*a*' as `predicate`)

    input $TM_i(t_i, t_j, r_i, r_j, a)$, set of (S_i, O_i)

    convert `association` as `predicate`

    $(t_i \equiv S_i) \cap (t_j \equiv O_i) \rightarrow (a \equiv p_i)$, where a_i is an `association` between t_i and t_j

    $(r_i \equiv S_i) \cap (r_j \equiv O_i) \rightarrow (a \equiv p_j)$, where

       • r_i and r_j are connected with a same `association` a_i

    output $RDF_1(t_i, a, t_j)$, $RDF_2(r_j, a, r_i)$

Rule 3. (Selecting '*r*' as `predicate`)

    input $TM_i(t_i, t_j, r_i, r_j, a)$, set of (S_i, O_i)

    convert `roles` as `predicate`

    $(t_i \equiv S_i) \cap (t_j \equiv O_i) \rightarrow (r_i \equiv p_i)$, where r_i is a `role` of t_i

    $(t_j \equiv S_i) \cap (t_i \equiv O_j) \rightarrow (r_j \equiv p_j)$, where r_j is a `role` of t_j

    output $RDF_3(t_i, r_i, t_j)$, $RDF_4(t_j, r_j, t_i)$

New `predicates` are needed to define relations between `topics` and `roles`. Rule 4 creates the new `predicates` and is defined as follows:

Rule 4. (Selecting '$_{new}p$' as predicate)

    input $TM_f(t_i,\ t_j,\ r_i,\ r_j,\ a)$, set of $(S_i,\ O_i)$

    create new $predicates$

        $(t_i \equiv S_i) \cap (r_i \equiv O_i) \rightarrow (_{new}p' \equiv p_i)$, where r_i is a $role$ of t_i

        $(t_j \equiv S_j) \cap (r_j \equiv O_j) \rightarrow (_{new}p'' \equiv p_j)$, where r_j is a $role$ of t_j

    output $RDF_5(t_i,\ _{new}p',\ r_i)$, $RDF_6(t_j,\ _{new}p'',\ r_j)$

Two issues are founded from these conversion rules' outputs. Rule 2 creates $RDF_1(t_i,$ $\underline{a},\ t_j)$ and $RDF_2(\underline{r_j},\ \underline{a},\ r_i)$. These RDF_1 and RDF_2 generates a same relation between $topics$ and between $roles$. Rule 2 creates $RDF_1(\underline{t_i},\ a,\ \underline{t_j})$ and Rule 3 generates $RDF_3(\underline{t_i},\ r_i,\ \underline{t_j})$. These RDF_1 and RDF_3 create duplicated $predicates$ between the same $topics$.

It's an obstacle to make RDF binary relation. These problems come from relation between $topic$ and $role$ where $topic$ is an instance of $role$. To solve these issues, an $association$ is used only as $predicate$ between $roles$ and a composed $predicate$, $association.role$ is created to make more precise $predicate$ between $topics$. The above is refined as the Table 2.

Table 2. Refinement of issued results of RDF statements

Issued RDF statements	Refined RDF statements
$RDF_1(t_i,\ \underline{a},\ t_j)$, $RDF_2(\underline{r_j},\ \underline{a},\ r_i)$	$RDF_1(t_i,\ \underline{a},\ t_j)$ -> change as a follow $RDF_2(r_j,\ \underline{a},\ r_i)$ -> select
$RDF_1(\underline{t_i},\ a,\ t_j)$, $RDF_3(\underline{t_i},\ r_i,\ t_j)$	$RDF_1(\underline{t_i},\ a.r_i,\ t_j)$ -> refine as a more specific predicate

Rule 2 and Rule 3 are respectively substituted into Rule 2-1, Rule 3-1.

Rule 2-1. (Refining Rule 2)

    input $TM_f(t_i,\ t_j,\ r_i,\ r_j,\ a)$, set of $(S_i,\ O_i)$

    convert $association$ as $predicate$

        $(r_i \equiv S_i) \cap (r_j \equiv O_i) \rightarrow (a \equiv p_j)$, where r_i and r_j are connected with same $association\ a_i$

    output $RDF_2(r_j,\ a,\ r_i)$

Rule 3-1. (Refining Rule 3)

    input $TM_f(t_i,\ t_j,\ r_i,\ r_j,\ a)$, set of $(S_i,\ O_i)$

    compose $association$ and $role$ as $predicate$

        $(t_i \equiv S_i) \cap (t_j \equiv O_i) \rightarrow (a.r_i \equiv p_i)$, where r_i is a $role$ of t_i

    output $RDF_1(t_i,\ a.r_i,\ t_j)$

(3) Step 3. Adding an exception rule

Through Rule 1 to Rule 4, Fig. 3 is converted RDF statements as follows:

$$R1(t1, a.r2, t2),\ R2(t2, a.r1, t1),\ R3(r1, a, r2),\ R4(t1, newp', r1),\ R5(t2, newp'', r2)$$

Therefore, all meanings are extracted from the sample in Section 3.2. RDF has an important property that must be considered. The `topic, association` and `role` of Topic map express 'thing'. This 'thing' can be addressable resource that have URI or non-addressable concept that expressed by literal(string) [14]. But, RDF's resource must have URI, addressable resource[7]. `Subject` of RDF means `resource`. Therefore, RDF's `subject` must become an addressable `resource` among of data elements of Topic map. `Object` is `resource` or literal value, so all of addressable `resources` and non-addressable concepts among of data elements of Topic map can become `object` of RDF. A rule to solve this issue must be attached to the predefined conversion rule set because the rule set prevent from convert of non-addressable concept to RDF `subject`.

Rule 5. (Exception rule to prevent converting non-addressable `concepts` to `subject`)
    input $TM_i(t_i\,t_j\,r_i\,r_j\,a)$, set of candidate $RDF_i(S_i\,P_i\,O_i)$
    exclude $(s_i,*,*)$, where :
    • s_i is a literal
    output complete set of $RDF_i(S_i,\,P_i,\,O_i)$

3.5 Case Study

This section shows a case study to verify converting quality of the proposed method with the sample in Fig. 3. The candidate pairs, (`subject, object`) are identified by Rule 1. `Topics` and `roles` can become `subjects` or `objects`.
Candidate pairs (`subject, object`)
    = {(Puccini,Tosca), (Tosca,Puccini), (Puccini,Composer),
      (Tosca,Opera), (Composer,Opera)}

Next, `predicate` elements are selected and added to the above `subject-object` pairs. The `roles` and `associations` become `predicates` by Rule 2, Rule 3-1, and Rule 4.

$R = (S,P,O)$ ={(Puccini,compose.opera,Tosca),
               (Tosca,compose.composer,Puccini),
               (Puccini,is-a,Composer), (Tosca,is-a,Opera),
               (Composer,compose,Opera)}

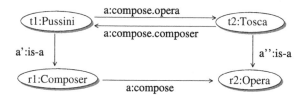

Fig. 6. Conversion result with the proposed method

Finally, an exclusion rule, Rule 5 must be added to prevent non-addressable `subject`.

4   Evaluation

4.1   Evaluation Model

Three evaluation criteria are used in our paper. The first is the loss rate of meanings after conversion, and the second is the structural complexity of conversion results. The last is the query efficiency about converted RDF tree.

Loss Rate of Meanings
The loss rate of meaning after conversion can be analized from the number of RDF statements that is created from conversion results. The calculation model is as follows:

$$LossMean(M) = \frac{\sum originTMmean - \sum extractRDFstat}{\sum originTMmean},$$

where $\Sigma extracRDFstat$ means Number of meanings from extracted RDF after conversion; $\Sigma originTMmean$ means Number of meanings from source Topic map

Structural Complexity of Extracted RDF
A complexity of conversion results can be analized from the number of nodes and arcs of converted RDF tree. It is also calculated as follows:

$$Compx(M) = \frac{\sum extractNewRDFnode}{\sum extractAllRDFnode},$$

where $\Sigma extractNewRDFnode$ is Number of new nodes from extracted RDF after conversion; $\Sigma extractAllRDFnode$ means Number of all nodes from extracted RDF after conversion

Query Efficiency
Query efficiency is in inverse proportion of query processing time about converted RDF tree. Query processing time can be decided by the number of arcs of RDF tree to pass to find a value.

$$QueryEff = \frac{1}{QueryprocessTime},$$

where QueryprocessTime : The Number of Arcs of RDF tree to pass to find answer.

4.2   Comparison with Related Research

[2] and [3] are used as comparison targets between related studies of Section 2 to evaluate our method. [1] and [4] are excluded because these methods use the extended vocabularies.

(1) Loss Rate of Meaning
[2]'s method is used as a comparison target about the number of extracted RDF statements. Fig.3 has five meanings if the duplicated meanings are eliminated. In [2],

nodes of Topic map are mapped to resources of RDF and arcs of Topic map are mapped to statements of RDF. Fig.7 shows the conversion result for the Topic map in Fig. 3 by the method [2]. This method extracts only two RDF statements with priority given to `association`.

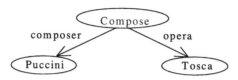

Fig. 7. Result of Lacher's method about Fig. 3. This is a conversion result for the Topic map in Fig. 3 by the method [2].

On the other hand, our method extracts five RDF statements. The loss rates of meaning of our method and [2]'s method are as follow:

$$LossMean(Our\ Method) = \frac{5-5}{5} = 0.00, \quad LossMean([2]'s\ Method) = \frac{5-2}{5} = 0.60$$

Our method offers conversion that there is no loss of meaning. The difference of the number of extracted RDF statements between [2]'method and our proposed method is more increased accoding to Topic map's volume as Fig. 8.

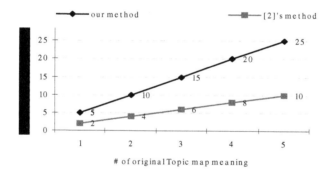

Fig. 8. Experiment result about the number of extracted RDF statements. Our method extracts five RDF statements from Fig. 3 but [2]' method extracts only two RDF statements.

(2) Structural Complexity of Extracted RDF

The method of [3] is used as a comparison target about the structural complexity of converted RDF. [3] defined conversion relations between Topic map and RDF as follows: RDF statement: `association` in Topic map; RDF identity: SubjectIndicatorReference in Topic map; RDF `resource`: `topic` entity; RDF `subject`: `role` playing `topic` (topic map); RDF `object`: `role` playing

topic (topic map); RDF *subject*: *role* defining *topic* (topic map); RDF
object: *role* defining *topic* (topic map)

Fig. 9 shows the conversion result of Fig. 3. It contains seven RDF statements but
two RDF statements of them have no means and create three additional-unnecessary
nodes.

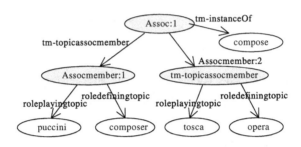

Fig. 9. Result of Moore's method about Fig. 3. This is a conversion result for the Topic map in
Fig. 3 by the method [3].

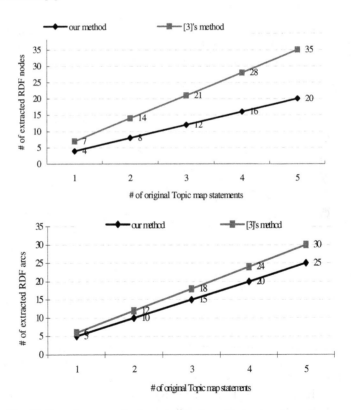

Fig. 10. Experiment result about the number of extract nodes and arcs

Our method creates four nodes and five arcs, but [3]'s method creates eight nodes and seven arcs. Our method creates no new nodes among four nodes, but [3]'s method creates three new nodes, *Asso:1*, *Assocmember:1*, *Assocmember:2,* among eight nodes such appear in result of Section 4.1. [3] creates complicated result because of new additional and unnecessary nodes. The complexity of each method is as follows:

$$Compx(Our\ Method) = 0/4 = 0.00, \quad Compx([3]'s\ Method) = 2/7 = 0.29$$

The more Topic map's volume increase, the more important this issue becomes. The difference of the number extracted RDF nodes and arcs are more increased accoding to Topic map's volume as Fig. 10.

(3) Query Efficiency to Extract Knowledge
Let's assume a sample query: *"Who is a composer of the Tosca?"*. In case of our method's output Fig. 6, three steps take to find a correct node about this query.

Fig. 11. An automate expression to solve sample query in our method's result tree

RDF has difficulty in backward search because of direction of arcs, but backward search supposes possible thing in this paper to analize query stpes of other related researches. [2]'s conversion requires four steps as Fig. 12 for precess the query.

Fig. 12. An automate expression to solve sample query in [2]'s method result tree

Fig. 9, the RDF that is converted from [3] passes six steps as Fig. 13 for the query.

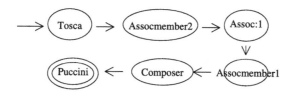

Fig. 13. An automate expression to solve sample query in [3]'s method result tree

The query efficiency of each method is as follows: Queryeff(Our Method) = 1/3 = 0.33; Queryeff([2]'s Method) = 1/4 = 0.25; Queryeff([3]'s Method) = 1/6 = 0.17. The difference of query efficiency is more increased accoding to Topic map's volume as Fig. 8.

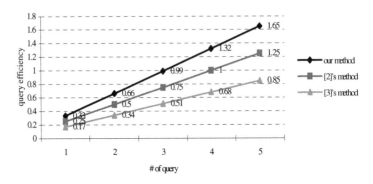

Fig. 14. Query efficiency experiment result

4.3 Discussion

The evaluation results in Section 4.2 show the efficiency of our method. 1) Our method extracts five RDF statements but [2]'s method extracts two RDF statements about Fig. 3. It means that our method offers more efficient conversion than [2] in terms of loss rate of meaning. 2) Our method creates four nodes and five arcs, but [3]'s method creates eight nodes and seven arcs. Therefore, our method offers more clear conversion than [3] in terms of complexity of extracted RDF results. 3) Our conversion requires passes three steps to find correct node about the query of Section 4.2's (3). [2]'s method passes four steps and [3]'s method passes six steps about same query. It also shows that our method is more efficient about query efficiency.

Table 3. Evaluation Results of Section 4.2

Items / Methods	Loss rate	Complexity	Query Efficiency
Proposed method	Low (0.0)	Low (0.0)	High (0.33)
[2]'s method	High (0.6)	-	Middle (0.25)
[3]'s method	-	High (0.29)	Low (0.17)

5 Conclusions and Future Work

This paper proposed a method to convert topic map to RDF for interoperability between both that are leading standard techniques to describe Web metadata. Our method is based on semantics and relations between resources. There are some loss of meanings in existent methods when convert topic map's n-ary relation to RDF's binary relation. However, our method converts possible all relations of topic map to RDF binary relations, minimizing loss of meanings. Proposed method recognized `role`s as important `subject`s and converted all relations and meanings of `role`s to RDF. It can contribute to promote of effective management and usage of information resources in the semantic web.

The Semantic web is composed of RDFS and OWL with RDF for more detailed expression of metadata. Therefore, it is needed to study on a relation of Topic map and RDF scheme, and OWL. Our method will be adapted to more complex Topic map instances. It will help a formalization of our method to consider various Topic map types.

A study on automatic conversion tool is also required. One solution to solve this issue is to use XSLT. XSLT provides the conversion between different file formats. Our method will be more formalized and implemented by XSLT script.

References

1. Garshol, L.M., Living with topic map and RDF, Proceeding of XML Europe 2003 (2003)
2. Lacher, M.S. and Decker, S., On the Integration of Topic Maps and RDF Data, Proceeding of Semantic Web Workshop (2001)
3. Moore, G., RDF and Topic Map-An Exercise in Convergence, Proceeding of the XML Europe 2001 Conference (2001)
4. Ogievetsky, N., XML Topic Map through RDF Glasses, Journal of Markup Languages :Theory and Practice Vol.3. Issue3, MIT press (2001)
5. Lacher, M.S. and Decker, S., RDF, Topic Map, and the Semantic Web, Journal of Markup Languages:Theory and Practice, Vol. 3, Issue 3, MIT press (2001)
6. Garshol, L.M., RTM: An RDF-to-TM mapping, http://psi.ontopia.net/rtm
7. Resource Description Framework(RDF) :Concepts and Abstract Syntax, W3C Recommendation (2004)
8. RDF Vocabulary Description Language 1.0: RDF Schema, W3C Recommendation, (2003)
9. OWL Web Ontology Language series, W3C Recommendation (2003)
10. The Standard Application Model for Topic map, ISO/IEC JTC1 SC34 N0396 (2003)
11. Topicmap.net's Processing Model for XTM 1.0, http://www.topicmap.net/pmtm4.htm, (2001)
12. ISO/IEC 13250 Topic Map : Information Technology Document Description and Processing Languages, ISO/IEC JTC1 (1999)
13. XML Topic Map (XTM) 1.0, http://www.topicmap.org/xtm/1.0/, TopicMap.Org (2001)
14. Prudhommeaux, E. and Moore G., RDF and Topic Map Mapping, http://www.w3.org/ (2002)

An Integrated Software Development Environment for Web Applications

Byeongdo Kang

School of Computer and Information Technology,
Daegu University, Republic of Korea
bdkang@daegu.ac.kr

Abstract. In recent years, the World Wide Web has become an ideal platform for developing Internet applications. World Wide Web service and application engineering is a complex task. Many web applications at present are large-scale and involve hundreds or thousands of web pages and sophisticated interactions with users and databases. Thus, improving the quality of web applications and reducing development costs are important challenges for the Internet industry. One way to resolve the difficulty is to provide web application developers with an integrated development environment. In this paper, I propose an efficient methodology and development environment for web application programs. This environment includes a design model to represent data and navigational structure, a modeling language for the notation technique of the design model, and a process model to define development stages.

1 Introduction

As the technologies of networks and the Internet improve rapidly, most software at present is being developed for World Wide Web[1] applications. Therefore, time and efforts are also on the rise as the size and complexity of web applications continue to increase. By reason of these managerial and technical issues, many researchers are studying web engineering. The goals of web engineering are to improve the quality and productivity of web applications[2]. One way to accomplish this is to provide web application developers with an integrated development environment.

The development environments for web applications can be built to a certain degree on software engineering environments. Designing the conceptual data model and abstract navigational model can benefit directly from software engineering approaches. However, differences in fundamental characteristics of applications make a direct transposition of techniques difficult. Large web applications containing many documents and complex interactive services need a more sophisticated engineering approach[3, 4]. Web application engineering is a complex task and comparable with the software engineering process. Web page and document editors that are similar to CASE(Computer-Aided Software Engineering)[5] environments are successful products.

A web application is an information system based on web and hypermedia technology. The large information system requires a development methodology and a set of tools for its development processes. There has been much research and development on methodologies and tools in web applications. These works lay emphasis on

W. Dosch, R.Y. Lee, and C. Wu (Eds.): SERA 2004, LNCS 3647, pp. 138–155, 2005.
© Springer-Verlag Berlin Heidelberg 2005

hypertext data model and characteristics such as information structure, navigation behavior, and presentation of structure and navigation. However, most of the previous works are for specific hypertext application domains and do not present how their methods and models can be adapted to different domains[6].

In this paper, I will present a development environment including a software process model for general web applications. The goal of this environment is to improve the quality and productivity of software. I will propose a process model for web applications and provide an integrated environment for the development phases from analysis through implementation. The documents from the analysis and design phases are used for generating the skeleton of source codes. Therefore, this environment helps developers to reduce the errors in the analysis and design phases and to improve the quality and productivity of web applications.

This paper is organized as follows. Section 2 introduces the general characteristics and architecture of World Wide Web applications. In Section 3, I explain briefly the previous related works in development methodology for web applications. In Section 4, I present the development methodology and functional structure of a web application development environment. Finally, I come to a conclusion with a summary in Section 5.

2   World Wide Web(WWW) Applications

Because of the rapid growth of the Internet, the World Wide Web has been the most popular platform for developing Internet applications. Since HTTP protocol[7] and the first WWW servers were introduced, a great number of computers and web servers have been connecting and are offering multimedia information. Web applications that are simply showing static HTML pages[8] are already outdated, and multimedia contents and active components are very popular.

2.1   Characteristics of Web Applications

Modern web applications are described as a hybrid between a hypermedia[9] and an information system. The integration of heterogeneous information, universal access by users, and real-time responses make web applications highly complex. Because of this hybrid structure, we should consider a number of the technical and managerial requirements of web applications[10]:

- Contents: The contents included in the web application may consist of static media(e.g., formatted data, text strings, images, and graphics) and active media(e.g., video clips, sound tracks, and animations).
- Structure: The organization of data contents.
- Navigational Interfaces: How users interact with individual pieces of information and move among them.
- Presentation: How web application contents and functions are shown to users.
- Dynamic Data Integration: The customization and flexible adaptation of content structure, data update, navigation interfaces, and presentation styles.

- Multilingual Concepts: International web applications are required to offer their contents in several languages.
- Evolution and Maintenance: Changes of requirements may cause the revision of web applications.

In addition to the above-mentioned requirements, we should consider the issues of security, scalability, and interoperability.

2.2 Architecture of Web Applications

The software architecture is one of the important factors in design and implementation and reflects the spatial arrangement of application programs and data. The minimal spatial configuration of a web application is the so-called two-tier architecture, shown in Fig. 1, which closely resembles the traditional client-server paradigm. Clients have web browsers and lightweight applications that are responsible for rendering the contents. Application programs and data reside on the server side. A more advanced configuration, called three- or multi-tier architecture shown in Fig. 2, separates the application programs from data. More tiers insure the scalability, reliability, security, and better performance of architecture[11].

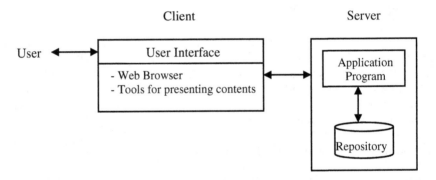

Fig. 1. Two-tier architecture

Web applications provide users with a graphic interface including a web browser. Users can communicate with web applications by entering commands for requesting what they want and receiving the results of the request. Web applications usually operate in the order of the following steps[12]:

- Step 1. Users enter commands and data into the user interface to request services on the web server. The user's commands are called query.
- Step 2. As soon as the input of the commands and data to the user interface is complete, the query is sent to a web server.
- Step 3. The web server processes the user's query using its application program. If the query processing needs data on the data server, the application program of the web server accesses the repository in the data server.
- Step 4. The results of the processed query are returned to the client.

- Step 5. The data returned to the client is displayed through the user interface. The display may be as simple as interpreting HTML or as complex as performing calculation or manipulation of data.

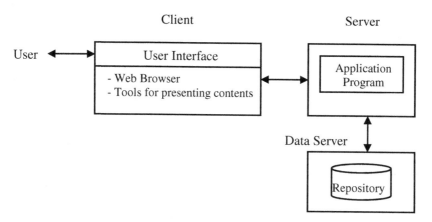

Fig. 2. Three-tier architecture

3   Related Works

Web engineering is a research field of which the goal is applying the technologies of software engineering to the development of web applications. Standard development methodologies and project management in software engineering can be applied to developing web applications. But researchers consider web engineering an emerging field. The early stage of study on web engineering was concerned with developing a good graphic user interface for web sites. Today, system and navigation structure are of great importance to the logical design for web applications.

The previous methods can be classified into five categories[13]: object-oriented approaches, entity-relationship approaches, component-based approaches, hybrid approaches, and open hypermedia approaches. In this section, I will introduce an overview of the popular related research on hypertext or hypermedia design environment and explain briefly their different methods.

3.1   HDM(Hypertext Design Model)

The hypertext design model(HDM)[14, 15] is a first towards defining a general purpose model for hypertext development. Some of the most innovative features of HDM are the notion of perspective, the identification of different categories of links with different representational roles, the distinction between hyperbase and access structures, and the possibility of easily integrating the structure of a hypertext application with its browsing semantics. HDM provides useful design primitives such as entities to represent information elements and three categories of links to connect the information elements together.

An HDM application consists of structures of information chunks called entities. Entities denote a physical or conceptual object of the domain and are grouped by entity types. An entity is the smallest autonomous piece of information that can be introduced or removed from an application, meaning that its existence is not conditioned by the existence of other information objects.

An entity is a hierarchy of components. Components are in turn made of units. In HDM, only entities are autonomous while components and units are not. Each unit shows the content of a component under a particular perspective. In hypertext applications, the same topic needs to be presented in several alternate ways. HDM provides the concept of perspective for the same content that needs to have multiple presentations.

HDM information structure can be interconnected by links. HDM provides three categories of links for designers. Structural links connect together components belonging to the same entity. Perspective links connect together the different units that correspond to the same component. Application links denote arbitrary domain-dependent relationships among entities or components and are chosen by the designer. All perspective links and most structural links do not need to be defined explicitly by the designer because they can be derived automatically from the structure of entities. Application links are organized into link types. An application type is specified with a name, a pair of source and target entity types, and a symmetry attribute.

An HDM specification of a hypertext application consists of defining a schema and a set of instances. A schema definition specifies a set of entity types and link types. Instances can be inserted into the application only if they obey the constraints specified in the schema. Access structures provide readers with entry points to directly access information structures in an instance of a schema.

According to HDM terminology, a hypertext application can be divided into two portions: a hyperbase and a set of access structures. The hyperbase represents the core of the application. It consists of entities, components, units, and links. The purpose of access structures is to allow the reader to properly select the entry points for further navigation.

The actual use of a hypertext application is defined by its browsing semantics. The browsing semantics specify how information structures are visualized to the readers and how they can navigate across information structures.

3.2 OOHDM(Object-Oriented Hypermedia Design Method)

The object-oriented hypermedia design method(OOHDM)[16] is a direct descendant of HDM. It differs from HDM in its object-oriented nature in that it includes special purpose primitives for both navigational and interface design. OOHDM is a model-based approach for building hypermedia applications. It comprises four different activities: conceptual design, navigational design, abstract interface design, and implementation. These activities are performed in a mixed pattern of incremental, iterative, and prototype-based development. During each activity except implementation, a set of object-oriented models[17] are built or enriched from previous iterations.

During conceptual design, a model of the application domain is built with object-oriented modeling principles, augmented with some primitives such as attribute perspectives and subsystems. Conceptual classes may be built with aggregation and generalization/specialization hierarchies. The main concern during this step is to capture the domain semantics as neutrally as possible. The product of this step is a class and instance schema built out of subsystems, classes, and relationships.

In order to have an application that can be utilized by users who want to accomplish a certain set of tasks, it is necessary to reorganize the information in the conceptual model. In OOHDM, this is achieved by defining a navigational model that is a view of the conceptual model. Different navigational models may be built from the same conceptual schema for different sets of users and tasks.

Navigational design is expressed with two schemas, the navigational class schema and the navigation context schema. The navigation class schema defines the navigable objects of a hypermedia application. The classes reflect the view chosen over the application domain. In OOHDM, there is a set of predefined types of navigational classes: nodes, links, and access structures. Nodes are defined as object-oriented views of conceptual classes during conceptual design. Links reflect relationships among nodes and are also defined as views on relationships in the conceptual schema. Access structures represent possible ways of accessing nodes.

Once the navigational structure has been constructed, the abstract interface model is defined. A clean separation between navigational and abstract interface design enables the building of different interfaces for the same navigational model and provides a higher degree of independence in the user interface.

To obtain a running system, the designer has to map the navigational and abstract interface models into concrete objects available in the chosen implementation environment. The models can be implemented in a straightforward way by using many of the hypermedia platforms such as Hypercard, Toolbook, Director, and HTML.

3.3 RMM(Relationship Management Methodology)

One data modeling approach is the entity-relationship(ER) model[18]. The ER model is suitable for modeling simple and small-scale hypermedia applications. The relationship management methodology(RMM)[19, 20, 21] models hypermedia applications by using the ER approach and represents an application with links among entities and the attributes of entities. RMM provides a computer-aided environment called RMCase[22] that includes a structured design methodology for the development and maintenance of a large class of hypermedia applications.

RMM has three different levels for modeling a web application. At the top, the presentation level deals with how the information is presented. Hyperlinks and information that groups together or separates are selected for presentation units such as web pages at this level. The storage level describes how information is organized physically. Between the storage and presentation level, the logical level maps the information in the storage level of web servers onto the actual web pages seen by users in the presentation level. Graphic designers who are interested in screen format work at the presentation level. System developers are more interested in the physical storage level. RMM provides a modeling language to represent the information domain and navigational structure of web applications at the logical level.

RMM provides developers with a design process. The developer begins with a requirements analysis to determine what the information domain is, what the application will do, who will use the application, and how the users will use the application.

Next, the developer creates the ER diagram to model the information structure of the application. The following step involves designing the application diagram in a top-down fashion. The application diagram depicts the entire application and embraces both a top-down and a bottom-up approach. Then the developer decomposes the application diagram into its building blocks called m-slices and designs each one separately. The function of the m-slice is to combine elements from any entities in the ER diagram. By combining all the m-slices, the developer generates the application diagram in bottom-up fashion and then compares the two versions, thereby debugging and refining the diagram in an iterative fashion. After the m-slices and application diagram are reconciled with each other, the developer designs the user interface and implements the design models.

4   The Web Application Development Environment(WDE)

In this section, I will present a web application development environment(WDE). The WDE provides a methodology for web applications and a tool environment specifically tailored for the methodology.

4.1   WDE Methodology

Even though HDM defines useful design primitives, it is deficient in extensibility and flexibility because it only provides a static set of structures of information chunks and link types. HDM provides design models but does not define a process model for design stages. The main advantage of RMM is the use of a simple ER design approach. However, it seems better suited for simple or small-scale applications. It cannot support applications that require complex structures among information items because it has difficulty handling the large number of entities in the large document. If a large document needs to be updated, the designer must repeat the steps of the navigation design to update the content of the hypermedia developed by the RMM. OOHDM seems to be suited for most of the application types. Although it has been used for developing several hypermedia applications[23], OOHDM lacks a complete implementation environment.

In general, a web application is described with three different design parts[24]:

- Structure: Describing the organization of the information that forms the application
- Navigation: Specifying the actions for moving across the application contents and accessing information
- Presentation: Defining the way that application contents are displayed to the users and the users can interact with an application.

In order to develop a web application, designers have to design the three requirements specifications of structure, navigation, and presentation. The WDE provides designers with a methodology including the following:

- A design model to describe the application precisely
- A modeling language that is the notation technique for the design model
- A process model to define the sequence of development phases.

The design model of WDE consists of three main diagrams: the architecture design diagram, the navigation design diagram, and the page detail design diagram. The contents of the diagrams are expressed in the modeling language. All of the design activities in each development step are defined in the process model.

For describing the structure of an application, the WDE provides modeling primitives to design the types of information components that constitute an application and semantic relationships among components. The structure of an application in WDE is described in the architecture design diagram. The architecture design diagram consists of various components and connectors representing semantic relationships.

The modeling primitives for designing the navigation express the various ways of exploring and moving among information components within a web application. The navigation model in WDE is described in the navigation design diagram. The navigation design diagram represents the relationships among web pages.

To display visual information through the application interface, a presentation model is developed. The basic unit of presentation is a web page. A web page includes the information about the layout and data contents of an application. The specifications of web pages in WDE are described in the page detail design diagram.

4.2 Functional Structure of WDE

The WDE supports development activities from analysis through implementation phases for web application programs. The WDE consists of three main functional modules: graphic editors, transformers, and a source code generator. Fig. 3 shows the

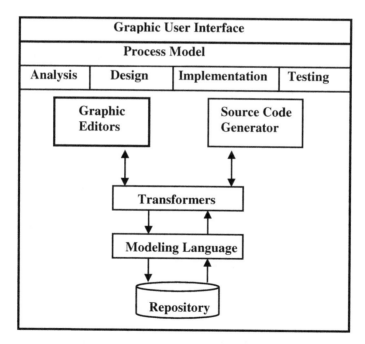

Fig. 3. The Functional Structure of WDE

functional structure of WDE. Graphic editors provide the diagramming notations to represent the design model for the data and navigational structure for web applications. The contents of diagrams are described through a web modeling language used by the transformer. The web application modeling language(WML) is used to store the semantics of the diagrams. The design model is finally transformed into the source codes for web programs.

Graphic Editors. Designers have to develop data and functional structures from the requirements specifications of web applications. In analysis and design phases, they need graphic tools to draw diagrams in terms of the predefined graphic notations. The graphic notations are based on components and connectors in WDE. Designers can define components, attributes, and relationships between components.

The WDE provides three kinds of diagrams: the architecture design diagram, the navigation design diagram, and the page detail design diagram. The architecture design diagram represents the overall structure of web applications to be developed. The navigation design diagram represents the navigation relationships between web pages. The page detail design diagram represents the detail contents of web pages. The project for one web application consists of one architecture diagram, one navigation design diagram, and one or more page detail design diagrams.

Transformers. The graphic diagrams are described in WML before they are stored into the repository. The WML formalizes the contents such as components, connectors, and attributes in the diagrams. To show the diagrams in the repository, graphic editors retrieve information about diagrams from the repository. Transformers help the translation between graphic editors and the repository.

The Source Code Generator. The source code generator automatically produces the skeleton of executable codes for the web pages from the analysis and design information in the previous phases. To produce web pages, the code generator uses the

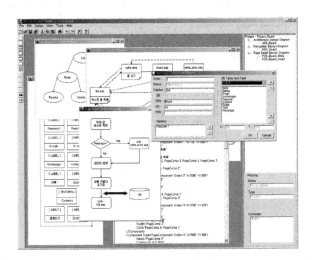

Fig. 4. The Graphic User Interface of WDE

information about the diagrams including the components, the attributes of components, and the relationships between components. Application developers can add additional functions to the skeleton of source codes. The WDE generates the codes of scripts, applets, and ActiveX for web programs.

Fig. 4 shows the graphic user interface of WDE. This figure shows the windows for editing diagrams, code generation, and other development activities.

4.3 Development Process Model of WDE

The development process model for web applications includes six phases: requirements analysis, architecture design, navigation design, page design, code generation, and implementation and testing. Fig. 5 shows the entire development cycle of WDE. This process model is iterative between phases to support feedback. The iterative feedback improves the design quality through recursive review and evaluation.

Requirements Analysis. Developers define the goals and functions of the web application. The purpose of the requirements analysis phase is to analyze the application domain through the viewpoint of users. Therefore, the communication between developers and users is very important. The success or failure of a project is dependent on the degree of understanding the user's requirements.

In this phase, developers define the target users who will use the web application. They also analyze the content and functions required, constraints, and who is going to provide the new content. The product of this phase is requirements specification.

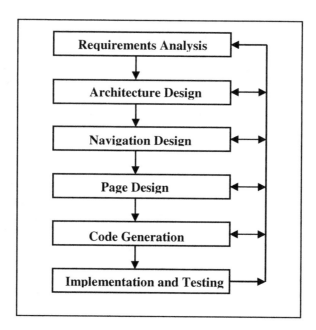

Fig. 5. The Development Process Model of WDE

Architecture Design. Developers determine the most suitable architecture according to the result of the requirements analysis phase. Developers divide the application domains into sub-applications. Well-defined architecture can reduce the complexity of the system and provide the work boundaries for developers. The product of this phase is the architecture design diagram.

Navigation Design. Developers define navigation relationships between web pages of the web applications. The navigation relationship includes the link relationship and data migration between the web pages and makes the web applications different from general applications. The web application program generally consists of more than one web page. Users of web applications navigate the web pages to retrieve some information or to accomplish what they want to do. The product of this phase is the navigation design diagram.

Page Design. Developers design the screen layouts and functions for each of the web pages. The web pages can be classified into static pages and dynamic pages according to their functions. The function of static pages is to show their contents. The function of dynamic pages is to accomplish tasks such as data processing or accessing databases. The products of this phase are page detail design diagrams.

Code Generation. The source code generator in WDE produces the skeleton of source codes for web pages. The source code generator uses the information about analysis and design specifications developed in the previous phases. To make the source codes complete and executable, developers can refine the skeleton of source codes generated from the code generator.

Implementation and Testing. The analysis and design specifications can be implemented in a straightforward manner by programming all of the page detail design diagrams. Above all, developers have to establish the directory structures and file naming conventions for version control. The application contents, such as text, graphics, or video clips, and the web site must be prepared before being tested and evaluated. After launching the web application, some faults and errors may occur during operation. Developers have to correct malfunctions, adopt new functions, or adapt new operation environments continuously.

4.4 Notations

The WDE provides web developers with two main notations-the component and the connector-for modeling analysis and design diagrams. Components represent the functional modules of the system while connectors represent the interactions between components. Fig. 6 displays the notations of the diagrams for modeling web applications.

Components in the diagrams include the architecture component, the page component, the passive component, the active component, the database component, the group component, and the condition component.

The architecture component is used to represent the structure of web applications in the architecture diagram and represents a function of a web application. The page component represents a web page in the navigation design diagram. The passive component represents a static functional module. The active component represents a dynamic module. The database component represents a data repository. The group component can be used to combine a set of components into one group of functions. The condition component is used to specify a condition. All of these components are used in the page detail design diagram.

Connectors in the diagrams include the general link, the indirect link, the direct link, the data link, the DB link, and the sequence link.

The general link represents the existence of any relationships between two components in the architecture design diagram. The indirect link and the data link represent the transitions occurred by a user's clicking on a button. The indirect link does not contain the data transmission between two components. But the data link contains the data transmission between two components. The direct link represents an automatic page link in the program. The DB link represents a data transmission between a functional module and a database. The sequence link represents the sequence of the activation of components. The DB link and the sequence link are used in the page detail design diagram.

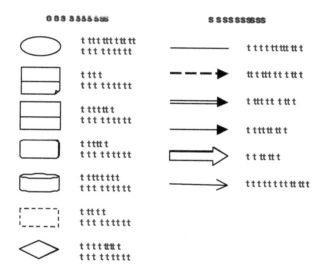

Fig. 6. Graphic Notations for Design Diagrams

4.5 Diagrams

The WDE provides developers with the following three kinds of diagrams to analyze and design a web application program:

• The architecture design diagram
• The navigation design diagram
• The page detail design diagram.

The Architecture Design Diagram. The architecture of software is defined by computational components and interactions among components. The well-defined structure makes it easy to integrate and maintain the parts of a large web application. The architecture design diagram shows the vertical and horizontal structure between functions of web applications and does not include the information about the detail algorithms. This diagram is concretized in the navigation design diagram and the page detail design diagram.

Fig. 7 shows an example of the architecture design diagram. This figure is the architecture design diagram for the log-in function. The log-in function includes three computational components: Register, Success, and Failure. The component Register processes the enrollment of users and keep data for users. The two components, Success and Failure, process the validation of users. The architecture design diagram includes architecture components and general links. The attributes of components and connectors are also defined separately.

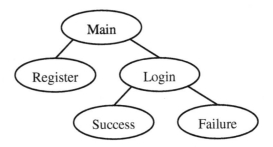

Fig. 7. The Architecture Design Diagram

The Navigation Design Diagram. The most important characteristic of web applications is the navigation feature. Because web applications consist of web pages, users of web applications have to explore web pages to search for information or accomplish what they want to do.

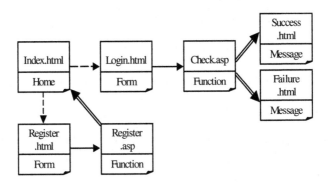

Fig. 8. The Navigation Design Diagram

The navigation design diagram represents the navigation among web pages. It shows the link relationships and data transformation between web pages. Fig. 8 shows the navigation design diagram for the architecture design diagram in Fig. 7. Fig. 8. represents the navigation relationships between web pages for the log-in function by using the page component, the indirect link, the direct link, and the data link. The attributes of components and connectors are also defined separately. The component in this diagram is concretized in the page detail design diagram.

The Page Detail Design Diagram. The page detail design diagram represents each web page in detail. The web pages are classified into static pages or dynamic pages according to their tasks. Some pages may include the characteristics of both.

The static pages display their contents and are described by the design patterns. On the other hand, the dynamic pages perform tasks and are described by the functional flows to represent the algorithms for the tasks.

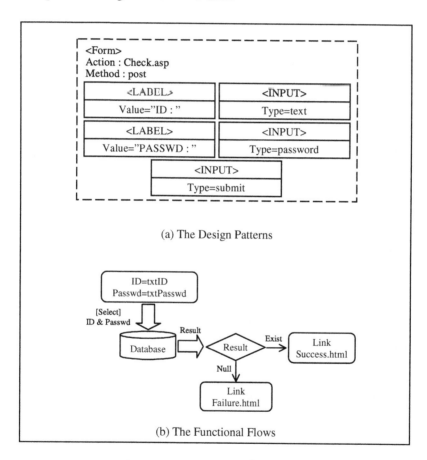

(a) The Design Patterns

(b) The Functional Flows

Fig. 9. The Page Detail Design Diagram

Fig. 9 shows the page detail design diagram for Fig. 8. Fig. 9(a) is an example of the design patterns of the static page, Login.html. Fig. 9(b) represents the functional flows of Check.asp and includes the passive component, the active component, the database component, the group component, the condition component, the DB link, and the sequence link.

4.6 Web Application Modeling Language(WML)

The WML describes the information about the contents and semantics of design diagrams. The WML description is automatically generated from the diagrams by transformers. All of the design diagrams are described by WML. The contents of these descriptions are then stored into the repository.

Fig. 10 shows the WML description of the architecture design diagram in Fig. 7.

```
<Diagram Type="ArchitectureDesignDiagram" Name="archBoard">
  <Component Type="ArchitectureComponent" Order="1" x="70" y="10" width="50" height="30">
    Name = "ac1"
    Caption = "List"
    Comment = "Start Page & List"
  </Component>
  <Component Type="ArchitectureComponent" Order="2" x="40" y="100" width="50" height="30">
    Name = "ac2"
    Caption = "Read"
    Comment = "Read"
  </Component>
  <Component Type="ArchitectureComponent" Order="3" x="100" y="100" width="50" height="30">
    Name = "ac3"
    Caption = "Write"
    Comment = "Write"
  </Component>
  <Connector Type="GeneralConnector" Order="4" x1="85" y1="40" x2="105" y2="40'>
    Name = "cnt1"
    Relation = "ac1→ac2"
  </Connector>
  <Connector Type="GeneralConnector" Order="5" x1="65" y1="100" x2="125" y2="100">
    Name = "cnt2"
    Relation = "ac1→ac3"
  </Connector>
</Diagram>
```

Fig. 10. Diagram Contents described by WML

4.7 Web Page Generation

A web application program consists of many web pages. The source code generator produces the skeleton of the web pages from the diagrams developed in analysis and design phases. In order to produce web pages, the code generator references the information about the diagrams from the repository. The WDE supports the codes of scripts, applets, and ActiveX for web programs.

Fig. 11 shows the source codes generated automatically from the diagrams of Fig. 9. Fig. 11(a) and Fig. 11(b) are generated from Fig. 9(a) and Fig. 9(b), respectively.

```
<html>
<head>
</head>
<body>
   <form action="Check.asp" method="post" name="frmLogin">
   <center>
   <br>
   ID :
   <input type="text" name="txtID" maxlength="10" size="10">
   <br>
   PASSWD :
   <input type="password" name="txtPasswd" maxlength="10" size="10">
   <br>
   <input type="submit" name="smOK" value="register">
   </center>
   </form>
</body>
</html>
```

(a) Login.html

```
<%
Id = Request.Form("txtID")
Passwd = Request.Form("txtPasswd")
Set Dbcon = Server.CreateObject("ADODB.Connection")
Dbcon.Open ("DSN=entrance;UID=sa;PWD=")
SQLString = "Select Id From entrance where Id='" & Id & "'
and Passwd='" & Passwd & "'"
Set Result = Dbcon.Execute(SQLString)
if Result.EOF then
Response.Redirect("Failure.html")
Dbcon.Close
Set Dbcon = Nothing
else
Response.Redirect("Success.html")
Dbcon.Close
Set Dbcon = Nothing
end if
%>
```

(b) Check.asp

Fig. 11. Source Codes in the Log-in Web Page

5 Conclusion

The rapid growth of the Internet makes the World Wide Web the most popular platform for developing Internet applications. Because of this, the size and complexity of
web applications continue to increase. There has been much research and development on the methodologies and tools in web applications. However, most of the previous works are for specific hypertext application domains and have not presented
how the methods and models can be adapted to different domains. One way to tackle

this problem is to provide web application developers with an integrated development environment.

In this paper, I presented a web application development environment(WDE). The WDE helps developers to reduce the errors in the analysis and design phases and to improve the quality and productivity of web applications. It also provides a methodology for web applications and a tool environment specifically tailored for the methodology. This methodology includes a design model, a modeling language, and a process model. The design model of WDE consists of three main diagrams: the architecture design diagram, the navigation design diagram, and the page detail design diagram. The contents of the diagrams are expressed in the modeling language. The process model includes six phases: the requirements analysis, the architecture design, the navigation design, the page design, the code generation, and the implementation and testing. The tool environment of the WDE supports development activities from analysis through implementation phases for web application programs. The WDE consists of three main functional modules: graphic editors, transformers, and a source code generator. Graphic editors provide the diagramming notations to represent the design model for the data and navigational structure for web applications. The contents of diagrams are converted to the web modeling language by transformers. The design model is finally transformed to the source codes for web programs. The source code generator produces the skeleton of the web pages from the diagrams developed in analysis and design phases.

Acknowledgement

This research is supported by Daegu University.

References

1. Berners-Lee, T., Cailliau, R., Loutonen, A., Nielsen, H. F., Secret, A.: The World Wide Web. Communications of the ACM, vol. 37, no. 8. (1994) 76-82
2. Powell, T. A., Jones, D. L., Cutts, D. C.: Web Site Engineering: Beyond Web Page Design. Prentice-Hall. (1998)
3. Nanard, J., Nanard, M.: Hypertext Design Environments and the Hypertext Design Process. Communications of the ACM, vol. 38, no. 8. (1995) 49-56
4. Schranz, Markus W.: Engineering Flexible World Wide Web Services. Proceedings of the 1998 ACM Symposium on Applied Computing. Atlanta, Georgia, United States. (1998) 712-718
5. Rock-Evans, R.: CASE Analyst Workbenches. Ovum. (1989)
6. Lowe, B. D., Webby, R. G.: Improving Hypermedia Development: a Reference Model-Based Process Assessment Method. Proceedings of the tenth ACM Conference on Hypertext and Hypermedia, Darmstadt, Germany. (1999) 139-146
7. Berners-Lee, T., Fielding, R. T., Nielsen, H. F.: Hypertext Transfer Protocol. World Wide Web Consortium, Informational RFC 1945, http://www.w3.org/Protocols (1996)
8. Berners-Lee, T.: HyperText Markup Language(HTML). World Wide Consortium, http://www.w3.org/MarkUp/. (1993)

9. Nielsen, J.: Hypertext and Hypermedia. Academic Press Prof., Inc., San Diago, CA., U.S.A. (1990)
10. Garzotto, F., Mainetti, L., Paolini, P.: Hypermedia Design, Analysis, and Evaluation Issues. Communications of the ACM, vol. 38, no. 8. (1995) 74-86
11. Fraternali, P.: Tools and Approaches for Developing Data-Intensive Web Applications: A Survey. ACM Computing Surveys, vol. 31, no. 3. (1999) 227-263
12. Introduction to the Web Application Development Environment, http://www.wdvl.com/Authoring/Tutorials. (2004)
13. Christodoulou, S. P., Styliaras, G. D., Papatheodorou, T. S.: Evaluation of Hypermedia Application Development and Management Systems. ACM Hypertext'98 Conference, Pittsburgh, USA. (1998) 1-10
14. Garzotto, F., Paolini, P., Schwabe, D.: HDM - A Model-Based Approach to Hypertext Application Design. ACM Transactions on Information Systems, vol.11, no. 1. (1993) 1-26
15. Garzotto, F., Mainetti, L.: HDM2: Extending the E-R Approach to Hypermedia Application Design. Proceedings of the 12th International Conference on Entity Relationship Approach, Dallas, Texas, USA. (1993) 178-189
16. Schwabe, D., Rossi, G., Barbosa, S. D. J.: Systematic Hypermedia Application Design with OOHDM. Proceedings of the ACM International Conference on Hypertext, New York, USA. (1996) 116-128
17. Rumbaugh, J., Blaha, M., Premerlani, W., Eddy, F., Lorensen, W.: Object Oriented Modeling and Design. Prentice Hall Inc. (1991)
18. Chen, P. P.: The Entity-Relationship Model-toward a Unified View of Data. ACM Transactions on Database Systems, vol. 1, no. 1. (1976) 9-36
19. Isakowitz, T., Stohr, E. A., Balasubramanian, P.: RMM: A Methodology for Structured Hypermedia Design. Communications of ACM, vol. 38, no. 8. (1995) 34-44
20. T. Isakowitz, A. Kamis, M. Koufaris, The Extended RMM Methodology for Web Publishing, Working Paper IS-98-18, Center for Research on Information Systems, 1998.
21. Balasubramanian, V., Bang, M. M., Yoo, Joonhee.: A Systematic approach to designing a WWW application. Communications of ACM, vol.38, no.8. (1995) 47-48
22. Diaz, A., Isakowitz, T.: RMCase: Computer-Aided Support for Hypermedia Design and Development. International Workshop on Hypermedia Design (1995) 1-15
23. Lee, Seung C.: IDM: A Methodology for Intranet Design. Proceedings of the International Conference on Information Systems. Helsinki, Finland (1998) 51-67
24. Fraternali, P., Paolini, P.: Model-Driven Development of Web Applications: The Autoweb System. ACM Transactions on Information Systems, vol. 28, no. 4. (2000) 323-382

On the Design and Implementation of
Parallel Programs Through Coordination

Chia-Chu Chiang[1], Roger Lee[2], and Hae-Sool Yang[3]

[1] Department of Computer Science, University of Arkansas at Little Rock,
2801 South University Avenue, Little Rock, Arkansas 72204-1099, USA
cxchiang@ualr.edu
[2] Software Engineering and Information Technology Institute, Central Michigan University,
Mount Pleasant, Michigan 48859, USA
lee@cps.cmich.edu
[3] Graduate School of Venture, HoSeo Univ., A_San, Chang-Nam, 336-795, Korea
hsang@office.hoseo.ac.kr

Abstract. The current state of art in existing middleware technologies does not support the development of distributed applications that need processes to complete a task collaboratively. What is needed in the next generation of middleware is synergy of heterogeneity, distribution, communication, and coordination. We are proposing to augment the existing middleware technologies to provide collaboration support through Multiparty Interaction (MI) protocol rather than design a new programming language for distributed coordinated programming. In this paper, a 4-layered interaction model will be presented to decouple the applications and their underlying middleware implementations including coordination protocols by providing a set of generic interfaces to the applications. The decoupling of applications and middleware technologies by isolating computation, communication, and coordination promotes reuse, improves comprehension, and eases maintenance due to software evolution.

1 Introduction

Existing middleware has been used to aid the development of distributed applications in heterogeneous computing environments. However, the current state of art in existing middleware technologies mainly supports client-server programming model. The language construct supported is, by large, remote procedure call (RPC). This simple RPC-based client-server programming model is not adequate to develop distributed applications that need three or more processes to work together collaboratively.

To support the development of heterogeneous distributed applications for coordination, we are proposing to augment the existing middleware technologies to provide collaboration support through Multiparty Interaction (MI) protocol rather than design a new programming language for distributed coordinated programming. A 4-layered interaction model will be presented to decouple the applications and their underlying middleware implementations including coordination protocols by providing a set of generic interfaces to the applications. The decoupling of applications and middleware technologies by isolating computation, communication, and coordination promotes reuse, improves comprehension, and eases maintenance due to software evolution.

W. Dosch, R.Y. Lee, and C. Wu (Eds.): SERA 2004, LNCS 3647, pp. 156–170, 2005.

2 First-Order Multiparty Interactions in IP

Joung and Smolka [1] write that "A multiparty interaction is a set of I/O actions executed jointly by a number of processes, each of which must be ready to execute its own action for any of the actions in the set to occur." N. Francez and I. R. Forman [2] present IP (Interacting Process) as the basis of programming languages for multiparty interaction.

2.1 Synchronization

In this section, we use the dining philosophers problem to illustrate how multiparty synchronization works. It consists of four philosophers sitting at a table who do nothing but think and eat. There is a single fork between each philosopher, and each philosopher needs to pick both forks up in order to eat. A solution using IP is presented in Figure 1.

```
DINING_PHILOSOPHERS  ::  [Philosopher₀  ||  Philosopher₁  ||
Philosopher₂ || Philosopher₃ || Fork₀ || Fork₁ || Fork₂ ||
Fork₃], where

Philosopherᵢ :: i = 0,...,3
sᵢ := 'thinking';
*[sᵢ = 'thinking' → sᵢ := 'hungry'
  □
  sᵢ = 'hungry' & get_forkᵢ[sᵢ := 'eating'] →
      release_forkᵢ[]
]

Forkᵢ :: i = 0,...,3
*[get_forkᵢ[] → release_forkᵢ[]
  □
  get_fork₍ᵢ₊₁₎ ₘₒ𝒹 ₄[] → release_fork₍ᵢ₊₁₎ ₘₒ𝒹 ₄[]
]
```

Fig. 1. A solution to the dining philosophers problem in IP

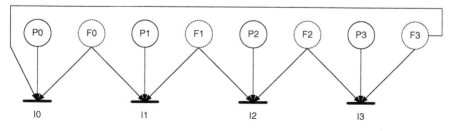

Fig. 2. Bipartite graph of the dining philosophers problem

In Figure 1, the participants of interaction, get_fork$_i$, are the fork processes Fork$_i$, Fork$_{(i-1) \bmod 4}$, and Philosopher$_i$ (we assume that index arithmetic is cyclic, i.e., $0 - 1 = 3$ and $3 + 1 = 0$). When all the dining philosophers are hungry and all the forks are available on the table, the coordination among all the processes is illustrated by the bipartite graph in Figure 2. The thick bars I$_i$ in the graph represents the multiparty interactions get_fork$_i$ and the circles the coordinating processes. The edge represents the possible participations and a process can participate in only one interaction.

2.2 Communication

In this section, we use the leader election problem to illustrate communication in IP. The leader selection problem is quite simple. There are $n \geq 1$ processes P_i $(0 \leq i < n)$ and each of them is supposed to have a different natural weight W_i. The leader is the process P_i satisfying that $W_i = \max(W_j)$ where $0 \leq j < n$. A solution to the leader election problem is shown in Figure 3.

```
LEADER :: [P₀ || P₁ || ... || Pₙ₋₁], where

Pᵢ :: i = 0, ..., n-1
Elect[leaderᵢ := (Wᵢ = max ₀≤ⱼ<ₙ(Wⱼ))]
```

Fig. 3. A solution to the leader election problem in IP

The multiparty interaction *Elect* synchronizes all of the processes, allowing them to exchange information and determine which participating process becomes the leader. The participating process that finds itself having the maximum weight will be the leader.

3 Related Work

A good start for a comprehensive study of multiparty interaction is the paper written by Joung and Smolka [1]. The paper introduces a taxonomy of languages for multiparty interaction that covers the complexity of the multiparty interaction implementation problem. There are several other specification languages for multiparty interaction, TROLL [3], LCM [4], and CAL [5], which are not discussed in [1]. Several algorithms for implementing IP have been described in [6, 7].

Recent research on coordination can be found in the notions of synchronizers [8, 9], regulated coordination [10], programmable coordination media [11], intercepting messages [12], strong interaction fairness via randomization [13], and dependable multiparty interactions [14]. Radestock and Eisenbach [12] developed a coordination model based on intercepting messages in a very similar way to the work described in [11].

4 A 4-Layered Model for Distributed Coordination

Radestock and Eisenbach [12] present the concerns in developing coordinated distributed applications that interact with each other. The concerns are separated into four parts: the communication part, the computation part, the configuration part, and the coordination part. The communication part defines how components communicate with each other. The computation part defines the behavior of a component which also determines what is being communicated. The configuration part indicates which components exist, which components can communicate with each other, the method of communication, and where data come from and where the data are sent to. The coordination part determines when certain interactions will occur. The dependencies of these four concerns yield a 4-layered protocol structure in Figure 4.

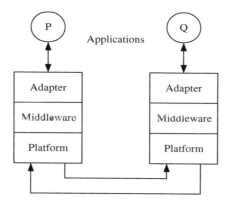

Fig. 4. Structure of communicating components through adapters

4.1 Development of Distributed Coordination for Coordination

IP [2] is the programming language adopted to develop heterogeneous distributed coordinated applications. For example, Figures 1 and 3 contain two examples of IP programs. IP programs are allowed to be realized under any general programming environment. The approach we use is to analyze an IP program and generate a multi-party interaction description that is a data structure to describe the properties of the multiparty interactions in IP. Our IP language mapping approach allows a multiparty interaction description written in any target programming language to be automatically generated from an IP program. Application developers then write a program in the target language to include the multiparty interaction description in the program. A function in the Adapter layer will be invoked to represent the caller (participating party) to interact with other participants for coordination. A set of APIs will be developed to facilitate the process to obtain the multiparty interaction information in the multiparty interaction description. The multiparty interaction description contains the information needed by the participating processes to resolve the concerns of communication, computation, configuration, coordination, and parallelism at run time.

The overall IP approach to developing applications is shown in Figure 5. Application developers write an IP program. An interface description in the target language and a global copy file are generated from the IP program by an IP compiler. An application program including the interface description and the global copy file is compiled and linked with the adapter library to produce a fully functioning independent executable file. Therefore, the only thing a programmer needs to do is to write an IP program for the problem and an application program to include the multiparty interface description in the application program.

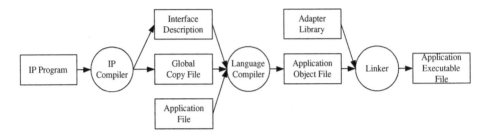

Fig. 5. Steps for developing applications in IP

To demonstrate the suitability of IP for parallel programming, we present three IP parallel programs in the following sections. They are parallel sum and parallel sorting. We present these three examples to demonstrate that programmers can specify distributed coordinated applications in IP for parallel processing through coordination without explicitly expressing parallelism.

Parallel Sum. A parallel sum algorithm originally presented in [15] adds $n = 2^m$ values on the SIMD-CC (Single Instruction stream, Multiple Data stream – Cube Connected) model. Processor P_j processes local variable a_j for all j such that $0 \le j \le n-1$. When the algorithm begins execution, the a_j's contains the values to be added. At its termination, a_0 contains the sum. In Figure 6, we present an IP program to solve the problem for MIMD (Multiple Instruction stream, Multiple Data stream) computers.

```
PARALLEL_SUM :: [P₀ || P₁ || … || Pn-1], where

Pj (int n, int b[]) :: j = 0, …, n-1
   int aj = b[j];
   for (int i = log(n)-1; i <= 0; i--)
   {
      int d = pow(2, i); // d := 2ⁱ;
      [(j < d) & compj[aj = aj + b[j+d]] → []];
   };
```

Fig. 6. An IP program for the parallel sum problem

The *for* loop iterates log n times. Suppose we have 16 processes (n = 16) as shown in Figure 7. In the first iteration, processes 0 to 7 will first obtain the values from processes 8 to 15, respectively. Processes 0 to 7 then add the values to their own values and store the results to their own local variables a_j. All the operations will be executed in parallel. The interaction point, $comp_j$, determines which processes are allowed to get involved in the first iteration. In the second iteration, processes 0 to 3 obtain the values from processes 4 to 7, respectively. The processes then add the values to their own values and store the result to their own local variables a_j. In the third iteration, processes 0 and 1 obtain the values from processes 2 and 3, perform the sum operation, and store the results to their own local variables, a_0 and a_1, respectively. In the fourth iteration, process 0 obtains the value from process 1, performs the add operation, and stores the total sum to a_0. As process 0 terminates, a_0 contains the sum.

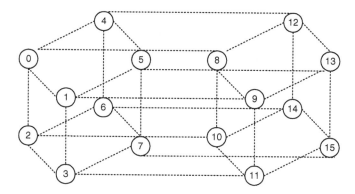

Fig. 7. Process numbers

The multiparty interface description corresponding to the parallel sum IP program defines the computation, configuration, coordination, and communication of the participating processes. For example, the following partial description describes the computation of P_i in the parallel sum problem.

```
struct parallel_sum_desc {
    ...
    struct symbol_00019 {
    ...
    struct symbol_00020 {
        kind symbol_kind;
        kind statement_kind;
        int predecessor;
        int successor;
        int index;
        struct stmt_attr {
            int used_symbol;
            int modified_symbol;
            ...
    };
    struct symbol_00021 {
...
};
```

Node 00020 describes a statement of a process. *Symbol_kind* indicates the types the symbol nodes such as statement, declaration, process name, etc. *Statement_kind* indicates the types of statements including while, if , for, and sequence if the *symbol_kind* is a statement type. *Predecessor* and *successor* nodes indicate the preceding and succeeding statements of the current statement. *Index* points to the context of the current statement in the statement table. The structure *stmt_attr* describes the properties of the statement including the variable names, which variables are used in this statement, and which variables are modified in this statement.

Once the multiparty interface description is created, the application program invokes the following adapter API to initiate the execution.

EXECOPR(INOUT &OperationArgumentBuffer,
OUT &UserExceptionBlock);

The *OperationArgumentBuffer* parameter is the beginning address of the multiparty interaction description. The multiparty interface description is passed down to the adapter, so the adapter can execute the operations for the process at runtime. The *UserExceptionBlock* parameter is used to return any user exceptions that are raised during runtime.

Parallel Sorting. The odd-even transposition sort in [15] was originally designed for the SIMD-MC (Single Instruction stream, Multiple Data stream - Meshed Connected) model, in which the processing elements are organized into a one-dimensional array. Assume that $b = [b_0, b_1, ..., b_{n-1}]$ is the set of n elements to be sorted, n is even, and for all i, $0 \le i \le n-1$, process P_i contains array elements b_i.

The algorithm requires n/2 iterations. Each iteration has two phases. In the first phase, called odd-even exchange, the value of a_i in every odd-numbered processor i (except process n-1) is compared with the value of a_{i+1} stored in even-numbered processor (i+1). The values are exchanged, if necessary, so that the lower-numbered processor contains the smaller value. In the second phase, called even-odd exchange, the value of a_i in every even-numbered processor i is compared with the value of a_{i+1} in processor (i+1). As the first phase, the values are exchanged, if necessary, so that the lower-numbered processor contains the smaller value. After n/2 iterations the values are sorted.

The algorithm can be easily implemented in IP with n parallel processes, each of which holds a data element. The data comparisons and exchanges are done through the multiparty interactions between neighboring processes. An IP program for the parallel sorting is as follows, assuming the type of data to be sorted is char:

```
OESort :: [P₀ || P₁ || … || Pₙ₋₁], where

 Pⱼ(int n, char b[])  :: j = 0, …, n-1
   char aⱼ = b[j];
   for (int i = 1; i <= [n/2]; i++)
   {
     //odd compare and exchange
     [(j < n-1 ∧ odd(j)) & compⱼ[aⱼ = min(aⱼ, aⱼ₊₁)] → []
     ▯
      (j > 0 ∧ even(j)) & compⱼ₋₁[aⱼ = max(aⱼ₋₁, aⱼ)] → []
     ];
     //even compare and exchange
     [(j < n-1 ∧ even(j)) & compⱼ[aⱼ = min(aⱼ, aⱼ₊₁)] → []
     ▯
      (j > 0 ∧ odd(j)) & compⱼ₋₁[aⱼ = max(aⱼ₋₁, aⱼ)] → []
     ];
   };
```

Fig. 8. An IP program for the odd-even transposition sort problem

Each process P_j holds a data element, a_j. The odd-numbered process P_j compares and exchanges the data element through the multiparty interaction $comp_j$ (j is odd, i.e. $odd(j)$ is true) with the process P_{j+1}. All these comparisons and exchanges are done in parallel, because they use different multiparty interactions $comp_j$ (j is odd). The even numbered processes are doing the same tasks. Figure 9 illustrates the execution of the IP program for a char array: $b[] = \{ 'S','R','Q','P' \}$. The boxes in the figure represent the three multiparty interactions, $comp_0$, $comp_1$, and $comp_2$. The dotted vertical lines show the progress of the processes (from top to bottom).

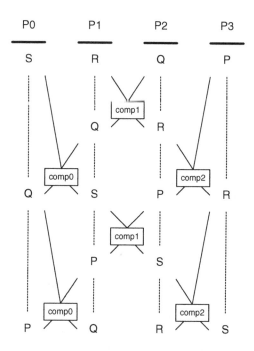

Fig. 9. Odd-even transposition sort of four values

It can be shown that after passing through k pairs of odd and even multiparty interactions, the data hold by each process is no farther than n − 2k positions away from its final sorted position. After process P_j finishes [n/2] iterations, the data that it holds in a_j must have passed through [n/2] pairs of odd and even multiparty interactions. Therefore, the array is sorted when all processes are terminated. Note that there is no global barrier synchronization across all processes in this program. The multiparty interactions and their synchronization are restricted between adjacent processes.

4.2 Coordination Support in the Adapter Layer

The implementation of our distributed multiparty interactions consists of three phases: synchronization, data exchange, and computation. In the synchronization phase, enabled interactions are detected and one is selected for execution. In the data exchange phase, data are exchanged among participating processes through the underlying middleware. In the computation phase, upon receiving all the needed data, the processes participating in an interaction continue their executions on the interaction bodies. For example, in the dining philosophers problem shown in Figure 1, $Philosopher_0$, $Fork_0$, and $Fork_3$ need to synchronize at the interaction point get_fork_0 in the synchronization phase. Next, they start to exchange data in the data exchange phase. In this problem, however, there is no need for data exchange among $Philosopher_0$, $Fork_0$, and $Fork_3$. Following the data exchange phase, these three participants enter the computation phase, $Philosopher_0$ needs to execute the body of get_fork_0 by assigning *'eating'* to s_0 which is a local variable declared in the $Philosopher_0$ process.

After synchronization, data exchange takes place. Thread managers inform their participating processes which interactions have been selected for execution. The participating processes exchange the data they are responsible for with their corresponding thread managers by means of *PutData(INOUT &OperationArgumentBuffer)* and *GetData(INOUT, &OperationArgumentBuffer)*. The implementation of *GetData()* and *PutData()* is placed in the Adapter layer of the protocol structure shown in Figure 4. *GetData()* and *PutData()* transmit data through the invocation of middleware functions implemented in the Middleware layer. At this moment, no participating processes can continue until they all have completed data exchanges.

The format of the *OperationArgumentBuffer* is defined in the interface description in the target language. The interface description is compiled from an IP which describes the interfaces of a coordination module. This interface description was designed to allow an adapter to examine the signature of the requested services at runtime such as operation names, parameters orders, parameters types, and parameters sizes.

5   Implementation of the Coordination Support

The heart of the design and implementation of multiparty interactions is the distributed guard scheduling problem described as follows:

Given n multiparty interactions I_i (i=1,..., n), each of which has l_i parties to be participated by distinct processes form m participating processes P_j (j=1,...,m) whose identifiers are not know until run-time, the guard scheduling problem is to select at subset of the multiparty interactions for execution, subject to the following constraints,

1. Each interaction selected for execution must have all its parties participated by distinct processes.
2. No process can participate in executions of more than on interaction.
3. If there are interactions which can be selected for execution, the selection must be finished in finite time.

Constraints 1 and 2 above are the safety requirement and Constraint 3 the liveness requirement of the problem.

For each interaction I_i, we create an interaction process, denoted as I_i. If P_j is ready to participate in k interactions I_{i1}, ..., I_{ik}, we create (1) thread manager M_j and (2) one proxy thread $T_{j,ir}$ for each of I_{i1}, ..., I_{ik}. The proxy thread $T_{j,ir}$ is used to communicate with interaction process, I_{ir}. Thread manager M_j serves as the manager of all the proxy threads $T_{j,i1}$, ... $T_{j,ik}$ which it spawns.

The basic idea of the protocol for $T_{j,ir}$ is as follows: It sends message *Request* to I_{ir} to notify its intension to participate. When I_{ir} receives all the *Requests* needed, it sends back a message *All-Met* to $T_{j,ir}$, telling $T_{j,ir}$ that I_{ir} is ready to be activated. After receiving message *All-Met*, $T_{j,ir}$ may do one of the following three tasks: (1) if none of the other $T_{j,ir'}$ has committed, $T_{j,ir}$ may proceed to commit itself to I_{ir} by sending a *Commit* message to it and makes transition to "commit-sent" state (2) if a $T_{j,ir'}$ with higher priority has committed to $I_{ir'}$, $T_{j,ir}$ withdraw its participation by sending a *Withdraw* message to I_{ir} and makes transition to "re-try" state, or (3) if a $T_{j,ir'}$ with lower priority has committed to $I_{ir'}$, $T_{j,ir}$ makes transition to "pending" state waiting to commit in case the commitment of $T_{j,ir'}$ does not realize the actual activation of $I_{ir'}$ (due to withdrawals of other participants of $I_{ir'}$). The information about the commitment or pending of all proxy threads is stored in a shared array accessed through critical sections. Once in "commit-sent" state, $T_{j,ir}$ is waiting for *Succeed* message from I_{ir} when it receives commitment from all of its participants. After $T_{j,ir}$ receives *Succeed* message, it sends a *Finish* message to thread manager M_j to register the activation of I_{ir} and make transition to "success" state.

The protocol for interaction process, I_{ir}, is a simple two-phase locking protocol with three states: "meeting", "all-met" and "success". In the "meeting" state, I_{ir} receives *Request* message or *Abort* message from its participants, incrementing or decrementing its request counter, respectively. When the request counter reaches the total number of participants, I_{ir} sends *All-met* message to all of the participants, and makes transition to "all-met" state. In the "all-met" state, it waits for either a *Commit*, *Withdrawal* or *Abort* message from each of its participants. A commit counter and a withdrawal counter are used to track the numbers of the corresponding participants to decide whether it can transit to "success" state (when all participants committed) or "meeting" state to start over again for the next round of coordination (when all responded, but the number of committed falls short of the total number of participants).

The protocol for thread manager M_j is to coordinate its all the proxy threads. It also intercepts and relay messages between proxy threads and its corresponding interaction process. In particular, it will discard all the messages to $T_{j,ir}$ after it is killed by M_j. The main function of M_j is to synchronize the transitions of $T_{j,i1}, \ldots T_{j,ik}$. After it spawns the proxy threads $T_{j,i1}, \ldots, T_{j,ik}$, it waits for either *Retry* message or *Finish* message from each of them. Upon receiving a *Finish* message from $T_{j,ir}$, it sends *Stop* message to all the other proxy threads so that they can send *Withdrawal* or *Abort* message to its corresponding interaction manages before make transition to 'ready-to-die" state. If all proxy threads send *Retry* message, M_j sends *TryAgain* message back and allow them to start the next round of coordination. The details of the above three protocols can be found in [16].

6 Correctness

In this section, we prove the correctness of the guard scheduling algorithm presented in the previous sections. A solution to the guard scheduling problem for coordinating first-order multiparty interactions must satisfy the requirements of safety, liveness, and progress.

6.1 Safety

The safety requirement of the guard scheduling problem defined in Section 5 demands that

- no interaction be selected to execute unless all its parties are participated by distinct processes (interaction safety), and
- no process participates in more than one interaction at a time (process safety).

The interaction safety requirement can be derived from the protocol of I_r directly. In particular, process I_r will not enter into state 'all-met' unless it receives the requests for participation from q (i.e. l_r) processes. Furthermore, it will not enter into state 'success' unless it receives the commitments from all these processes. The process safety is ensured by Theorem 1 as follows.

Theorem 1. Among the proxy threads $T_{j,i1}$, ..., $T_{j,ik}$, started by P_j, only one can enter into state 'success'.

Proof: Thread $T_{j,ir}$ can enter into state 'success' only from state 'commit-sent'. It can enter into state 'commit-sent' either from state 'pending' or state 'request-sent'. Thread $T_{j,ir}$ moves from state 'request-sent' to state 'commit-sent' only when all the bits of bit map a[] are 0. If it moves into state 'pending', it will not enter into state 'commit-sent' until another thread sends it a *Continue* after leaving state 'commit-sent'. Therefore, there is only one thread in state 'commit-sent' at any time. After the thread enters into state 'success', all other threads will be killed.

6.2 Liveness

The liveness requirement of the guard scheduling problem demands that there be no deadlock in the system comprising all the threads and processes running the protocols of $T_{j,ir}$, M_j, and I_i. In particular, no process or thread is allowed to stay in a waiting state indefinitely. After I_i receives all the I_i requests it needs and enters into state 'all-met', it will receive the same number (l_i) of Commit(), Withdraw() or Abort(), provided that each thread $T_{j,ir}$ involved is live and responds eventually. After that, I_i will enter either into state 'meeting' again for the next round of coordination or into state 'success'. In other words, I_i is live as long as each thread $T_{j,ir}$ with which it communicates is live. Similarly, if every thread $T_{j,ir}$ ($1 \leq r \leq k$) is live, thread M_j is also live. In particular, thread M_j will remain in state 'working' and start the next round of coordination if all the k proxy threads $T_{j,ir}$ (r = 1, ..., k) are successful. If one thread succeeds, M_j will receive Finish() from it and enter into state 'finishing'. M_j will further receive (k-1) ReadyToDie()s from the remaining threads and enters into state 'success'. Therefore, the liveness of the entire system hinges on the liveness of the protocol of $T_{j,ir}$. The following lemma is used to prove the liveness of $T_{j,ir}$.

Lemma 1. If a thread $T_{j,ir}$ is in state 'pending' indefinitely, there must be another thread $T_{j,ir'}$ of P_j such that $r < r'$ in state 'commit-sent' indefinitely.

Proof: a[r] = 1 only if $T_{j,ir}$ is in state 'commit-sent' or 'pending', but the first thread $T_{j,ir}$ with a[r] = 1 must be in state 'commit-sent'. To simplify the notation, we rename

$T_{j,ir}$ to be $T'_{j,r}$. Let us assume that $T'_{j,r}$ stays in state 'pending' indefinitely. When thread $T_{j,ir}$ enters into state 'pending', $a[(r+1)...k] \neq 0$ must be held. Let $a[u_1]$, ..., $a[u_v]$ ($r+1 \leq u_1 < ... < u_v \leq k$) be all the bits that either are 1 when $T'_{j,r}$ enters into state 'pending' or ever become 1 when $T'_{j,r}$ is in state 'pending' (indefinitely). Thread $T'_{j,uv}$ must be in state 'commit-sent' when $T'_{j,r}$ enters into state 'pending'. Other threads $T'_{j,u1}$, ..., $T'_{j,uv-1}$ must be in state 'pending' first. We want to prove that based on the assumption above at least one of $T'_{j,u1}$, ..., $T'_{j,uv}$ must be in state 'commit-sent' indefinitely. Consider thread $T'_{j,uv}$ first. If it does not stay in state 'commit-sent' indefinitely, it must receive a Success() or a *Fail* in finite time. If it receives a Success(), $T'_{j,r}$ would leave state 'pending' in finite time. This would contradict the assumption above. If it receives a *Fail*, thread $T'_{j,uv-1}$ will enter into state 'commit-sent' in finite time. The same procedure will also apply to threads $T'_{j,uv-1}$, ..., $T'_{j,u1}$. Therefore, if none of $T'_{j,u1}$, ..., $T'_{j,uv}$ can stay in state 'commit-sent' indefinitely, $T'_{j,r}$ will leave state 'pending' in finite time. This proves the lemma. There are four waiting states in the protocol of $T_{j,ir}$: 'req-sent', 'commit-sent', 'pending', and 're-try' The waiting of $T_{j,ir}$ in state 'req-sent' is to ensure interaction safety and should not be considered as a problem for liveness. $T_{j,ir}$ in state 're-try' will enter into state 'init' after all the threads started by P_j send Withdraw()s to their interactions. Therefore, for the liveness of the protocol of $T_{j,ir}$, we only need to prove that no thread $T_{j,ir}$ will stay in state 'commit-sent' or 'pending' indefinitely. This is done in the following theorem.

Theorem 2. It is impossible for any thread $T_{j,i}$ in the system to stay in state 'commit-sent' or 'pending' indefinitely.

Proof: According to Lemma 1, we only need to prove that it is impossible for any thread $T_{j,i}$ to stay in state 'commit-sent' indefinitely. Let us assume that there is a thread $T_{j1,i1}$ staying in state 'commit-sent' indefinitely. This means that $T_{j1,i1}$ receives neither Success() nor *Fail* in finite time. Therefore, none of the threads coordinating interaction I_{i1} ever sends a Withdraw() or an Abort() to it. Furthermore, there is at least one of these threads that does not ever send a Commit() either. Let this thread be $T_{j2,i1}$. According to the protocol, $T_{j2,i2}$ from the same process P_{j2} such that it stays in state 'commit-sent' indefinitely and $i_1 < i_2$. Continuing this way, we will have an infinite series $T_{j1,i1}$, $T_{j2,i1}$, $T_{j2,i2}$, ..., $T_{jk,ik-1}$, $T_{jk,ik}$, ... such that $T_{jk,ik}$ ($1 \leq k$) and $T_{jk,ik-1}$ ($2 \leq k$) are indefinitely in states 'commit-sent' and 'pending', respectively, and $i_1 < i_2 < ... < i_k < ....$ On the other hand, there are only a finite number (m) of interactions and we must have $i_1 < i_2 < ... < i_k < ... < m$. Therefore, the series above cannot be infinite. We have reached a contradiction.

6.3 Progress

We have proved the liveness of the system. The next question is whether the system can make progress in selecting interactions. The liveness of the system guarantees that an interaction process in state 'all-met' will enter into state 'meeting' or state 'success' in finite time. The progress requirement demands that at least one of those interactions in state 'all-met' enter into state 'success'. This requirement is satisfied in our algorithm. In order to prove this, we need the lemma as follows.

Lemma 2. If thread $T_{j,ir}$ sends Withdraw() to I_{ir} in state 'req-sent' and enters into state 're-try', there must be another thread $T_{j,ir'}$ of P_j in state 'commit-sent' such that $r' < r$.

Proof: Thread $T_{j,ir}$ in state 'req-sent' sends a Withdraw() to I_{ir} only if it finds $a[1..(r-1)] \neq 0$. Let r' be the largest integer such that $r' < r$ and $a[r'] = 1$. According to the protocol, thread $T_{j,ir'}$ is either the first thread in state 'commit-sent' or a past pending thread which has been woken up by another thread and entered into state 'commit-sent'.

The following theorem shows that in each coordination at least one selectable interaction will be selected. This ensures the progress of our algorithm.

Theorem 3. Let $I_{u1}, ..., I_{uw}$ be the subset of all the interactions that enter into state 'all-met' after receiving all the requests they need. Then, at least one of them will enter into state 'success'.

Proof: Let $P_{v1}, ..., P_{vy}$ be all the processes involved to make $I_{u1}, ..., I_{uw}$ enter into state 'all-met'. Without loss of generality, we also assume $I_{u1} < ... < I_{uw}$, i.e. $u1 < ... <$ uw. Due to the liveness of the system, every interaction of $I_{u1}, ..., I_{uw}$ will receive a response, Commit(), Withdraw(), or Abort(), from each of its participating processes from $P_{v1}, ..., P_{vy}$ and enter into either state 'meeting' or state 'success'. Let us assume that none of $I_{u1}, ..., I_{uw}$ enters into state 'success'. According to the protocol, a thread $T_{vj,ui}$ ($1 \leq j \leq y$, $1 \leq i \leq w$) can send Withdraw() only in two states: 'req-sent' and 'pending'. But, based on the assumption above, it is impossible for $T_{vj,ui}$ to send Withdraw() in state 'pending'. This is because otherwise it must receive a Stop from M_{vj} and therefore there must be a thread $T_{vj,ui'}$ ($1 \leq i' \leq w$) that succeeds in its coordination. This would imply that $I_{ui'}$ enters into state 'success'. To simplify the notation, P_{vj}, I_{ui}, and $T_{vj,ui}$ are renamed P'_j, I'_i, and $T'_{j,i}$, respectively. Consider I'_w first. Because it enters into state 'meeting', it must have received at least one Withdraw() from, say $T'_{j1,w}$ ($1 \leq j_1 \leq y$). According to Lemma 2, there must be a thread $T'_{j1,i1}$ that has sent a Commit() to I'_{i1} such that $i_1 < w$. Since I'_{i1} also enters into state 'meeting', it must have received a Withdraw() from say, $T'_{j2,i1}$ ($1 \leq j_2 \leq y$). By using Lemma 2 again, we can find another thread $T'_{j2,i2}$ that has sent a Commit() to I'_{i2} such that $i_2 < i_1$. Continuing this way, we will have an infinite series $T'_{j1,w}$, $T'_{j1,i1}$, $T'_{j2,i1}$, ..., $T'_{jk,ik}$, $T'_{jk+1,ik}$, ... such that $... < i_k < ... < i_1 < w$. On the other hand, there are only a finite number (w) of interactions involved and we must have $1 < ... < i_k < ... < i_1 < w$. Therefore, the above series cannot be infinite. We have reached a contradiction.

7 Summary

First-order multiparty interaction is one of the abstractions in the distributed programming model, called Interacting Processes, proposed by N. Francez and I. R. Forman [2]. In this paper, we proposed an algorithm for coordinating first-order multiparty interactions on demand with the middleware support. By taking advantage of multi-threading supported by modern operating systems, this algorithm requires less messages than the algorithm proposed by Joung and Smolka [13]. In this algorithm, middleware serves as the underlying communication infrastructure. Data exchanges are done by middleware. Application developers can develop distributed applications without concerning about the issues of heterogeneity such as data marshalling/unmarshalling and data formats. Applications in different programming languages running on different machines can exchange information across different network systems. In addition, no specific language processor needs to be implemented in order to execute IP programs. Our model allows IP programs to be executed in any general programming environment. Finally, the concerns of heterogeneity, distribution, communication, and coordination are separated into a 4-layered interaction model. The model isolating computation, communication, and coordination promotes reuse, improves comprehension, and eases maintenance due to software evolution.

References

1. Joung, Y.-J., Smolka, S.: A Comprehensive Study of the Complexity of Multiparty Interaction. Journal of the ACM. Vol. 43. No. 1. (1996) 75-115
2. Francez, N., Forman, I. R.: Interacting Processes. Addison-Wesley (1996)
3. Jungclaus, R., Saake, G., Hartmann, T., Sernadas, C.: TROLL: A Language for Object-Oriented Specification of Information Systems. ACM Transactions on Information Systems. Vol. 14. No. 2. (1996) 157-211
4. Feenstra, R., Wieringa, R.: LCM 3.0: A Language for Describing Conceptual Models. Technical Report IR-344. Faculty of Mathematics and Computer Science. Vrije Universiteit, Amsterdam (1993)
5. Ruiz, A., Corchuelo, R., Pérez, J., Durán, A., Toro, M.: An Aspect-Oriented Approach based on Multiparty Interactions to Specifying the Behavior of a System. Proceedings of the International Conference on Principles, Logics, and Implementations of High-Level Programming Languages (PLI'99). (1999) 56-65
6. Garg, V., Ajmani, S.: An Efficient Algorithm for Multiprocess Shared Events. Proceedings of the 2nd Symposium on Parallel and Distributed Computing. (1990)
7. Joung Y.-J., Smolka, S.: A Completely Distributed and Message-Efficient Implementation of Synchronous Multiprocess Communication. In Yew, P.-C. (ed.): Proceedings of the 19th International Conference on Parallel Processing. Vol. 3. (1990) 311-318
8. Frolund, S., Agha, G.: A Language Framework for Multi-object Coordination. Proceedings of ECOOP'93. Vol. 707. Lecture Notes in Computer Science, Springer-Verlag, (1993)
9. Frolund, S.: Coordinating Distributed Objects: An Actor-Based Approach to Synchronization. MIT Press, (1996)
10. Minsky, N., Ungureanu, V.: Regulated Coordination in Open Distributed Systems. In: Garlan, D., LeMetayer, D. (eds.): Proceedings of 2nd International Conference on Coordination Languages and Models. Spring-Verlag, (1997)
11. Denti, E., Natali, A., Omicini, A.: Programmable Coordination Media. In: Garlan, D., LeMetayer, D. (eds.): Proceedings of 2nd International Conference on Coordination Languages and Models. Spring-Verlag, (1997)
12. Radestock, M., Eisenbach, S.: Component Coordination in Middleware Systems. Proceedings of IFIP International Conference on Distributed Systems Platforms and Open Distributed Processing. Springer-Verlag, (1998) 225-240
13. Joung, Y.-J., Smolka, S.: Strong Interaction Fairness via Randomization. IEEE Transactions on Parallel and Distributed Systems. Vol. 9. No. 2. (1998) 137-149

14. Zorzo, A., Stroud, R.: A Distributed Object-Oriented Framework for Dependable Multi-party Interactions. Technical Report No. 671. University of Newcastle upon Tyne. United Kingdom (1999)
15. Quinn, M. J.: Designing Efficient Algorithms for Parallel Computers. McGraw-Hill, (1987)
16. Chiang, C.-C., Tang, P.: Middleware Support for Coordination in Distributed Applications. Proceedings of the Fifth IEEE International Symposium on Multimedia Software Engineering. (2003)

Reusability Analysis of Four Standard Object-Oriented Class Libraries

Saeed Araban[1] and A.S.M. Sajeev[2]

[1] Department of Computer Science and Software Engineering,
The University of Melbourne, Carlton, VIC 3010, Australia
`araban@unimelb.edu.au`
[2] School of Mathematics, Statistics and Computer Science,
University of New England, Australia
`sajeev@turing.une.edu.au`

Abstract. Class libraries play a key role in object oriented paradigm. They provide, by and large, the most commonly reused components in object-oriented environments. In this paper, we use a number of metrics to study reusability of four standard class libraries of two object-oriented languages; namely Java and Eiffel. The purpose of the study is to demonstrate how different design philosophies of the two languages have affected structural design and organization of their standard libraries that in turn might have affected their reusability with regards to *Ease of Reuse* and *Design with Reuse*. Our study concludes that within limits of our measurements, the Java libraries are easy to reuse whereas Eiffel libraries are better designed with reuse. We observe that whilst *design with reuse* may make class libraries extensible and maintainable, but it does not necessarily make them easy to reuse.

1 Introduction

Reuse is one of the major advantages of Object-Oriented (OO) paradigm [16, 12]. *Object-based* middleware technologies, such as SUN's J2EE, Microsoft's .net and OMG's CORBA, are also improve reusability of commercial-off-the-shelf (COTS) components by providing greater interoperability across different hardware/software platforms. We believe that such technologies will lead to a much more competitive, democratized, quality driven component market with far less emphasis on the programming language and/or runtime environment of the components. In the context of OO class libraries, that means libraries of high quality classes that are well designed, well organized, regardless of their programming language, are more likely to compete and survive. It is thus increasingly important that class libraries are designed and organized more carefully, in such a way that makes them easier to develop, maintain and reuse.

The most basic unit of reuse in Object-Oriented Programming (OOP) is called *Class*. A class may be defined as implementation of an abstraction of an entity in the system. Each class encapsulates relevant data and valid operations on that data for an entity. In other words, a class is an implementation for an

W. Dosch, R.Y. Lee, and C. Wu (Eds.): SERA 2004, LNCS 3647, pp. 171–186, 2005.

Abstract Data Type (ADT). Once defined, a class can potentially be reused in different object-oriented systems.

There are different types of software reuse including *Black-* and *white-box* reuse [6]. *Black-box* reuse (a.k.a. *verbatim* reuse) is when software components are reused without any modification [18, 2]. *White-box* reuse is the reuse of components through modification and adaptation [18]. White-box reuse usually requires access to the source code of the components and intimate knowledge about their design and implementation. Compared to black-box, white-box reuse can be more flexible; however, it can also be more expensive and difficult to develop and maintain.

OOP supports both black- and white-box reuse. White-box reuse is achieved through the *inheritance* relation, where a class may inherit features of its parent class(es). Black-box reuse is achieved through *client-supplier* relation, where a class relies on services provided by other class(es).

Class libraries are the main source of reusable components in OO Languages (OOL) that provide essential building blocks and frameworks for constructing software systems from common data structures (e.g. lists and stacks) to those handling networking and security protocols. Domain specific class libraries are also available for applications ranging from numerical analysis [19, 17] to particle physics [3] and even agricultural modelling [13]. Therefore, learning various class libraries in modern OOLs may well take more time and effort than learning syntax and semantics of the language itself. The large number of available classes and the complexity of the relationship among them may in fact hinder the learning process.

In this paper, we argue that both designers and re-users of class libraries may benefit from metrics that help them to measure, analyse and compare various quality attributes, such as reusability and maintainability, of the class libraries.

Our hypothesis here is that an OO class library is easier to reuse if it reduces the amount of effort needed by a programmer to find and understand the class that she needs. Here, we try to establish links between the effort required for learning and understanding a class library to its number of classes, the amount of similarity between classes, and the complexity of classes in terms of the number and complexity of their methods and the number and complexity of their relationships with other classes.

The rest of the paper is organized as follows. In the next section, we develop our criteria and method of evaluation. In Section 3, we give a brief description of the organization of Java and Eiffel libraries. In Section 4, we analyse and compare the structure of the two languages libraries based on the criteria developed in Section 2. Section 5 draws some conclusions and discusses future work.

2   Criteria and Method of Evaluation

In this paper, we analyse and compare standard class libraries of two prominent OOLs, Eiffel [16] and Java [11] to assess how easy they are to be reused by programmers (*Ease of Reuse*) and to what extent they practice reuse in their own construction (*Design with Reuse*).

Eiffel is chosen since it is considered to be one of the purest OOLs [14]. It is widely appreciated among OO researchers for its simple syntax and rich semantics. Java, on the other hand, is a popular OOL which is widely used in the commercial world. Both these languages support basic OO concepts, such as *classes* and *objects, inheritance, strong typing* and *late binding*, and automatic memory management and *garbage collection*.

However, Java and Eiffel follow different design philosophies and offer different degrees of support for the above concepts (e.g. single vs. multiple-inheritance), which makes them good representatives for the OOLs family. Also, these different design philosophies may have affected organizational structure of the class libraries, which in turn may have affected the complexity, flexibility, and consequently reusability of each class library.

Our method of evaluation is based on measuring various attributes of the class libraries. There are many software metrics – both general (e.g. [1], [7]) and OO specific metrics [9] – in the literature. Among those metrics, we have chosen a subset of Chidamber and Kemerer's metrics suite for object-oriented design [4] because of their sound theoretical foundation, clear and widely accepted definitions, and their ease of measure. Furthermore, in our view, those metrics can measure attributes that are relevant to reusability of class libraries.

We use two criteria for analysing the reusability aspects of class libraries. They are: Ease of Reuse, and Design with Reuse.

2.1 Ease of Reuse

Ease of reuse analyses how classes are designed, structured and distributed into libraries so that they can be reused easily. It also looks at how easy it is for a programmer to incorporate a library class into a program once they have located the right class. A straightforward way to evaluate the latter criterion is to compare the steps required to use a library class in a program.

However, a more interesting problem in *ease of reuse* is the difficulty for a programmer to choose the required class. The design of the class library and the support provided to search the library are important aspects in evaluating this criterion. In order to study how the structure of the library affects *ease of reuse*, we use the following metrics.

Weighted Methods per Class (WMC). *Definition*: Consider a class C_1, with methods $M_1, \cdots, M_n$ that are defined in the class. Let $c_1, \cdots, c_n$ be the complexity of the methods [4]. Then:

$WMC = \sum_{i=1}^{n} c_i$

This metric is an indication of the complexity of a class based on the complexity of its methods (c_i). However, for simplicity purposes, we consider all methods to be of unity complexity:

$WMC = n$

The original metric takes all methods in a class into account. However, in order to reuse a class, only its public methods are needed to be learned and understood. Therefore, we only include public methods in our WMC measurement.

Classes with smaller number of methods are likely to be easier to understand and learn and therefore be reused. Also, classes with large number of methods are likely to be more application specific, limiting possibility of wider reuse. But, with the same token, higher WMC values can indicate more functionality. Thus, one may conclude that higher WMC is good for highly specialised and domain specific classes/libraries, whereas lower WMC is more suitable for general purpose classes/libraries.

Depth of Inheritance Tree (DIT). *Definition*: The length from a class (node) to the root of the inheritance hierarchy is the depth of inheritance of the class. In the case of multiple inheritance, the DIT will be the maximum length from the node to the root of the hierarchy [4].

Inheritance provides white-box reuse. To fully understand a class, a programmer needs to understand its ancestors. Greater DIT means larger number of ancestors. Therefore, harder to understand and learn the class. Furthermore, greater DIT implies greater specialization of the class that again may limit the possibility of wider reuse.

2.2   Design with Reuse

Class libraries can be considered as development frameworks for their application domain. In the context of class libraries, *Design with Reuse* may be defined as: reusing library classes by the other classes within the library. Hence, the degree of design with reuse for a library can be considered as an indication of its effectiveness as a framework for the intended application domain.

As mentioned before, both white- and black-box reuse are supported in OOLs through inheritance and client-supplier relations. Therefore, measuring these relations among classes of a library can be a good indicator of the level of design with reuse within the library.

Depth of Inheritance Tree (DIT). As defined in 2.1.2, DIT can also be used as an indicator for level of white-box reuse within a library. Higher DIT values may be interpreted as greater white-box reuse amongst classes of a library.

Number of Children (NOC). *Definition*: NOC =number of immediate subclasses subordinated to a class in the class hierarchy [4].

Higher NOC value indicates more reuse in the library itself through inheritance. NOC is also a measure for the degree of impact a class has on other classes and the library. Libraries with high NOC value can be more sensitive to changes in their classes, which can be an important factor in the library design and maintenance. Therefore, new and less stable class libraries would try to minimize this number. On the other hand, more stable libraries may have higher values for NOC without compromising their maintainability.

Coupling between object Classes (CBO). *Definition*: CBO for a class is a count of the number of other classes to which it is coupled. Two classes are coupled when methods declared in one class use methods or instance variables defined in another class [4].

Coupling can be measured at two distinct levels, interface and implementation. *Interface coupling* refers to those dependencies between classes, which are visible through their public interfaces (e.g. inheritance and public methods' signature). On the other hand, *Implementation-coupling* cannot be seen through the public interface of coupled classes (e.g. private state variables and methods' signatures).

Coupling is a measure of design with reuse. Higher the coupling, higher the number of use of other classes. It is also a measure of maintainability.

One might argue that lower the coupling the higher the independence of a class, and therefore higher the ease of reuse. Unlike inheritance metrics, we have not used CBO as an "ease of reuse" measure because, as far as a programmer is concerned, coupling is an internal matter of the class and the programmer does not have to study the behavior of the server classes to understand a client class. For example, a Car class may be a client for an Engine class, but a driver only needs to know the behavior of the Car class, and not the Engine class. On the other hand, if a Car class inherits from a Vehicle class and if the steering behavior (which is common to all vehicles) is defined in the Vehicle class, a driver needs to understand both Car and Vehicle classes.

2.3 Compared Libraries

A meaningful comparison can only be made between class libraries within similar application domains that provide similar set of functionalities.

This study is limited to subsets of Java and Eiffel standard libraries. Compared standard libraries are fallen into two main categories: *Basic* and *GUI* (see Table 1). The Basic category includes the most widely used libraries, such as mathematical, I/O and text processing libraries. Some of these libraries, such as Lang in Java and Kernel in Eiffel, provide basic data types, data structures that are essential for programming in the corresponding language.

The GUI category provides another set of widely used Eiffel and Java libraries that support design and implementation of graphical environments.

The following is a very brief introduction to each of the target libraries.

Java Libraries. Java standard library is organized over several packages, such as *java.lang, java.io, java.awt*. In this study, we used the following subset of JDK^{TM} standard class library:

- IO: This package contains three groups of classes and interfaces:
  1. classes for building data streams.
  2. classes and interfaces for serialization.
  3. classes and interfaces for dealing with the file system.
- Lang: This package contains classes that are essential to the Java language, such as class Object, Throwable, Exception and Thread.

Table 1. Compared Eiffel and Java Libraries

Java	Eiffel
Basic:	
Lang	Kernel
IO	Structure
Math	Iteration
Util	Thread
Text	Lex
	Parse
GUI:	
AWT	Vision

- Math: This package contains classes for performing arithmetic and bit manipulation on decimal and integer numbers.
- Text: This package contains classes and interfaces for handling text, dates, numbers, and messages.
- Util: This package contains useful utility classes (e.g. data structures, random number generator, string tokenizer, date and time).
- AWT: This package contains classes for creating graphical environments and user interfaces.

Eiffel libraries. ISE Eiffel provides a set of class libraries for a wide range of applications. ISE Eiffel (for MS-Windows) that is used in this study comes with Eiffel *Base* and *vision* libraries, which consist of the following libraries:

- Eiffel Base libraries:
  - Kernel: Covers fundamental concepts close to the language, such as basic structures, general purpose classes, and execution mechanisms such as garbage collector.
  - Data Structure: Provides fundamental data structures and algorithms. It is the largest and probably the most important library in Base collection.
  - Iteration: Provides ways for systematic traversal of some data structures. It can be considered as a part of the Data Structure library.
  - Lex: Provides lexical analysis services.
  - Parse: Supports syntactical analysis.
- Eiffel Vision: provides graphical classes, which can be mapped into any supported windowing system (e.g. X11 and Windows) that can guarantee source level compatibility.

3   Analysis of the Libraries

3.1   Ease of Reuse

Both Eiffel and Java classes are easy to reuse provided that one knows exactly what classes are provided and how to find and integrate them. In Java, standard class libraries are organized into packages, which can be imported into classes of a Java program using import statements. Similarly, Eiffel libraries are organized into clusters of related classes. However, in Eiffel, libraries are imported at the system level using compiler directives. The advantage of the Eiffel approach is that each class within a system does not need to explicitly specify where the library classes are coming from, which not only makes them simpler, but also immune to changes to the libraries.

Weighted Methods per Class (WMC). The percentage of classes corresponding to each WMC values for different libraries are shown in Figures 1 to 4.

According to the above figures, Java libraries have lower WMC values than their Eiffel counterparts, which is more evident in the Base libraries than the GUI ones. This means that, on average, there is less number of methods to go through to understand a class in Java libraries than a corresponding class in an Eiffel library. Based on this observation, one may conclude that Java libraries are better designed for reuse (in terms of ease of understanding) within limits of this measure. On the other hand, higher WMC values for Eiffel libraries implies more functionality provided by Eiffel classes that can make them more rewarding for reuse. Eiffel's design philosophy of separating query methods (that return a value about the current state of an object) and command methods (that change the state of an object) could have contributed to higher WMC in its libraries.

Depth of Inheritance Tree (DIT). Figures 5 to 8 show the percentage of classes in Eiffel and Java libraries with different depth of inheritance tree values.

From the DIT values it's clear that Java libraries have a flatter inheritance structure where as Eiffel libraries have a deeper inheritance structure. In Eiffel Base, nearly 10% of the classes have 10 or more ancestors which means, to be able to reuse one of these classes, a programmer needs to understand 10 other classes in its ancestry. On the other hand, in Java Base, no class has more than 6 ancestors. Looking at the GUI libraries, in Java GUI, only 38% of the classes have more than one ancestor, whereas, for Eiffel Vision, more than 80% of the

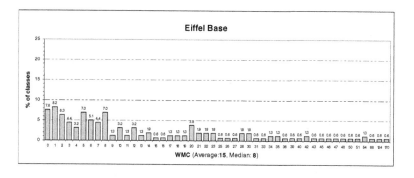

Fig. 1. WMC for Eiffel Base class libraries

classes have more than one ancestor. Looking at the average figures, Java classes have 50% or less ancestry than Eiffel classes. On this measure, Java libraries are easier to reuse since understanding a class is less dependent on understanding its ancestors. GUI libraries are one of the heavily used libraries since modern applications are almost always GUI based. The average depth of inheritance tree of Eiffel Vision is nearly three times more than the average DIT of Java GUI.

Looking at the DIT and WMC figures together, in order to reuse a Java class (as opposed to an Eiffel class), a programmer needs to be familiar with less number of other (ancestor) classes, and each of these other classes have less number of weighted methods thus favoring understandability considerably.

3.2   Design with Reuse

Depth of Inheritance Tree. Let's look at the DIT graphs (Figures 5 to 8) again, this time wearing a different hat: our purpose now is to study design with reuse that is how a library reuses its own classes. We observe that Eiffel's inheritance trees are much deeper than their corresponding Java trees indicating that an Eiffel library class tend to reuse more of other classes as its ancestors. Some Eiffel Base classes have up to 13 ancestors, whereas no class in Java Base has more than 6 ancestors. In OO design, it is well established that inheritance should only model the *is-a* relation and not any haphazard or convenient reuse. This means that the library needs to be very carefully designed in order to be able to use acceptable inheritance relation to the level Eiffel has achieved. It could also mean that since the inheritance hierarchy is designed to a much deeper level, there is possibility of reusing classes at levels up in the hierarchy to start up other branches (in a multiple inheritance language such as Eiffel this is straightforward) to expand the library in future with lesser effort than in a flatter structure as in Java.

Number of Children (NOC). Unlike a DIT that shows how many ancestors a class has, an NOC shows how many children a class has. Measurement of Eiffel

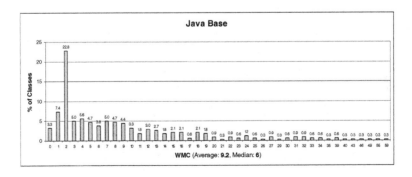

Fig. 2. WMC for Java Base class libraries

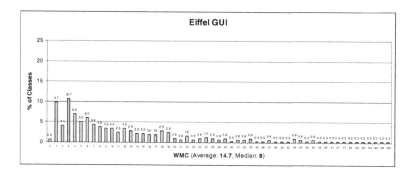

Fig. 3. WMC for Eiffel GUI class libraries

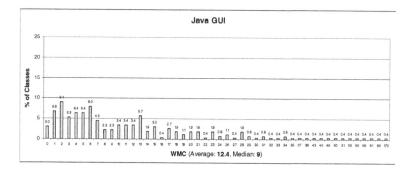

Fig. 4. WMC for Java GUI class libraries

Base and GUI libraries (Figures 9 and 11) shows a similar pattern: more than 50% of the classes have one or more children and on average, the same level of dependencies among classes (less than 2 children per class). These figures suggest that Eiffel classes are reused more by subclassing classes in the libraries.

Therefore, Eiffel class libraries are more sensitive to changes made to a class since it could affect relatively larger number of children. Eiffel handles this by defining pre- and post-conditions and invariants for methods and suggesting that changes made to a class should satisfy these conditions on which other classes rely on.

On the other hand, more than 80% of classes in both Java Base and GUI libraries (Figures 10 and 12) have no child (i.e., they are terminal nodes) and their average NOC values are well under 1. Therefore, changes to classes in Java libraries have little effect on other classes suggesting easier library maintenance.

The flatter inheritance structure of Java means there is a small number of classes with a large number of children with a class having up to 128 children in Java Base, where as Eiffel's more deeper inheritance structure means that the number of children are divided more uniformly between classes, thus the largest number of children for a class is only 7 in Eiffel base. The average values are

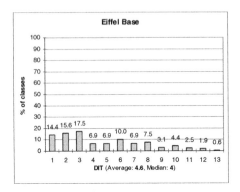

Fig. 5. *DIT* for Eiffel Base class libraries

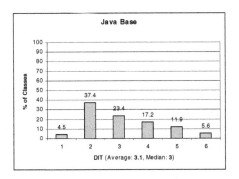

Fig. 6. *DIT* for Java Base class libraries

similar for Java and Eiffel (with Eiffel value being slightly higher), however, the average values do hide the difference in the distribution that is observable in the graphs.

Coupling Between Object Classes (*CBO*). The coupling between object classes is shown in Figures 13 to 16. Java libraries have a higher *CBO* value than Eiffel libraries. A quarter of Eiffel base classes have no coupling, where as only 4% of Java Base classes are coupling free. While coupling does not exceed beyond 7 classes for Eiffel Base, it can go up to 21 classes in Java Base.

The average coupling values are higher in the GUI libraries than in Base libraries, indicating that GUI classes need to use other classes more often than the Base classes. A small percentage of classes (0.2%) in Eiffel Vision has the highest coupling value of 43, as opposed to only 7 in Eiffel Base, and similarly 0.4% of Java GUI classes have the highest coupling value of 53 as opposed to 21 in Java Base. Here again, Eiffel has less average coupling (3.1%) than Java (4.7%). Furthermore, 35% of Eiffel Vision classes do not have coupling where as only 7% of Java GUI classes are coupling free.

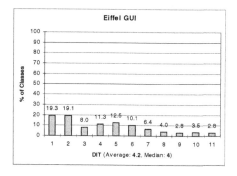

Fig. 7. *DIT* for Eiffel GUI class libraries

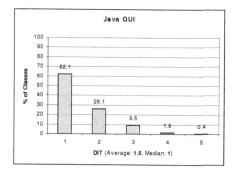

Fig. 8. *DIT* for Java GUI class libraries

Here we observe trends that are opposite to those observed in the case of *DIT*. It seems that the lower the *DIT* the higher the *CBO* value. It is possible that Java libraries are compensating the smaller inheritance hierarchy by using higher coupling between classes.

As discussed before, coupling through client/server relation is a more common method of reuse than inheritance, since client/server coupling can be used for any relation other than *is-a*. It may be worth investigating Java libraries further to see whether *is-a* relations are also implemented using client-server coupling in Java to get these higher values.

4   Conclusions

Several surveys comparing OOLs are published (e.g. [8], [20]). There are also several studies on reusability of object-oriented systems (e.g. [10], [5]). However, studies on reusability of class libraries are rare.

We have analysed class libraries of two object-oriented languages, Eiffel and Java, to better understand them in terms of Ease of Reuse and Design with

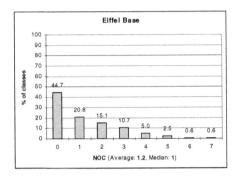

Fig. 9. *NOC* for Eiffel Base class libraries

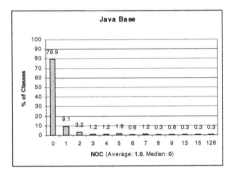

Fig. 10. *NOC* for Java Base class libraries

Reuse. We took a set of libraries representing basic and graphical user interface classes. The metrics we used were from Chidamber and Kemerer.

Ease of Reuse tells us whether the library is structured in a way that it is easy for programmers to understand, locate and use the classes. Design with Reuse, on the other hand, examines the level of reuse of classes within the library itself. Our observations are summarized in Table 2. In the table a plus sign indicates that the corresponding language favors the criteria, and a minus indicates the opposite.

Table 2. Summery of reusability analysis of Eiffel and Java libraries

Language	Ease of Reuse			Design with Reuse		
	Ease of Coding	Class Size	Deep Hierarchy	Number of Ancestors	Number of Children	Coupling Between Classes
Eiffel	+	-	-	+	+	-
Java	+	+	+	-	-	+

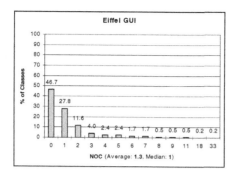

Fig. 11. *NOC* for Eiffel GUI class libraries

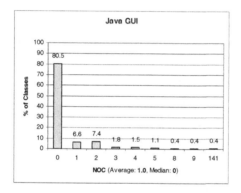

Fig. 12. *NOC* for Java GUI class libraries

Java class libraries get a plus for all three criteria we examined for Ease of Reuse, while Eiffel libraries get a plus for only one of the three criteria. This is because Eiffel libraries tend to have higher weighted methods per class and deeper inheritance hierarchy of classes, thus requiring more effort on the programmer's part to understand the library. For example, while Eiffel libraries with many closely related classes (e.g. Dynamic_List, Arrayed_List, Multi_Array_List, Part_Sorted_List, Sorted_List, Two_Way_List, Part_Sorted_Two_way_List, Sorted_Two_Way_List, etc.) [15] may increase the probability of a programmer finding exactly the class she wants, in general, they may increase the time and effort required to understand all these variety provided.

On Design with Reuse, Eiffel class libraries get a plus for two of the three criteria we employed, where as Java libraries get a plus for only one of the three. This is again because, Eiffel employs reuse by inheritance heavily in its library. A typical class in Eiffel has a large number of ancestral and/or descendent classes, whereas a large number of classes in Java have no child. Java libraries, however, tend to have a higher reuse in the form of client/supplier relations. Since reuse by inheritance can only model the *is-a* relation, it requires much care to design

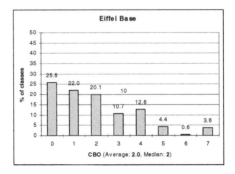

Fig. 13. *CBO* for Eiffel Base class libraries

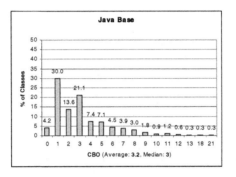

Fig. 14. *CBO* for Java Base class libraries

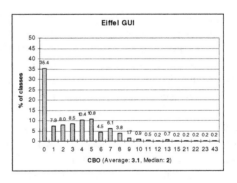

Fig. 15. *CBO* for Eiffel GUI class libraries

libraries with heavy use of inheritance; otherwise, one could end up with spurious classes with no use other than being an intermediary between ancestors and descendants. Clever use of inheritance hierarchy allows the library to be easily extendible by starting new branches in the hierarchy.

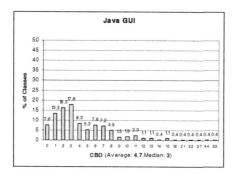

Fig. 16. *CBO* for Java GUI class libraries

In summary, Eiffel and Java libraries have employed different design principles which have resulted in giving different kinds of benefits to their users. While it is not easy to state which principles are better, it may be worth conducting a further study to see whether these principles played a role in Eiffel being better appreciated by the research community, and Java being better accepted by programmers of the commercial world.

Acknowledgments

We would like to thank the anonymous referees for their comments during the evaluation process of this paper. This work was supported in part by an ARC Discovery Grant (grant number DP0209483).

References

[1] A.J. Albrecht. Measuring application development productivity. In *IBM Applications Development Symp*, 1979.

[2] J. Bieman and S. Karunanithi. Candidate reuse metrics for object oriented and ada software. In *IEEE-CS 1st International Software Metrics Symposium*, 1993.

[3] R. F. Boisvert, J. Dongarra, R. Pozo, K. Remington, and G. Stewart. Oops: an object-oriented particle simulation class library for distributed architectures. *Concurrency: Practice and Experience*, 10(11-13):1117–1129, 1998.

[4] S.R. Chidamber and C.F. Kemerer. A metrics suite for object oriented design. *IEEE Transactions on Software Engineering*, 20(6):476 – 493, 1994.

[5] R.G. Fichman and C.F. Kemerer. Object technology and reuse: Lessons from early adopters. *IEEE Computer*, 30(10):47–59, 1997.

[6] William Frakes and Carol Terry. Software reuse: Metrics and models. *ACM Computing Surveys*, 28(2):415–435, 1996.

[7] T.E. Hastings and A.S.M. Sajeev. A vector based approach to software size measurement and effort estimation. *IEEE Transactions on Software Engineering*, 27(4):337–350, 2001.

[8] R. Henderson and B. Zorn. A comparison of oo programming in four modern languages. *Software Practice and Experience*, 24(11):1077–1095, 1994.

[9] B. Henderson-Sellers. *Object-Oriented Metrics: Measures of Complexity*. Prentice-Hall, 1996.

[10] M. Hitz. Measuring reuse attributes in object-oriented systems. In *Int. Conf. on Object Oriented Info. Systems*, Dublin,Ireland, 1995.

[11] C.S. Horstmann and G. Cornel. *Core Java*. Sunsoft Press, Mountain View, California, 1997.

[12] I. Jacobson. *Software Reuse: Architecture, Process and Organization for Business Success*. ACM Press, 1997.

[13] H. Kage and H. Sttzel. Hume: An object oriented component library for generic modular modelling of dynamic systems. In M. Donatelli, C. Stockle, F. Villalobos, and J. Villar, editors, *Modelling cropping systems*, pages 299–300, Lleida, 1999. European Society of Agronomy.

[14] B. Meyer. *Eiffel: The Language*. Prentice-Hall, 2nd edition, 1992.

[15] B. Meyer. *Reusable Software: The Base Object-Oriented Component Libraries*. Prentice-Hall, 1994.

[16] B. Meyer. *Object-Oriented Software Construction*. Prentice Hall PTR, Upper Saddle River, New Jersey, 2nd edition, 1997.

[17] R. Pozo. Template numerical toolkit. Technical report, National Institute of Standards and Technology, 2002.

[18] R. Prieto-Diaz. Status report: software reusability. *IEEE Software*, pages 61–66, 1993.

[19] John V. W. Reynders, David W. Forslund, Paul J. Hinker, Marydelland Tholburn, David G. Kilman, and William F. Humphrey. Developing numerical libraries in java. *Computer Physics Communications*, 87(1-2):212–224, 1995.

[20] H.W. Schmidt and S. Omohundro. Clos, eiffel and sather: A comparison. Technical report, International Computer Science Institute, 1991.

Validation of an Approach for Quantitative Measurement and Prediction Model

Ki-won Song, Jeong-hwan Park, and Kyung-whan Lee

School of Computer Science and Engineering, Chung-Ang University, Korea
{kwsong, jhpark, kwlee}@object.cau.ac.kr
http://www.object.cau.ac.kr

Abstract. Software organizations are in need of methods to understand, structure, and improve the data they are collection. We have developed an approach for use when a large number of diverse metrics are already being collected by a software organization. The Approach combines two methods. One looks at an organization's measurement framework in a goal-oriented fashion and the other looks at it in the performance pyramid by quantitative method. We present model-based performance prediction at software development time in order to optimize a project of organization and strengthen control of it and thus, accomplish its objectives by determining its process capability and project capability through the proposed three models(PCM, ECM, PPM) by developing strategies to improve the process and, by planning the most suitable project to its vision with Project Prediction Model (PPM).

1 Introduction

Recently, S/W companies have tried to have an edge on other competitors in securing more extensive market and maximizing financial profits.

To this end, they should develop strategies suitable to their vision and implement projects to measure performance attributes. Lynch and Cross suggested a performance pyramid for developing strategies needed to accomplish an organization's vision and measuring whether the organization accomplished its vision.

This paper measures quality and delivery attributes for an organization's external effectiveness and, cycle time and waste attributes for its internal efficiency. It also measures process capability and project capability through PCM by completing and analyzing a questionnaire based on GQM (Goal Question Metrics) to find a way to improve the process.

Based on the analysis of results, ECM (Earned Value Calculation Model) can be designed to analyze financial performance (earned value) through which effective process improvement plan and project plans suitable to the organization's vision can be developed.

In order to predict the project suitable to the organization's vision and optimize the process with analysis results gained through the ECM, this paper also suggests PPM which can predict, based on the organization's project-performing capability, how much manpower, time and capital should be invested to the project and what degree of quality the developed product will have.

W. Dosch, R.Y. Lee, and C. Wu (Eds.): SERA 2004, LNCS 3647, pp. 187–200, 2005.

2 Basic Study

2.1 Why is Earned Value Needed for IT Business?

Promoting resources-managing ability to effectively invest IT resources and maximize their effect is becoming an essential field in the IT industry [2] [3].

   IT emerged as a key area to reengineer and improve business process, along with using computers. Large corporations including IBM, Ford, and GE are enjoying 80% more effect from business process reengineering using IT than from the improvement just using computers.

2.2 Calculation Procedure for Earned Value

The best way to calculate earned value is to accumulate data on the project to be implemented and conform to the following procedures[2].

Calculation Procedures for Earned Value

(1) Set objectives suitable to your organization's vision.
(2) Complete the questionnaire to find out the attributes helpful to improve the process
(3) Develop models and methods to measure attributes for evaluating accomplishment of the objectives.
(4) Identify the alternatives and measures through analysis

2.3 GQM (Goal-Question-Metrics) Process

GQM process is a series of procedures as follows:

   Set an organization's goals through GQM approach, Set goals of project in each area, Make questions and develop metrics measure accomplishment of the goals using the metrics. As shown in <Figure 1>, GQM process is generally composed of vision, objectives, and areas belonging to external effectiveness or internal efficiency [10].

   For example, if an organization's vision is improvement of public recognition on it, it should concentrate on market shares rather than on financial performance, and put its priority on customer satisfaction and flexibility rather than on flexibility and productivity[1].

Fig. 1. *Lynch and Cross's Performance Pyramid*

In order to satisfy customers, quality and delivery should be more emphasized than cycle time and waste.

Quality and delivery is goals to measure external effectiveness while cycle time and waste is to measure internal efficiency [1].

Here, goals are set again in each area, strategies for process improvement are developed through GQM approach, and measurement is carried out [11].

2.4 GQM Approach

GQM approach involves three steps.

First is conceptual step. It consists of elements such as object, purpose, viewpoint and focus. In this step, major goal are set. Second is operational step. In this step, questions are derived from the goals that must be answered in order to determine if the goals are achieved. Third is quantitative step in which proper answers are given to the questions.

Through the three steps, metrics system is made. These metrics can be used as a measurement tool [10] [11] [17] [18].

3 PCM (Project Capability Model)

This section suggests PCM which can measure an organization's capability through completion and analysis of questionnaire.

PCM calculates project-performing capability of an organization with GQM approach regarding each of 4 performance attributes in the performance pyramid (Lynch and Cross).

GQM process is a series of procedures as follows:

Set an organization's goals through GQM approach
Set goals of project in each area

Make questions and develop metrics measure accomplishment of the goals using the metrics. Based on the performance pyramid, GQM quantitative questionnaire is made which enables calculation of an organization's capability and earned value by using GQM approach. GQM quantitative questionnaire is composed of items with which external effectiveness and internal efficiency of an organization can be measured. For evaluation of external effectiveness, performance attributes like quality and delivery are analyzed and for evaluation of internal efficiency, cycle time and waste are analyzed. In each area above, project goals are set again, strategies for process improvement are developed through GQM approach and measurement is carried out.

For each of 4 goals including quality, delivery, cycle time and waste, questions are made and then metrics are completed.

3.1 Data Collecting Method

This paper uses data from questionnaires on 20 tasks of corporations which are collected from SPICE (SW Process Improvement & Capability determination) assessment. Data gained from the answers to the questionnaires are revised according to some defined rules to secure reliability of data on the assumption of T-distribution.

Considering possible miscommunication between respondents and questionnaires and problem of representing quantitative data, data out of confidence intervals are revised according to revision rules.

3.2 GQM Quantitative Questionnaire from Project Meta Data

This section proposes GQM quantitative questionnaire made from general meta data.

Procedures for making the questionnaire involving three steps: setting goals; giving questions; gaining metrics.

First is conceptual step. It consists of elements such as object, purpose, viewpoint and focus. In this step, major goal are set.

Second is operational step. In this step, questions are derived from the goals.

Third is quantitative step in which proper answers are given to the questions.

Through the three steps, metrics system is made. 20 measurable metrics were made for 8 questions. GQM results gained though three steps are shown in <Table 1>

Table 1. Metric Results based on GQM

Goal	Question	Metric
Quality (To improve quality of product up to level of satisfying customers)	Defect density (In the project, how densely defect are found and properly dealt with.)	Defect rate of products
		Defect rate of technical documents.
		Defect rate of codes
		Defect management rate.
	Impact requirement (How much impact customer's requirement of change has on project?)	Requirement change rate
Delivery (Shorten time needed to deliver product to customers)	Delivery time (Are products delivered to customers on schedule?)	General on-schedule-rate
		On-schedule-rate at planning/analysis stage
		On-schedule-rate at design stage
		On-schedule-rate at implementation stage
		On-schedule-rate at test stage
Cycle time (Shorten total processing time)	Man-Month: Effort distribution (To shorten cycle time, optimal MM is needed. Is MM optimized at each stage?)	Man-Month rate at planning/analysis stage
		Man-Month rate at design stage
		Man-Month rate at implementation stage
		Man-Month rate at test stage
Waste (Reduce waste of available resources when proceeding project)	Productivity (What is current productivity of project?)	Code productivity per person
		Documentation scale per code
		Documentation scale per person
	Reuse (How many codes are reused?)	Code reuse rate
	Rework (How much time is spent for rework?)	Rework hours

Meta data is deprived from questions and metrics gained through GQM approach. Each factor of measure method of PCM model needed to calculate metrics is meta data. And measure method of each metric is a capability measure model factor of PCM. Meta data gained like this compose answers to GQM quantitative questionnaire.

3.3 Project Capability Measurement Model

This section proposes PCM to calculate project capability in terms of external effectiveness and internal efficiency of an organization.

Input data of this model is data collected from GQM questionnaire as suggested in 3.2. Factors of PCM to measure a project capability of an organization for 4 goals are shown in <Table2>

Table 2. Factors of PCM to measure a project capability in terms of external effectiveness of an organization

Question	Metric	Capability Measure Factor
Defect density (Quality)	Defect rate of products	Total number of defects
	Defect rate of technical documents.	(Requirement specification + design specification) number of defects and total number of pages of outcome
	Defect rate of codes	Number of code defects, total SLOC
	Defect management rate.	Number of complete correcting defects.
Impact requirement (Quality)	Requirement change rate	Number of requirement change, total number of requirement
Delivery time (Delivery)	General on-schedule-rate	Total delivery days, planned delivery days
	On-schedule-rate at planning/analysis stage	Actual delivery days, planned delivery days at planning/analysis stage
	On-schedule-rate at design stage	Actual delivery days, planned delivery days at design stage
	On-schedule-rate at implementation stage	Actual delivery days, planned delivery days at implementation stage
	On-schedule-rate at test stage	Actual delivery days, planned delivery days at test stage
Man-Month : Effort distribution (Cycle time)	Man-Month rate at planning/analysis stage	MM at planning/analysis stage
	Man-Month rate at design stage	MM at design stage
	Man-Month rate at implementation stage	MM rate at implementation stage
	Man-Month rate at test stage	MM at test stage
Man-Month ; Effort correspondence (Cycle time)	General effort correspondence	Actual MM and planed MM, general MM
	Effort correspondence rate at planning/analysis stage	Actual MM and planed MM at planning/analysis stage
	Effort correspondence rate at design stage	Actual MM and planed MM at design stage
	Effort correspondence rate at implementation stage	Actual MM and planed MM at implementation stage
	Effort correspondence rate at test stage	Actual MM and planed MM at test stage
Productivity (Waste)	Code productivity per person	Effort SLOC
	Documentation scale per code	Number of document's page
	Documentation scale per person	Total distributed effort
Reuse (Waste)	Code reuse rate	Number of reused SLOC
Rework (Waste)	Actual output to planned output ratio	Actual SLOC, Planned SLOC
	Rework rate cause by defects	Rework hours, total spent hours

Calculation forms to measure a project capability of an organization in terms of external effectiveness and internal efficiency for 4goals are shown in <Table3>

Table 3. Calculation forms to measure a project capability of an organization in terms of external effectiveness and internal efficiency

External effectiveness $PCM(qd) = (PCM(q)+PCM(d))/2$	PCM(q): quality effectiveness score	$\sum((100 - each\,defect\,rate) + defect\,management\,rate)/4$
	PCM(d): schedule effectiveness score	$\sum(100 - on\,schedule\,rate\,at\,each\,stage)/5$
Internal efficiency $PCM(c,w)=(PCM(c))+PCM(w))/2$	PCM(c): effort efficiency score	$\sum(effort\,correspndence\,rate\,at\,each\,stage)/4$
	PCM(w): resource efficiency score	$\sum(all\,factors) - (2\times(100 - [rework\,per\,code]))/6$

By calculating PCM for external effectiveness (q, d, quality and delivery) and PCM for internal efficiency(c, w, cycle and waste), benchmarking other competitors becomes possible. In addition, it also shows the degree of external effectiveness improvement.

But effective process strategies cannot be developed with organization's capability alone.

For example, in the case that PCM(q):85>PCM(d) : 75, no matter what you select out of two strategies(to heighten quality capability from 85 to 90 or to heighten time capability from 75 to 80) in order to increase external effectiveness, PCM result is same because both strategies is to increase 5.

But if you can get 1000 won from increased quality of 5 and get 500 won from increased delivery time of 5, it is not effective to increase external effectiveness by simply improving factors with lower figure. That is because it excludes the cost/profit the organization can get.

Therefore, in order to decide which capability should be strengthened by comparing quality capability and delivery capability of PCM, earned values should be calculated in fields of quality and delivery.

4   ECM (Earned Value Calculation Model)

This section suggests ECM with which project's cost for external effectiveness can be calculated, using the project capability results gained from PCM. Calculation procedure of ECM is as follows and the composition is shown in <Figure 2>

Calculation procedures of ECM

1. Calculate project capability with PCM.
2. Measure cost factors of quality and delivery belonging to external effectiveness of organization.
3. Design and calculate ECM for external effectiveness by using the measured values above.
4. Calculate expected cost for project improvement through analysis of the calculated results above.

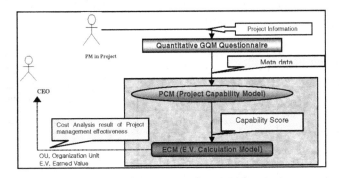

Fig. 2. Composition of ECM

<Table 4> provides ECM to analyze project cost, using PCM value of organization, with project input from GQM quantitative questionnaire.

By using PCM results and expected gains from improvement, effective strategies for external effectiveness of organization can be developed.

All that PCM and ECM can calculate is only current project capability and expected gains from improvement.

For example, when a strategy to increase delivery time by 5 is selected because the gains from shortened delivery time by 5 is larger than gains form improved quality, you cannot expect how much cost will be spent or how much days will be needed for the project.

Therefore, this paper also suggests PPM(Project Predict Model) which can calculate schedule and manpower for future project by analyzing PCM and ECM results.

Table 4. ECM for project cost analysis

Goal	Earned Value	ECM Calculation model
Quality	Total cost for defect management	Rework hours/ 184 x average monthly salary
	Cost per defect	Total cost for defect management/ total number of defects
	Sigma level of current process	NORMSNIV(1-code defect rate/100)+1
	Number of defects which should be found to heighten sigma level of current process by one sigma.	Total number of SLLOC x code defect rate - (total number of SLOC(code defect rate-(1-NORMSDIST(sigma level of current process-1.5+1)))
	Cost for managing the defects found for 1 sigma level-up	Number of defects which should be found to heighten sigma level of current process by one sigma. Cost per defect
Gains from improvement	Cost/profit gained when a person to manage 100% increased number of defects	Rework hours/368 average monthly salary
Delivery	Total project cost	Project cost per day x total actual project days + total defect management cost
	Project cost per day	Average salary/23((total MM 23) /total actual project day)
	Total loss caused by difference between plan and actual result	Sum of loss at each stage + total schedule difference project cost per day
	Loss caused by difference between plan and actual result at planning/analysis stage	Schedule difference at planning/analysis stage * Project cost per day
	Loss caused by difference between plan and actual result at design stage	Schedule difference at design stage * Project cost per day
	Loss caused by difference between plan and actual result at implementation stage	Schedule difference at implementation stage * Project cost per day
	Loss caused by difference between plan and actual result at test stage	Schedule difference at test stage * Project cost per day
Gains from improvement	Gains caused when project is implemented on schedule.	Total project cost – total loss caused schedule difference
Cycle Time	Project cost at planning/analysis stage	(MM and average salary at planning/analysis stage)+ cost for defect management at planning/analysis stage
	Project cost at design stage	(MM and average salary at design stage)+ cost for defect management at design stage
	Project cost at implementation stage	(MM and average salary at implementation stage)+ cost for defect management at implementation stage
	Project cost at test stage	(MM and average salary at test stage)+ cost for defect management at test stage
	Gain/loss cause by difference between plan and performance at planning/analysis stage	(Planned MM – actual MM at planning/analysis stage) average salary
	Gain/loss cause by difference between plan and performance at design stage	(Planned MM – actual MM at design stage) * average salary
	Gain/loss cause by difference between plan and performance at implementation stage	(Planned MM – actual MM at implementation stage) * average salary
	Gain/loss cause by difference between plan and performance at test stage	(Planned MM – actual MM at test stage) * average salary
	Total gain/loss cause by difference between plan and performance	(Total planned MM – actual MM) * average salary
Gains from improvement	Gains caused by improved productivity	Total MM: total cost = 1MM: x (x= cost when reducing number of people by one) 100:272 = 1:Y (1% is for how may people?)
Waste	Earned value from reuse	Total SLOC number-Effort SLOC number)/400* (Total project days/184) * * average salary
	Cost caused by not doing reuse	Earned value from reuse + total project cost
	Earned value from reuse of 1SLOC	Total earned value from reuse
Gains from improvement	Gains caused by distributing manpower as planned	Gains when project is implemented 100% as planned/capability to be increased for hitting the target of 100%

4.1 PPM (Project Predict Model)

This section suggests PPM which can predict schedule, cost, manpower, and quality of future project by using PCM results.

This model is designed to predict schedule, cost, and manpower when an organization plans a new project by using PPM and PCM results and earned value from ECM.

Calculation Procedures and Composition of PPM are provided in <Table 5> and <Figure 3>

Table 5. Calculation Procedure of PPM

1. Calculate project capability through designed PCM model. 2. Calculate expected gains from improved project by using ECM for external effectiveness. 3. Design a project predict model for schedule, cost, manpower, based on PCM and ECM results 4. Calculate project predict value for effective strategies to improve quality and delivery, based on experience of individual organization

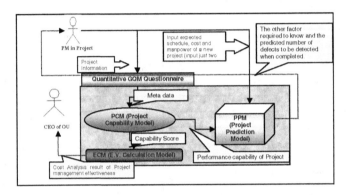

Fig. 3. Composition of PPM

PPM basically has assumptions as follows.

Assumptions of PPM

Assumption 1: a new project is planned through PPM Assumption 2: The organization to implement the new project already answered GQM quantitative questionnaire and thus has PCM and ECM results. Assumption 3: The new project belongs to the same team within the organization as the project for which GQM questionnaire was answered. Assumption 4: Scale of the project is predicted. (expected SLOC) Assumption 5. 2 out of 3 factors(schedule, cost, manpower) has been determined.

Ex) implement the project whose scale is 17, 721 SLOC with 50M/M within 6 months.(manpower and schedule has been determined) How many days will be spent? (Cost has not been determined)

On the assumption like this, PPM (project predict model) can be used in following 3 cases. It is assumed that SLOC has been determined for all cases.

Cases in which PPM can be used

Case 1 : total expected cost and man-month have been known, but total expected schedule has not been known.
Case 2 : total expected schedule and man-month have been known, but total expected cost has now been known.
Case 3 : total expected schedule and cost have been known, but total expected man-month has now been known.

PPM for expected schedule, cost, manpower of a project is described in <Table 6>

Table 6. PPM (Project Predict Model)

PPM(Project Predict Model)		
Case 1: total scheduled days $= \dfrac{\dfrac{total\ expected\ SLOC}{400}}{expected\ MM \times \dfrac{man-month\ rate\ at\ implementation\ strategy}{100} \times 23} \times \dfrac{1}{\dfrac{MM\ rate}{100}}$		
Case 2: total expected cost=project cost per day x total scheduled days		
Case 3: total expected manpower=project cost per day x total scheduled days/average salary		
Additional values	**Calculation Model**	
Predicted number of defects	Total expected SLOC (product defect rate/1000) [to calculate as KSLOC]	
Defect management cost	Total expected cost (product defect rate/1000) [to calculate as KSLOC]	
Rework hours	Total predicted defects/defect management rate per hour	
Pure project cost	Total predicted cost - defect management cost	
Project cost per day	Case 1	Total expected cost/total scheduled days
	Case 2	Project cost per day= (salary/23) (total MM 23)/total schedule days [(salary/23): daily pay per person]

5   Case Study of PCM and ECM, and Verification of Reliability for PPM

5.1   Case Study of PCM and ECM

This section verifies reliability of PCM and ECM through case study using data on GQM quantitative questionnaires collected from SPICE assessments during 2003 to 2004 period.

This paper uses data of three organizations as project data.<Table 7> provides specifics of each of the three organizations

Table 7. Specifics of each organization

	A company	B company	C company
Nature of task	Development task	Commercialization task	Development task
Existence of mother task	Exist	Exist	Not exist
Project Cost	About 80 million won (about 70 thousand USD)	About 500 million won	About 100 million won
Motive of project	For commission from other organization.	For commission from other organization.	For internal study of the organization
Project domain	Mobile	Computer	Multimedia

This paper used Excel as a tool for case study

5.2 Verification of Reliability Using PCM and ECM Cases

For case study, this paper used data which were collected from GQM questionnaires of three companies by using Excel as an automation tool.

For example, calculation result of A company is shown in <Figure 4>

GQM Quantitative Maturity Questionnaire

Profile		Unit
1	Project name	A Company
	Project feature	Development
	Period of Priect performance	
	Schedule	
	Start date	2001-12-03	Day
	Completion date	2002-06-29	Day
	Start date at project's planning/Req. analysis phase	2001-12-03	Day
	Completion date of planning & Req. analysis phase	2002-03-11	Day
	Start date of basic design + Detail design phase	2002-01-28	Day
	Completion date of basic design + Detail design phase	2002-04-24	Day
	Start date of construction phase	2002-05-02	Day
	Completion date of construction phase	2002-05-27	Day
	Start date of test phase	2002-05-28	Day
2	Completion date of test level	2002-06-29	Day
	Result	
	Start date	2001-12-03	Day
	Completion date	2002-07-19	Day
	Start date at project's planning/Req. analysis phase	2001-12-03	Day
	Completion date of planning & Req. analysis phase	2002-03-13	Day
	Start date of basic design + Detail design phase	2002-01-30	Day
	Completion date of basic design + Detail design phase	2002-06-22	Day
	Start date of construction phase	2002-05-02	Day
	Completion date of construction phase	2002-07-05	Day
	Start date of test phase	2002-06-05	Day
	Completion date of test level	2002-07-19	Day
	Project Size	
	Plan	
	Number of Total SLOC in project	15400	SLOC
	Man-Month of Total Plan in project	30.9	MM
	Result	
3	Number of new SLOC	10228	SLOC
	Number of modified SLOC	0	SLOC
	Number of reused SLOC	8275	SLOC
	Number of deleted SLOC	0	SLOC
	Man-Month of Planning/Req. analysis phase	10.5	MM
	Man-Month of High design / Detail design phase	16.9	MM
	Man-Month of Development phase	14.5	MM
	Testing of Development phase	3.5	MM
	Result of Project performance	
	Number of total Requirement	29	Num.
	Number of Chaned Requirement	0	Num.
	Number of finally Requirement	29	Num.
	Number of total pages of Work product	544	Page
4	Number of defect in design document	155	Num.
	Number of solved defect in document	155	Num.
	Number of Code defect	34	Num.
	Number of solved defect in source code	34	Num.
	Number of to solve of defect per hour by 1 man	1	Num.
	Average pay in project	2,000,000	w

PCM : Project Capability Model

Goal	Question	Metrics	Vaulue	Unit		
Quality	Defect density	Degree of defect in product	10,21	%		
		Degree of defect in document	0,28	%		
		Degree of defect in code	1,84	%		
		Degree of solved defect in project	100,00	%		
	Impact of Req.	Degree of changed Req.	0,0	%	Number of day by plan	Number of actually day
Delivery	Delivery time	Deviation of total schedule	20	day	206	226
		Deviation of Planning/Req. analysis phase	2	day	98	100
		eviation of High design / Detail design phase	56	day	86	142
		Deviation of Development phase	38	day	25	63
		Deviation of testing phase	13	day	31	44

Project Capability Value	82, 09	Point
Quality Capability Value	97, 53	Point
Delivery Capability Value	66, 64	Point
Process Capability (A hitting ratio of each perise)		
total schedule	90, 29	%
Planning/Req. analysis phase	97, 96	%
High design / Detail design phase	34, 86	%
Development phase	52, 00	%
testing phase	56, 06	%

Result day of total performance	226	day
Number of total defect	189	Num,
Number of total SLOC	18503	SLOC
New SLOC %	0, 55	%
Modified SLOC %	0, 00	%
Reused SLOC %	0, 45	%
Deleted SLOC %	0, 00	%
Rework Time	169	hour

Goal	Question	Metrics	Vaulue	단위
Cycle Time	Man-Month : Effort distribution	MM distribution percent of Planning / analysis phase	23,13	%
		MM distribution percent of design phase	37,22	%
		MM distribution percent of construction phase	31,94	%
		MM distribution percent of Test phase	7,71	%
	Man-Month : Effort correspondence	Hit percentage of MM Result	53,07	%
		Human hit percentage of Planning/Analysis phase	91,75	%
		Hit percentage of design phase human	-19,48	%
		Human hit percentage of Construction phase	16,46	%
		Human hit percentage of Test phase	59,32	%
Waste	Productivity	Code Productivity by People	56,32	%
		Document Productivity by Code	105,37	%
		Document Productivity by People	59,91	%
	Reuse	Code Reused percentage	44,72	%
		Hit percentage of product in Project	79,85	%
	Rework	Rework percentage	10,45	%

Project Capability Value	50,21	point
Cycle Time Capability Value	63,40	point
Waste Capability Value	37,01	point

Metric	Vaulue
Code Productivity by People	100,00
Document Productivity by Code	6,37
Document Productivity by People	59,91
Reused percentage of Code	44,72
Hit percentage of SLOC	79,85
Percentage of Reused	89,55

Capability Value of PCMc	63,40
Capability Value of PCMw	37,01
Capability Value of PCMcw	50,21

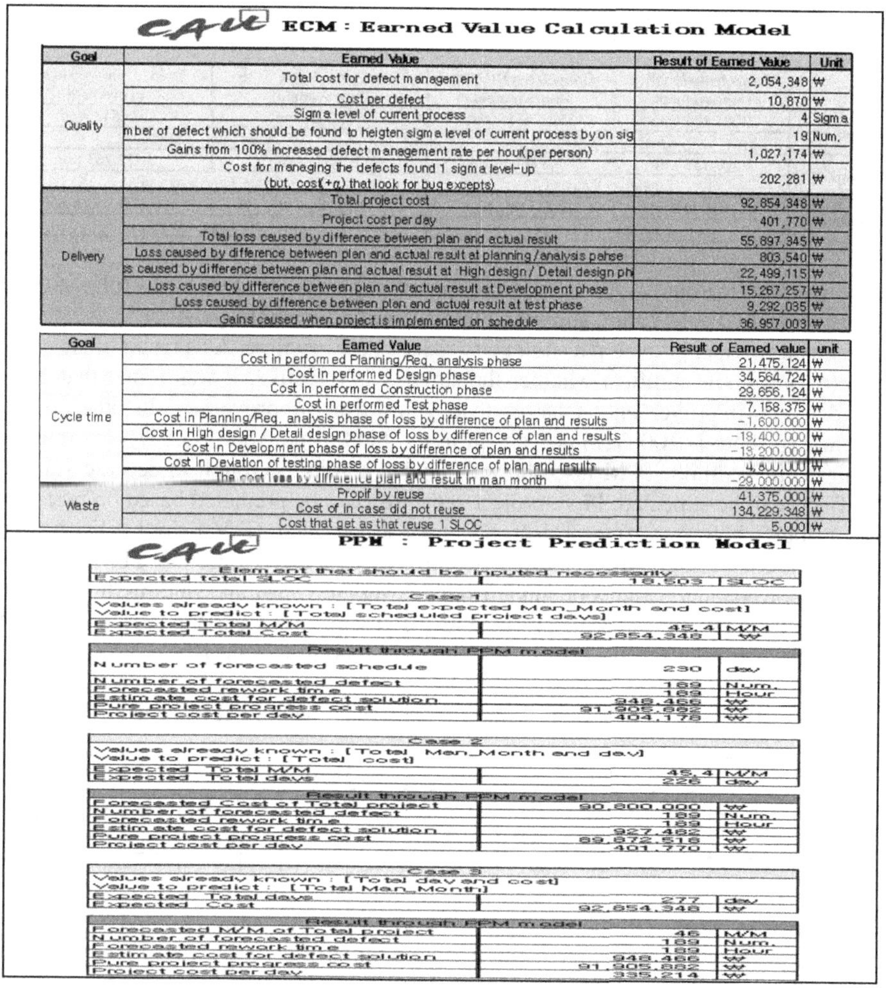

ECM : Earned Value Calculation Model

Goal	Earned Value	Result of Earned Value	Unit
Quality	Total cost for defect management	2,054,348	₩
	Cost per defect	10,870	₩
	Sigma level of current process	4	Sigma
	mber of defect which should be found to heigten sigma level of current process by on sig	19	Num.
	Gains from 100% increased defect management rate per hour(per person)	1,027,174	₩
	Cost for managing the defects found 1 sigma level-up (but, cost(+α) that look for bug excepts)	202,281	₩
Delivery	Total project cost	92,854,348	₩
	Project cost per day	401,770	₩
	Total loss caused by difference between plan and actual result	55,897,345	₩
	Loss caused by difference between plan and actual result at planning/analysis pahse	803,540	₩
	s caused by difference between plan and actual result at High design / Detail design ph	22,499,115	₩
	Loss caused by difference between plan and actual result at Development phase	15,267,257	₩
	Loss caused by difference between plan and actual result at test phase	9,292,035	₩
	Gains caused when project is implemented on schedule	36,957,003	₩

Goal	Earned Value	Result of Earned value	unit
Cycle time	Cost in performed Planning/Req. analysis phase	21,475,124	₩
	Cost in performed Design phase	34,564,724	₩
	Cost in performed Construction phase	29,656,124	₩
	Cost in performed Test phase	7,158,375	₩
	Cost in Planning/Req. analysis phase of loss by difference of plan and results	-1,600,000	₩
	Cost in High design / Detail design phase of loss by difference of plan and results	-18,400,000	₩
	Cost in Development phase of loss by difference of plan and results	-13,200,000	₩
	Cost in Deviation of testing phase of loss by difference of plan and results	4,800,000	₩
	The cost loss by difference plan and result in man month	-29,000,000	₩
Waste	Propif by reuse	41,375,000	₩
	Cost of in case did not reuse	134,229,348	₩
	Cost that get as that reuse 1 SLOC	5,000	₩

PPM : Project Prediction Model

Element that should be inputed necessarily		
Expected total SLOC	18,503	SLOC

Case 1		
Values already known : [Total expected Man_Month and cost] Value to predict : [Total scheduled project days]		
Expected Total M/M	45.4	M/M
Expected Total Cost	92,854,348	₩
Result through PPM model		
Number of forecasted schedule	230	day
Number of forecasted defect	189	Num.
Forecasted rework time	189	Hour
Estimate cost for defect solution	948,466	₩
Pure project progress cost	91,905,882	₩
Project cost per day	404,178	₩

Case 2		
Values already known : [Total Man_Month and day] Value to predict : [Total cost]		
Expected Total M/M	45.4	M/M
Expected Total days	226	day
Result through PPM model		
Forecasted Cost of Total project	90,800,000	₩
Number of forecasted defect	189	Num.
Forecasted rework time	189	Hour
Estimate cost for defect solution	927,482	₩
Pure project progress cost	89,872,518	₩
Project cost per day	401,770	₩

Case 3		
Values already known : [Total day and cost] Value to predict : [Total Man_Month]		
Expected Total days	277	day
Expected Cost	92,854,348	₩
Result through PPM model		
Forecasted M/M of Total project	46	M/M
Number of forecasted defect	189	Num.
Forecasted rework time	189	Hour
Estimate cost for defect solution	948,466	₩
Pure project progress cost	91,905,882	₩
Project cost per day	335,214	₩

Fig. 4. PCM, ECM, PPM results of A company

Table 8. Analysis results of case studies of PCM

	PCM capability score	Capability score of each goal	
A company	74.36	82.09	66.64
	PCM(QD)	Quality > Delivery	
	45.50	54	37
	PCM(CW)	Cycle Time > Waste	
B company	80.16	88.97	71.34
	PCM(QD)	Quality > Delivery	
	58.18	69.12	47.23
	PCM(CW)	Cycle Time > Waste	
C company	86.66	87.42	85.9
	PCM(QD)	Quality > Delivery	
	73.03	59.49	86.57
	PCM(CW)	Cycle Time < Waste	

Table 9. Analysis results of case studies of ECM

	Gains from Quality improvement	Gains from Delivery improvement	Gains from Cycle Time improvement	Gains from Waste improvement
A company	1,027,174 won	55,897,345 won	630,385 won	928,543 won
	Quality < Delivery		Cycle Time < Waste	
B company	4,500,152 won	398,897,460 won	1,638,600 won	5,522,763 won
	Quality > Delivery		Cycle Time > Waste	
C company	1,250,000 won	17,537,021 won	212,286 won	1,029,000 won
	Quality < Delivery		Cycle Time < Waste	

Reliability verification results of 3 companies through case studies are as follows. <Table 8> and <Table 9> are summarized results of case studies.

A company should develop a strategy to reduce delivery time. As a result of checking ECM (q,d)results to confirm whether the strategy is effective, it was found that gains from delivery improvement is larger than gains from improvement in other fields. Therefore, if there is 100 % improvement in the field of delivery, 55,897,345 won can be gained. In addition, PPM also showed reliable results. Through these case studies, two effects can be expected. First, project capability can be predicted based on performance attributes before starting project. Second, Earned value (E.V.)'s reliability can be verified by comparing the E.V. calculated from ECM and values for SPI (Software Process Improvement) effects obtained from answers to GQM and finding the cause of difference through difference analysis. Results through Comparison and analysis of ECM results and relevant SPI effects items are specified in <Table 10>

Table 10. Comparison results of ECM results and SPI effects items

	Capability score				Value for SPI effects from answers to GQM			
	Quality	Delivery	Cycle	Waste	Quality	Delivery	Cycle	Waste
A company	82.09	66.64	54	37	42%	35%	28%	20%
B company	88.97	71.34	69.12	47.23	45%	38%	32%	25%
C company	87.42	85.9	59.49	86.57	44%	42%	30%	43%

As shown in Table 10, the results measured through ECM model and SPI effects felt by the developers in the organization are the same.

The value flow of efficiency and effectiveness is as shown in <Figure 5>.

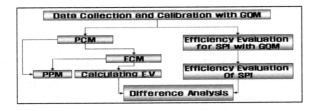

Fig. 5. Value Flow of efficiency and effectiveness

6 Conclusion and Hereafter Research

In this paper, case studies were implemented based on 3 data collections. Therefore, the reliability analysis was carried out on the assumption of T-distribution. If number of data collection exceeds 30, data reliability can be analyzed on assumption of F-distribution because data of all models that can be analyzed by F-distribution shows normal distribution. In this case, 4 performance attributes (quality, delivery, cycle time, and waste) are represented by using each typical performance variables.

By using GQM_based questionnaire we can analysis and define quality and delivery for the external effectiveness, and cycle time and waste for the internal efficiency to performance pyramid as the following equations.

Quality : Q = Rq (typical cost performance), Delivery : D = Rd (typical cost performance)
Cycle : C = Rc (typical cost performance), Waste : W = Rw (typical cost performance)

Rq, Rd, Rc and Rw are functional relation for each quality, delivery, cycle, and waste.

To maximize benefit of the equation for the external effectiveness, we can calculate the benefit by using the following partial differential equation.

$$\frac{\partial F}{\partial Rq \times \partial Rd} = 0$$

And to maximize benefit of the equation for the internal efficiency, we can calculate the benefit by using the following partial differential equation.

$$\frac{\partial F}{\partial Rc \times \partial Rw} = 0$$

References

1. Richard L.Lynch, Kelvin F. Cross, "Measure up!", 1995, Blackwell.
2. Kyung-whan Lee, "Modeling for High Depending Computing", The fifth Korea Information Science Society's Software Engineering Association,Feb.20. 2003
3. Kyung-whan Lee, "ROI of IT Business" , The federation of Korean Information Industries, 2003. 5
4. Kyung-whan Lee, "Quantitative Analysis for SPI" , Corporation seminar, Feb. 17. 2003.
5. Boehm, C. Abts, A.W. Brown, S. Chulani, B. Clark, E. Horowitz, R. Madachy, D. Riefer, and B. Steece, "Software Cost Estimation with COCOMO II", Prentice Hall, 2000.
6. Steece, B., Chulani, S., and Boehm, B., "Determining Software Quality Using COQUALMO," in Case Studies in Reliability and Maintenance, W. Blischke and D. Murthy, Eds.: Wiley, 2002
7. Mark C. Paulk et al, "The Capability Maturity Model Guidelines for Imporving the Software Process, CMU/SEI, 1994
8. ISO/IEC JTC1/SC7 15504: Information Technology-Software Process Assessment, ISO TR, ver.3.3, 1998
9. KSPICE (Korea Association of Software process Assessors), SPICE Assessment Report http://kaspa.org, 2002~2003
10. V. R. Basili, G. Caldiera, H. D. Rombach, "Goal Question Metric Paradigm", Encyclopedia of Software Engineering, John Wiley & Sons, Volume 1, 1994, pp. 528-532.
11. Frank Van Latum, Rini Van Soligen, "Adopting GQM-Based Measurement in an industrial Environment", 1998, IEEE software
12. Young-jun Yoon, "Easy 6 sigma- Renovation of management quality", Future management technique consulting, 1998.

13. Tim Kasse, "Action Focused Assessment for software process improvement", Artech House, 2002.
14. Williams A. Florac, Anita D. Carleton, "Measuring the software process", 1999, SEI Series, Addison Wesley.
15. Bohem, "Software Cost Estimation-COCOMOII , PH, 2000, pp34-40.
16. Tom Gilb, "Software Inspection", Addison-Wesley, 2001.
17. Ki-Won Song, "Research about confidence verification of KPA question item through SEI Maturity Questionnaire's calibration and SPICE Level metathesis modeling", SERA03, San Francisco, 2003.06
18. Boehm, IEEE Computer, March 2003.
19. Donald J. Reifer, "Making the Software Business Case", Addison-Wesley, 2002.

Slicing Java™ Programs Using the JPDA and Dynamic Object Relationship Diagrams with XML

Adam J. Conover and Yeong-Tae Song

Dept. of Computer and Information Sciences,
Towson University, Towson, MD, 21286
adam@adamconover.com, ysong@towson.edu

Abstract. Recent advances in object-oriented technology and computer networking have changed the way we maintain and develop software systems, i.e., you may need to maintain the system that is running in remote area. In this paper, we introduce a dynamic program slicing method applied to Java™ programs using the JPDA [1] (Java Platform Debugger Architecture) facilities. Our approach produces DORDs (dynamic object relationship diagrams) with respect to given slicing criterion in XML format, for export and graphical representations. The resulting slice is collectively called DORD-XML. The slicing algorithm keeps track of dynamic dependencies of objects so that it can compute a minimum set of objects with respect to given slicing criterion. By using DORD-XML and a graph-drawing tool, we attempt to reduce the complexity of Java programs and to make distributed, remote, and local systems more maintainable and understandable.

1 Introduction

In recent years, object-oriented software has been the dominant methodology in software development and maintenance. Most programming languages have already adopted object-orientation in their semantics or are in a process of adopting it. Object-orientation has brought us many benefits, such as reusability, maintainability, information hiding, and so on. While many developers are obsessed with object-orientation, many are still struggling with the complexity of object-oriented software systems. This is because object-orientated programs often contain inheritance and polymorphic hierarchies that may not be obvious by inspection of the objects in runtime environment. Another reason is that the dynamic behavior of a system usually precludes total comprehension of the system. Since objects can be created or destroyed at any time, it often makes programs difficult to understand, especially when there is dynamic dependency among objects at runtime. There have been numerous approaches, including Dwyer[2], Chen[3], and Li[4, 9], to analyze and decompose object-oriented software (especially Java programs) in an attempt to reduce the complexity to make it more tractable and easier to understand.

Program slicing is a technology that decomposes a program and extracts the portion of interest with respect to a certain criterion. According to Mark Wiser[5], a slice is an executable portion of the original program whose behavior is, under the

W. Dosch, R.Y. Lee, and C. Wu (Eds.): SERA 2004, LNCS 3647, pp. 201–213, 2005.
© Springer-Verlag Berlin Heidelberg 2005

same input, indistinguishable from that of the original program on a given variable v at given point p in the program. Here we extend the definition to an object-level slice to include object instances, fields, and method signatures instead of actual program statements.

Our goal is to develop a functional slicing technology and tool-set – based upon both existing and newly developed theory – to utilize slicing as a utility in the analysis and debugging of "real-world" applications. Though slicing theory has been explored in detail by various researchers in the past, very few tools presently exist that provide the casual software developer tangible benefits of this research. *Bandera*[6] from the SAnToS Laboratory (The Laboratory for Specification, Analysis, and Transformation of Software), is one such tool. *Bandera* relies upon compiling Java programs to *Jimple* code via the *Soot Java Optimization Framework*[7]. Our technique, however, attempts to produce meaningful slice results by dynamically monitoring the activities of an unmodified executing program in near real-time.[1]

The slicing algorithm we choose to implement here is loosely based upon the "forward slicing" algorithm described by Song and Huynh[8], which in turn is based on a technique initially described by B. Korel and S. Yalamanchili[9]. Korel and Yalamanchili describe forward program slicing as "... a dynamic program slicing technique. It computes slices as a program executes, unlike any other dynamic slicing techniques, which require the construction of the dependency graph after execution of a program to compute slices."

As a framework for representing program slices, we will be extending DORDs (Dynamic Object Relationship Diagrams) discussed by [8] to include an alternate XML representation. Since XML parsers and parser generators have been written for many modern programming languages/environments, the choice to use XML as a format for representing DORD graphs allows for significant portability and ease of both human and machine interpretation. For the sake of our research, we will be limiting our implementation to the Java programming language.

As a mechanism for dynamic runtime slice extraction in the Java programming language, we use the JPDA (Java Platform Debugger Architecture) facilities that exist as a standard feature of the JVM (Java Virtual Machine) distributed by Sun Microsystems®, Inc. Though specifically designed to facilitate runtime debugging and profiling, the generality of the architecture lends itself nicely to any kind of runtime tracing and inspection at the JVM level. Fig. 1 shows the relationship between our slicer and a target application.

Some benefits of slicing using the JPDA include:

- The availability of source code is not necessarily required to produce a meaningful and readable slice.[2]
- No preprocessing of the class files is necessary.
- Dynamic slices can be produced while the target application is actually executing.

---

[1] Building the Java application with the debugging symbols switched on greatly enhances the usefulness of this technique.

[2] Assuming the target class files have not been obfuscated in some way and symbols have not been stripped.

- Interactive programs can be sliced in near real-time, with only marginal performance degradation.[3]
- The program can be sliced remotely over a network connection.
- Slices can be generated against unit tests to aid in modification impact analysis.

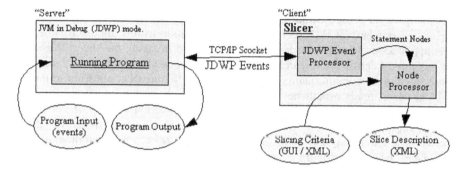

Fig. 1. Relationship between a running application and the slicer

2 A Brief Introduction to the JPDA

The JPDA consists of three layers[4]:

- JVMDI (Java Virtual Machine Debugger Interface) provides the low-level system interface to the JVM.
- JDWP (Java Debug Wire Protocol) is the transport-independent protocol for interfacing a JVM with a front-end application or library.
- JDI (Java Debug Interface) provides the high-level Java API to the JPDA. It is this last layer that we will use to create our runtime dynamic object slicer.

Essentially, JPDA functions in a client/server event driven model where the target application executes within a JVMDI-providing virtual machine; such as the reference JVM provided in Sun's *Java Developers Kit*. The client "debugger" can communicate via the JDWP directly, or – more commonly – use the JDI classes that exist as part of the *com.sun.jdi.** library. These classes serve as a wrapper around the lower level JDWP protocol.

The JPDA messages that we rely upon are the events generated by method entry/exit and the events generated by variable and field access. With these events, we can determine which methods are invoked from within an object and which fields are accessed from each method invocation. Furthermore, we can differentiate between

---

[3] Any performance degradation will be comparable to execution the application in a typical Java debugging environment.

[4] J2SE1.4 was used the time of this research. J2SE1.5 introduces a replacement for the JPDA known as JVMTI (Java Virtual Machine Tool Interface). Future development on the slicer engine will utilize this new technology as well.

field accesses that result in modification of the field versus those accesses that are purely read-only.

Depending on the underlying operating system, the JPDA offers several *connector* and *transport* options for connecting the client (the slicer) to the server (the target program), ranging from shared memory methods to TCP/IP Socket based connections. For simplicity and portability, we have chosen the *Socket Attaching Connector* method. This allows the program being sliced to start in a suspended "debugging server" mode within its own JVM, while awaiting the slicer application to attach via a standard TCP/IP socket. A minor limitation to this approach is that the target application must be launched manually prior to invoking the slicer. While this gives us more control for research purposes, we may wish to utilize the *Launching Connector* in a production quality tool, which starts the target application in its own JVM and transparently establishes the communication channel.

Once the slicer (client) is attached to the target application (server), the client can send the appropriate events to the server to indicate which events the server should generate. The client may also *start*, *stop*, *step*, *pause*, or *resume* program execution. Our slicer takes as input a `<slice_critera>.xml` file and generates a `<slice_descrption>.xml` file as output. These file formats will be discussed in more detail below.

2.1 Challenges

One of the greatest challenges in using the JPDA to perform program slicing is the mapping of JPDA events to specific source statements at specific points of execution. For example, when looking at the following lines of code, we can plainly see that line 2 is invoking a method in an object and line 3 is assigning that result to a field in another object.

```
         . . .
1.    Calculator c = new Calculator();
2.    int x = c.add(2,3);
3.    resultObj.sum = x;
         . . .
```

In the JPDA, events are generated at the statement being acted upon, not the statement performing the action and some events are generated in non-obvious ways. For example, Looking at line 2 above, the entry and subsequent exit from `c.add()` generates a *MethodEntryEvent* and a *MethodExitEvent*, respectively. However, the execution of line 3 will generate a *ModificationWatchpointEvent* from the `sum` field in `resultObj`, if and only if a watch point was actually set on that field. Though watch-points are not automatically set, this is easily resolved by utilizing Java's reflection mechanism to iterate though all of a class' fields and setting the appropriate watch-points in response *ClassPrepareEvent* events.[5]

Finally, in the current JPDA implementation, individual variables have no corresponding *Modification* or *Access* events associated with them. This precludes the

---

[5] We are using the traditional Java terminology conventions that define a field as a class or object attribute (object scoped) and a variable as a locally scoped method attribute (method scoped).

ability to do meaningful statement-level slicing from the JPDA alone, as we have no way of knowing for sure what variables (within a method) are being referenced or modified at any given time. As a result, we treat each method within an object as a "black-box" without any consideration of its internal behavior.

The following is a summary of the key limitations to slicing with the JPDA:

- Tracking intra-method variable access is extremely difficult, as no events are generated for the access or modification of any variable. The only things we can know for sure about the behavior of any given method pertain to invoked methods (including object constructors), corresponding return values of invoked methods, and fields that are read and/or modified.
- Without intra-method (statement) level slicing, we have no guarantees that any given access or invocation generates a true (minimal) dependency. However, this is not really a concern if we are only interested in the slice produced by inter-method analysis, as we implicitly assume that methods are the atomic units of code execution and are highly cohesive.
- Interfaces and abstract methods pose a special problem in the JPDA, as events are only generated by the implementing object. However, in the case of a static initializer in an interface, the interface "object" does generate the appropriate and expected events.
- Dependencies may be "swallowed" by any excluded and/or system libraries. Excluding standard libraries is generally necessary to prevent an explosion of irrelevant information, but a dependency has the potential not to resolve until the invocation of a library method.

3 Defining a Slicing Criterion

In defining a slicing criterion, we are interested relating the criterion to a feature of the program. In our current prototype slicer, a criterion can be defined by comparing a single field to a literal value or algebraic expression; or even by a simple "run to termination" of a program upon the processing of a unique input stream. In the latter case, every encountered field will have an associated slice related to the termination state of the program. Since unique input streams may trigger different execution paths, a unique set of object states will exist within the application upon termination. A slice can then be viewed as the union of all slices with respect to all the fields accessed in execution. This by itself does not really give us a useful slice, since it is nearly equivalent to a simple trace. However, it does still provide valuable information about the *potential* dependencies in a running program.

By definition, a slice must be restricted to the minimum essential states of a system required to implement a specific feature of the program. Though we may be able to throw out a lot of "superfluous" code in a simple "run to termination", the application will most likely enter many states that are irrelevant to the implementation of a specific feature of interest. Though a slice is generally computed with respect to a variable or variables, another useful slice criterion can be defined as the throwing of an unhanded exception. Since (in most software) we do not consider an unhandled exception to be an actual feature, we may wish to compute a slice with respect to the generation of an exception.

The biggest challenge in establishing a meaningful slicing criterion is the establishment of a formal relationship between a high-level feature that are interested in examining and the low level states of the running program. A full exploration of this formal relationship is beyond the scope of this paper (and will be a topic of future research). For the sake of example, we have created a very simple two-function postfix calculator program that is the basis of the subsequent discussion. The calculator contains several objects that represent functions, operators, operands, the input stack, intermediate/final results, etc. We can define one feature of the calculator as the ability to multiply two numbers.

If we wish to isolate a specific multiplication step we could – for example – define the feature as the ability to multiply 3 * 5 from the input stack of {2, 4, +, 5, 3, *, +}. Since the calculator knows how to perform two operations (addition and multiplication), our slice should only reflect the set of objects necessary to perform the desired multiplication step. With the above input, the result of the multiplication step is completely independent from the addition steps; therefore, the multiplication object should not be dependent on the addition object in any way.

For our purposes, a slicing criterion will be represented as an XML file. Shown in Fig. 2 is a preliminary DTD. As an example, Fig. 3 shows a short XML file (based upon the DTD) that defines a slice criterion. Though this example is intentionally very simple, XML provides the flexibility to represent expressions that are far more complicated.

```
<?xml version='1.0' encoding='UTF-8'?>

<!ELEMENT match EMPTY>
<!ATTLIST match placeholder CDATA #IMPLIED value CDATA
  #IMPLIED match_type CDATA #IMPLIED>

<!ELEMENT object (match)>
<!ATTLIST object object_name CDATA #IMPLIED>

<!ELEMENT package EMPTY>
<!ATTLIST package name CDATA #IMPLIED>

<!ELEMENT ignore (package)*>

<!ELEMENT slice_criterion (object|ignore)*>
<!ATTLIST slice_criterion version CDATA #IMPLIED>
```

Fig. 2. Simplified Slice Criterion DTD

Briefly, criterion shown in Fig. 3 states that we are looking for the program slice that makes the following conditions true:

- An object named (from its corresponding class definition) Multiplier must exist.
- A field in Calculator.Multiplier named lastResult must equal the ordinal value of 15.

- All objects from the *java.** and *com.sun.** trees should be ignored. This limits the scope of our slicing and prevents the internals of Java libraries from becoming part of dependency output.

```
<slice_criterion version="0.1">

  <ignore>
    <package name="java.*"/>
    <package name="com.sun.*"/>
  </ignore>

  <object object_name="Calculator.Multiplier.lastResult">
    <match match_type="literal" value="15"/>
  </object>

</slice_criterion>
```

Fig. 3. A Simple example of a Single Slice Criterion

The resulting slice should represent the dependency graph necessary to describe a minimal program capable of matching the above criterion under the same input. In other words, it should represent the minimal code necessary to multiply two numbers together that equal 15 under the same input to the application. In this example, the criterion is obviously very narrow and perhaps only useful in a limited debugging situation where you need to track the origin of an unexpected value. However, the DTD does allow much more elaborate criteria to be expressed. For example, the current incarnation of the slicer supports:

- The `match_type` attribute may be "`literal`" for a simple string or literal match.
- The `match_type` may be "`algebraic`" for an expression represented by a simple logical expression using a placeholder value for the object in question. For example, $X \Rightarrow 15 \&\& X < 20$ means match where the field value represented by placeholder X is greater than or equal to 15 and less than 20.[6]
- In the future, we will be expanding the criterion definition to include a wider range of options, such as pre/post conditions, etc.

4 The Slicer

In our slicer, we wish to monitor the objects, fields, and methods necessary to define a single slice and we attempt to mirror the DORD structure as closely as possible in our output. To prevent an overload of redundant information in the resulting XML, objects that appear more than once are referred to by their object ID on subsequent references. All dependencies from any one object to another are indicated in the dependency description for each object. The result is a list of all objects, fields and

---

[6] The algebraic parsing engine currently used is JEP (Java Mathematical Expression Parser) by *Singular Systems*: http://www.singularsys.com/jep/.

methods in the execution that are necessary to satisfy the given slicing criterion.[7] To summarize our slice description goals:

- The XML schema should be as clean and simple as possible. We are not concerned with "statement-level" slicing, so we only concern ourselves with tracking and representing dependencies at the object/method level.
- System (platform) libraries should be explicitly excluded from the slice. Though they are implicitly required for the program to execute, their decomposition is not generally in the scope of our analysis.
- Dependant objects and methods are fully described only once. Subsequent references should happen simply by object ID.
- Tracing the dependencies from the initial (entry) object will produce a dependency graph that maps to an appropriate slice based upon the slicing criteria.

The data format we propose should be sufficient to create a DORD graph from the resulting slice description. In addition, we assume that we are restricting our analysis to a program with a fixed entry point for a given execution instance. (A slice with respect to a variable is only valid for a single unique entry point.). The DTD is simply Fig. 1.

```
<?xml version='1.0' encoding='UTF-8'?>

<!ELEMENT node (node)*>
<!ATTLIST node  obj_id CDATA #IMPLIED line CDATA #IMPLIED
          method CDATA #IMPLIED signature CDATA #IMPLIED>
```

Fig. 4. DTD for slice resulting slice description

The DTD is extremely simple since the most useful information is contained in the nesting of the nodes. As nodes are nested within each other, all nodes beneath a given node represent the dependency a tree for that node. Fig. 5 shows a sample XML document for the slice defined in Fig. 3 based upon our sample calculator.

5   Building Dependency Tree

We treat each method within an object as a "black box" which may invoke other methods, read from fields, or modify field values. With this in mind a simple algorithm presents itself, based on several observations and derived rules and observations:

- The "state" of an object may be (loosely) defined as the union of all field states.
- A field's content may change only in response to the execution of a statement within a method.

---

[7] Given the current limitations of our technique, the slice remains a *naïve slice*.

```
 1:<node signature="Calculator.Multiplier.lastResult
         method="Calculator.Multiplier.operate(Calculator.SimpleInteger,
                 Calculator.SimpleInteger)"
         line="17" obj_id="75">
 2:  <node signature="Calculator.Multiplier.operate(Calculator.SimpleInteger,
                      Calculator.SimpleInteger"
        method="Calculator.Multiplier.operate(Calculator.SimpleInteger,
                Calculator.SimpleInteger)"
        line="16" obj_id="75">
 3:   <node signature="Calculator.Calculator.calculate(Calculator.Operation)"
           method="Calculator.Calculator.calculate(Calculator.Operation)"
           line="20" obj_id="46">
 4:    <node signature="Calculator.Calculator.popResult()"
            method="Calculator.Calculator.popResult()"
            line="35" obj_id="46">
 5:     <node signature="Calculator.Calculator.stack"
             method="Calculator.Calculator.[init](java.io.PrintStream)" line="6"
             obj_id="46">
 6:      <node signature="Calculator.Calculator.[init](java.io.PrintStream)"
              method="Calculator.Calculator.[init](java.io.PrintStream)" line="9"
              obj_id="46">
 7:       <node signature="Calculator.Calculator.main(java.lang.String[])"
               method="Calculator.Calculator.main(java.lang.String[])" line="56"
               obj_id="46">
 8:        <node signature="Root" method="[n/a]" line="0" obj_id="0"></node>
 9:       </node>
10:      </node>
11:     </node>
12:     <node signature="Calculator.Stack.pop()"
             method="Calculator.Stack.pop()" line="20" obj_id="52"></node>
13:     <node signature="Calculator.Operation.isOperator()"
             method="Calculator.Operation.isOperator()" line="21"
             obj_id="74">
        </node>
14:    </node>
15:   </node>
16:   <node signature="Calculator.SimpleInteger.value()"
           method="Calculator.SimpleInteger.value()" line="15" obj_id="67">
17:    <node signature="Calculator.SimpleInteger.simpleInteger"
            method="Calculator.SimpleInteger.[init](int)" line="8" obj_id="67">
18:     <node signature="Calculator.SimpleInteger.[init](int)"
             method="Calculator.SimpleInteger.[init](int)" line="7" obj_id="67">
19:      <node signature="Calculator.Calculator.initStack()"
              method="Calculator.Calculator.initStack()" line="48" obj_id="46">
20:       <node signature="Calculator.Calculator.stack" obj_id="46" />
21:      </node>
22:     </node>
23:    </node>
24:   </node>
25:  </node>
26:</node>
```

Fig. 5. A sample of the XML output for a the given slice. The line 1 is the criterion node. Line 8 is the program entry point, which is also a dependancy.

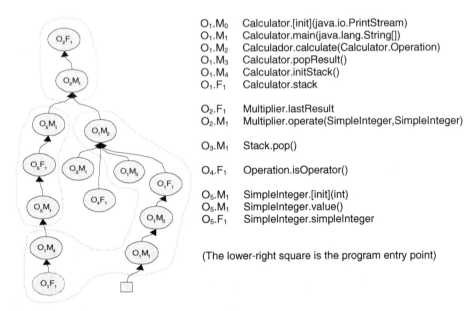

$O_1.M_0$ Calculator.[init](java.io.PrintStream)
$O_1.M_1$ Calculator.main(java.lang.String[])
$O_1.M_2$ Calculador.calculate(Calculator.Operation)
$O_1.M_3$ Calculator.popResult()
$O_1.M_4$ Calculator.initStack()
$O_1.F_1$ Calculator.stack

$O_2.F_1$ Multiplier.lastResult
$O_2.M_1$ Multiplier.operate(SimpleInteger,SimpleInteger)

$O_3.M_1$ Stack.pop()

$O_4.F_1$ Operation.isOperator()

$O_5.M_1$ SimpleInteger.[init](int)
$O_5.M_1$ SimpleInteger.value()
$O_5.F_1$ SimpleInteger.simpleInteger

(The lower-right square is the program entry point)

Fig. 6. Graphical representation of the slice XML Fig. 5

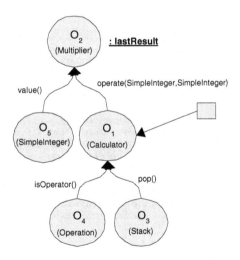

Fig. 7. DORD representation of the graphical hierarchy shown in Fig. 6

- Only one method (per thread) is executing at any given time.
- When a method alters the value of a field, the dependency graph of the field node becomes equal to the dependency graph of the setting method node.
- When a method reads a value from a field, the dependency graph of the method node becomes the union of the method's existing dependency graph and that of the field.

- When a (caller) method invokes another (callee) method with parameters, the invoked method inherits the active dependencies of the invoker.
- When a (callee) method returns a value to a (caller) method, the dependency graph of the caller method becomes the union of the method's existing dependency graph and that of the callee method.

Formalized Rules:

$$O_n.M_m \Rightarrow O_i.M_j \quad :: \quad Dep\{O_i.M_j\} \quad = \quad Dep\{O_n.M_m\} \quad \cup \quad O_n.M_m$$

$$O_n.M_m \Leftarrow O_i.M_j \quad :: \quad Dep\{O_n.M_m\} \quad \cup= \quad Dep\{O_i.M_j\} \quad \cup \quad O_i.M_j$$

$$O_n.M_m \Rightarrow O_i.F_j \quad :: \quad Dep\{O_i.F_j\} \quad = \quad Dep\{O_n.M_m\} \quad \cup \quad O_n.M_m$$

$$O_n.M_m \Leftarrow O_i.F_j \quad :: \quad Dep\{O_n.M_m\} \quad \cup= \quad Dep\{O_i.F_j\} \quad \cup \quad O_i.F_j$$

Where:

$O_n.M_m$	Method(m) in Object(n)
$O_n.F_m$	Field(m) in Object(n)
$O_n.M_m \Leftarrow O_x.F_y$	Method(m) in Object(n) **reads** a value from Field(y) in Object(x)
$O_n.M_m \Rightarrow O_x.F_y$	Method(m) in Object(n) **sets** value in Field(y) in Object(x)
$O_n.M_m \Rightarrow O_x.M_y$	Method(m) in Object(n) **invokes** Method(y) in Object(x) with parameters
$O_n.M_m \Leftarrow O_x.M_y$	Method(m) in Object(n) **receives** a return value from Method(y) in Object(x)
$Dep\{O_n.M_m\}$	The set of dependencies under $O_n.M_m$
$\cup=$	"Union Equals" assignment operator. Concatenates the left value with the right value and stores new left value.

As the program executes, the JPDA produces *method-entry, method-exit, field-access,* and *field-modification* events as the slicer grows a dependency graph for each node, until the given slice criterion is satisfied. Method invocations are tracked as objects on an invocation stack with all *potential* dependencies. All fields and related dependency graphs are stored in an association map as new fields are encountered. When a field's value is set or modified by a method, the current dependency tree is "attached" to the field overwriting any previous tree. This can be done since the setting method will have already inherited the necessary dependencies prior to modifying a field. At the end of execution, every visited field in the active block set exists in a map (providing the corresponding slices for each of those fields). "State explosion" is minimized by the fact that field dependency trees only ever exist with respect to the active block set and method dependency trees (by virtue of being stored on a call stack) only exist while the method is part of an active block.

Since each method is essentially being treated as a "black box" (i.e., we do not know how locally scoped variables are being modified or accessed), it must be assumed that any dependencies of a method becomes a potential dependencies of any field that is modified by the method. It also must be assumed that an active method potentially inherits all dependencies of any field that it reads. The same logic applies to method invocations containing formal parameters and subsequent return values. If parameters are passed to a method during a method invocation, the invoked method must inherit all potential dependencies from the invoking method. Likewise, if an invoked method returns a value to an invoking method, the invoking method must inherit the dependencies of the invoked method. Conversely, if no parameters are passed or values returned in a method invocation, then the dependency graphs of the respective methods do not directly affect each other. This technique effectively grows a dependency graph while the target application is executing, providing a valid slice for any field of interest at any given time.

6 Conclusions

We have examined the feasibility of using the Java Platform Debugger Architecture as a tool to perform object, method, and field level slicing dynamically on an executing Java application. While the JPDA does not provide – by itself – enough information about the internal workings of a running application to perform statement-level slicing, it does provide enough information to produce a useful slice with respect to a given field in an object. Though the resulting slice is inherently a naïve slice, it may still provide enough valuable information about the dynamic potential dependencies of an application to ease the debugging or refactoring of a large application. The limitations of this technique may be offset by the fact that very little preparation is needed by the target application. Invoking the target application with the appropriate JVM switches is often sufficient. The production of a platform neutral slice description in the form of an XML document will allow other tools, such as graph drawers or debuggers, to more easily make use of the data. Finally, a simple dynamic algorithm for maintaining potential dependency trees for each visited field in a running application was proposed.

7 Future Works

As the current slice descriptions are formatted as XML documents, they are easy for machines to understand, but rather difficult for humans to comprehend at a glance. Several "off-the-shelf" tools already exist to cleanly display graphs generated via formal API. One such tool is *Jgraph* (http://www.jgraph.com/). *JGraph* is a powerful open-source graphing tool licensed under the GNU Lesser General Public License[8]. The next logical step in DORD-XML visualization is the creation of a parser to process the resulting XML files for input into such a visualization tool. As of this writing, a prototype of a *JGraph* based visualizer is in progress. A more distant goal is to create an IDE plug-in application that will allow bi-directional consistency

---

[8] For a full description of the GPL/LGPL see: http://www.gnu.org/licenses/licenses.html.

mapping from a high level ADL to low level source code in such a way as to establish that a given implemented feature reflects the actual architecture and functionality specified by the high-level requirements.

References

[1] Java Platform Debugger Architecture (JDPA), http://java.sun.com/products/jpda
[2] M. Dwyer, J. Corbett, J. Hatcliff, S. Sokolowski, and H. Zheng. Slicing multithreaded java programs : A case study. Technical Report 99-7, Kansas State University, Department of Computing and Information Sciences, March 1999.
[3] Z. Chen and B. Xu. Slicing Object-Oriented Java Programs. *ACM SIGPLAN Notices*, 2001, 36(4), 33-40
[4] Bixin Li, Analyzing information-flow in Java program based on slicing technique. *ACM SIGSOFT Software Engineering Notes*, September 2002, 27 (5).
[5] Mark Weiser (July 1982) *Program slicing*. IEEE Trans. on Software Engineering, SE-10(4) 352-357
[6] Bandera, http://bandera.projects.cis.ksu.edu
[7] Soot: a Java Optimization Framework, http://www.sable.mcgill.ca/soot/
[8] Y. Song and D. Huynh, Dynamic Slicing Object-Oriented Programs using Dynamic Object Relationship Diagrams. *The Journal of Computer and Information Science*, 2 (1)
[9] B. Korel and S. Yalamanchili, Forward Computation of Dynamic Program Slices. *International Symposium on Software Testing and Analysis (ISSTA)*. August 1994

Infrastructures for Information Technology Systems: Perspectives on Their Evolution and Impact

C.V. Ramamoorthy[1] and Remzi Seker[2]

[1] Department of Electrical Engineering and Computer Sciences,
University of California Berkeley, Berkeley, CA 96720, USA
ram@cs.berkeley.edu
[2] Computer Science Department,
University of Arkansas at Little Rock, Little Rock, AR 72204, USA
rxseker@ualr.edu

Abstract. This paper attempts to clarify infrastructure's definition and its impact and reach. Despite the wide use of the term and the importance of the entities it represents, the notion of infrastructures has not been thoroughly addressed. We use different perspectives for defining infrastructures and investigate the intricate relationships a system has with its infrastructure. In order to deal with the complexity of the infrastructure notion, we provide a diverse set of classifications. We focus on the information technology infrastructure and its security and survivability. We investigate the design issues for building evolvable, resilient, disaster-hardened infrastructures.

1 Introduction

For any given system, the presence of an underlying infrastructure (I/S) is a necessary condition. According to Warren Buffet, a well-known stock market personality, an I/S is like oxygen. When it is there, we take its services for granted and do not even think about it. When absent, we will not survive. In the same way, when any essential service incurs a disruption due to a failure in the I/S, we feel its drastic effects in our daily activities. In Latin, the notion of I/S is "Sine qua non" (without which nothing exists); the I/S is an absolute necessity for any system to function.

An I/S is the set of basic underlying foundations, features, functions and resources that provide facilities on which the continuance and growth of a system, state, or community depends. We associate public I/Ss to include transportation systems, power grids (including power plants), clean air and water, communication systems supported by Information Technology (IT) etc. We generalize the notion of I/S to include essential processes, functions, systems, products, and services necessary to fulfill the system's intended mission by performing and sustaining specified activities at the desired levels.

Although the numerous definitions for I/S notion slightly vary in their comprehensiveness, all of them eventually emphasize that a system's I/S is the most vital element; without an I/S a system can neither function nor support its long-term existence. Despite its importance, the term I/S has been vaguely used to mean

W. Dosch, R.Y. Lee, and C. Wu (Eds.): SERA 2004, LNCS 3647, pp. 214–228, 2005.

different things in different contexts. Our aim is to clarify the I/S definition and its implications.

The motivation for this paper to focus on the I/S notion is as follows; commonly used systems, especially those like the power grid, weapon systems, and the I/S associated with IT systems are very expensive to build and they remain in commission for a long time. As an example, the B-2 bombers designed and deployed during World War II continue to remain in service today, and are projected to remain in operational service for the next fifty years. Regular maintenance on these I/Ss is needed in order to assure their correct functioning. We expand and extend current systems without consequent upgrading of their I/S's due to practical issues such as cost. The I/Ss provide essential public services, they stay around for a long time, and the society becomes dependent on them. These I/Ss have become increasingly vulnerable in our society and face continuously increasing service demands as well as unexpected threats. To summarize, we can say that an I/S is always associated with a specified system which has a purpose, functionality, and mission, operating predictably under specified constraints including environments and threats, during its lifecycle. Systems and services must be designed with due consideration of their required I/S in mind. The I/S also constitutes the life support system of the entity being designed. To put it strongly, we should co-design the system and its infrastructure. In many instances, parts of the necessary infrastructures may already be available.

This paper is concerned primarily with I/S issues of IT based systems. We shall consider some systems and engineering design perspectives. We shall discuss the current status of the I/S's based on our experience and summarize some salient problems and issues. We benefited from the pioneering presentation of our friend, Prof Herbert Weber, of the Technical University of Berlin in the International Conference on Integrated Design and Process Sciences, 1998, but regrettably we did not come across any comprehensive studies subsequently on this topic. We consider some future trends for I/S based on some potential advances in the software and the IT (including communications) as well as the perceived evolutions in consumer needs.

2 Fundamental Attributes of I/S Notion

The Webster's New World Dictionary defines an infrastructure as "the basic installations and functions on which the continuance and growth of a system, service, and state depends." Clearly, the definition implies that the infrastructure of any system includes the set of essential functions, activities, and services, which support the systems operations, current health, and future growth. An infrastructure is necessarily associated with a specific system, namely, with the system's purpose, functionality, and mission, while it is operating predictably during its life cycle under specified constraints, including the environment, known failure modes, and threats.

The importance of an infrastructure cannot be overstressed. It constitutes the foundation, generally the root of a massive tree and often the key stems and branches. Its strength, inherent in its design, will not only protect the derived systems from disasters but ensure sustainability, adaptability, growth, and evolution.

We slim down the I/S notion into three parts, based on the entity's lifecycle:

1. The I/S needed for the entity's creation, development, and implementation: when we have an idea that can be manifested as a new entity, we need appropriate tools, knowledge, man-power, and other resources to realize the idea, i.e., design, development and implementation of an artifact. These elements represent a part of the entity's infrastructure.
2. The I/S needed for the entity's operation and maintenance. A system cannot be expected to operate flawlessly under all conditions except those for which it was designed. The services and resources needed for these activities are another part of its I/S. The components under this category include the hardware, operating systems, etc. Fault corrections, performance improvements, etc. all require modifications of the existing system. These activities require support tools, knowledge about the system, its documentation, etc., to allow us make the desired changes.
3. The I/S needed to support system re-engineering for upgrading, platform migrations, adaptations due to technology advances, and evolution. These generally include the addition of new functionalities.

All three parts of the I/S we have stated above would ideally be there for a specific entity, operating under specified environments and failure modes which may include safety and security aspects. In summary, I/S consists of essential resources in the form of functions, activities, services, and systems needed for an entity's creation, development, and implementation, its operation and maintenance at an expected level, and its sustenance, evolution, and growth.

We classify, from the perspective of human life, I/S into two categories, namely, primary I/S and secondary I/S.

1. Primary I/S: this part of the I/S is the most basic, fundamental and essential. Air, water, food, shelter, etc. are most basic necessities and these are part of the primary I/S.
2. Secondary I/S: this is essential to the entity once the primary I/S elements are in place. Examples of secondary I/S are electric power, transportation, communications, computers, etc. The infrastructures required for proper operation of the IT entities belong to the secondary category under the implicit assumption that there exists the primary I/S in the background. In other words, electric power and transportation will not make any sense if there is no clean air and water for the people who will use them. In the subsequent discussions we will be only dealing with the secondary I/S structures which are IT-specific.

3 I/Ss for IT Systems

We shall now focus our attention on the IT I/S. We can model these I/S structures as consisting of some common base with several levels (layers) or tiers constructed around it, as shown in Fig. 1. The common base of the I/S can be visualized as the foundation of a building (the core elements of I/S) supporting other I/S elements layered above it.

An I/S can be considered like the roots and stem of a tree. Just like a good house is always built on a solid foundation, sound I/S is necessary for a system's (or service, function, or product's) sustainability, adaptability, growth, and evolution. The importance of I/S emphasizes the requirement that it must be protected from and during the disasters, as disruptions in I/S-based services can inflict severe damage on the society.

We shall examine the IT- I/S notions from the systems and engineering design viewpoints. The systems viewpoint includes considerations of the tools and utilities, operating systems, computer and communication systems, database management systems, and application systems. Engineering design viewpoint considers I/S as an entity that is being gradually developed, through the integration of independently developed subsystems around a common base. The primary I/S of an IT system tends to be rigid, expensive and often too difficult to change. Since the I/S helps in the creation, nurturing and evolution of the entities under its auspices, it has to be properly created, designed and grown. This then implies the system designer has to keep in mind the infrastructure needs of the products over their lifetime and help in the configuring a suitable I/S design to meet the perceived needs.

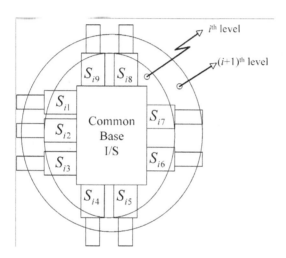

Fig. 1. I/S levels built upon the common base I/S. There can be different elements at each level.

3.1 Examples of I/S

We will provide some examples for the I/S elements within the context of IT. They can range from very abstract concepts, theories, design rules, hardware and software entities. Based on the definitions provided earlier, an I/S element can be an abstraction, a software process, a hardware artifact or an entity that manifests all of these. It has to be essential to the creation, operation, maintenance, and evolution of the system.

In a typical processor configuration the I/O unit, the memory sub-system, the register files, the arithmetic logic unit, execution unit, control and display hardware are essential for proper operation. These can be considered as parts of the total system infrastructure. In a communication system, the standards, protocols, etc., that provide rules to specify services are also elements of the IT system's infrastructure. In the programming language domain, the rules of syntax used in the production systems provide analyzability and the semantics of their vocabulary provide the expressive power of the language. These too are rules that govern programming languages. The Boehm-Jacopini conditions which establish the operational completeness requirements for programming languages can be considered as part of their I/S. Similarly the essential and necessary control functions that manage the computer systems are also parts of that operating system's I/S.

Tools like formal methods can help showing that the system's design satisfies the necessary and sufficient conditions for the desired operation. Software system development, an important part of the IT I/S, depends on languages, compilers, execution environment and operating systems, design and development tools (including the utilized process), communication environment (including the Internet), and also on the quality of engineers and designers.

Biological systems possess complex I/Ss as required for their maintenance. For example, a human hip joint is a single ball and socket structure, which uses cartilage dependent on glands and the blood supply. However, in order to keep the joint alive, the body has a complicated "factory" (I/S), which produces and purifies blood and maintains glands.

Our last example is from the oil industry and it shows the critical importance of the I/S notion. 'The US Energy Information Administration estimates that both petroleum production and consumption will raise by 2% a year from 2001 to 2025, arriving at 123M barrels a day by 2025. This steady increase will require an *exponential growth* in global infrastructure, capital, and personnel addition to the continuing productivity gains that should be achieved by technologically intensive oil industry" [1]. The important point in this example is that providing 2% increase in oil production requires an exponential increase in costs to create the additional infrastructure.

3.2 Functions of I/S

An entity's I/S consists of essential resources, services, and functions to fulfill the following objectives.

– To help create, develop, and implement the entity specified by functionality and performance requirements,
– To assure its operation at a desired level and support its maintenance, and
– To help the entity's evolution, sustainability, and survivability.

The above objectives are meant to support the entity's intended purposes (application needs) and its mission. These objectives are to be satisfied by the entity under specified conditions of operating environment, including failures resulting from specific threats.

3.3 The Immense Scope, Impact, and Reach of I/S

I/S breakdowns can create disasters. For example, a telecommunication satellite (PanAmSat's Galaxy 4) failed in May 1998 due to a solar storm and this failure disabled 90% of the pagers across US, crippled ATMs, some communication networks, and credit card systems worldwide. In addition, this failure also disabled airline-tracking services and created a 26-hour black hole effect, which stopped the air traffic between east and west coast of US for a few hours. Other examples for I/S failures, include the collapse of the Internet in 1997, when the Domain Name System failed due to operator error; the US-wide collapse of AT&T's frame relay network on April 13, 1998, due to faulty software upgrade, etc. For more examples, we refer the reader to Reference [2].

I/S has direct implications on designing and implementing new products. The following quote from Hewlett-Packard's (HP) CEO Carly Fiorina supports our point: "HP's collaborative approach is tailored to a customer's ecosystem to create adaptive infrastructures that use leading software products and architectures and leverage HP's own expertise in the creation of adaptive infrastructures" [3].

Infrastructures must evolve with the technological advances as well as the people's love for product variety. These are implied in the empirical observations as portrayed in Grove's multiplier effect [4] (after you use one product you buy many more products of the same technology family, e.g., PC's and handhelds) and Ross Ashby's rising tide effect (from his law on requisite variety) which emphasizes that the rising tide of knowledge and technology lifts (increases) our need for higher quality and more variety in products we use [5].

4   Classification of I/S

Classification helps structuring and organizing our knowledge. It also helps discovering subtle relationships on the matter for which the classification is being made. Therefore, in order to gain a better understanding of I/S concept, we will look at I/S classifications.

4.1   Structural: Levels/Layers and Rings (L/L&R)

The objectives of using levels/layers and rings are (a) to decompose the system into segments in form of levels/layers and rings, (b) understanding the system to make it easy to maintain, change, restructure, and enhance, and (c) to reduce "complexity" in representation and understanding. The layers/levels can be perceived as ways of vertically structuring while rings can be perceived as horizontally structuring the system. However, in the way that we represent them they can be equivalent.

A level is defined as an attribute or a position in a graded scale of values. For example, one thinks of levels of abstractions in a hierarchy. A layer is defined as arrangements of "material" laid out or spread over a surface, e.g. in a layered system, lower layer supports (services) the next higher layer. In practice, levels and layers are used interchangeably, unless instructed otherwise. The key point is that each layer supplies and supports the services needed by the layer just above it, e.g., the Open Systems Interconnection (OSI) protocol suite specifications.

There can be several layers of I/S. Some are essential for the products function; these are the primary I/S elements (e.g. air, food, and water being the primary I/S elements for existence of human life). Others depends on the primary I/S and they constitute the secondary I/S. Usually, for practical purposes, the primary I/S is assumed to exist and be pervasive; it is available anytime, anywhere. As indicated before, we will be concerned with the secondary I/Ss. These secondary I/Ss are usually associated with the IT aspects of systems (i.e., IT-specific components/systems).

There could be a layered hierarchy among the secondary I/S, as seen in Fig. 2. IT-I/S is the secondary I/S from a system point of view and includes the essential computer and communication-oriented functions encompassing hardware, software, operating systems, and supporting databases. It would include application specific essentials such as the interface systems, the front end, parts of middleware and specialized application services within the back end. These involve hardware, software, communications, etc. (Each layer, even within the secondary level can have a layered structure. This fact is depicted in Fig. 2.) The primary I/S, which includes physical services such as power, communication connectivity, etc. will be the bottom (lowermost) layer and its presence and availability is implicitly assumed. The primary I/S supports the secondary I/S.

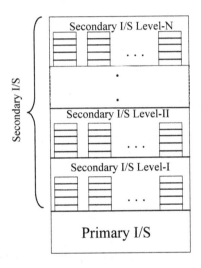

Fig. 2. A coarse layered representation of I/S with IT I/S in perspective

Vertical structuring (levels/layers) allows implementing functions at one level by using the functions at the level immediately below it (e.g., micro-operations, micro-programs, machine language instructions, etc.). In other words, the lower levels support the functions of the higher levels. Isolation between levels can be used to implement safeguards that could be necessary in some I/Ss.

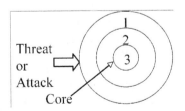

Fig. 3. Ring structured I/S

Horizontal structuring is based on the use of rings. The main idea of the horizontal (ring) structure is that the outer rings support or protect the functions of the inner rings. Some of the examples are security and protection rings, and firewalls. Historically, protection rings protected medieval castles using moats with moat-monsters, archers, hot-oil, and high castle walls. Fig. 3 shows a simple ring structure.

An egg could be given as an example of a ring structured biological entity. The embryo in an egg carries the minimum, essential function. The egg white provides the resources and serves as a "cushion" for the embryo. The membrane around the egg white also provides an additional protective cushion. The eggshell is the stronger wall, which protects the egg, and is the third layer. The I/S of an egg then provides protection against shocks and vibrations, and against intrusion. The I/S for an egg protects the embryo, and the layers provide the protection: if any of the I/S levels malfunctions, the egg will fail its mission.

The ideas used in rings and layers/levels are very similar. The implementations may be different. The main difference is that ring structure can picture levels of protection in addition to the representations achieved by layers/levels. In a ring structured I/S, if the core (primary I/S) fails, the whole system fails. Moreover, each ring can be partitioned into essential and nonessential functions thereby result in additional rings (e.g. rings that collectively form a ring, just like it is in the case of levels/layers). Fig. 4 shows rings and layer/level representations side by side.

In the usual security type of ring structure, an outer ring doesn't service/support the functions of the next inner ring, but provides security and protection, which is essential for proper operation of the next inner ring. In the traditional layered structures (e.g. OSI protocol scheme), the lower layers provide service/support to the functions of the next upper layer. Fig. 5 shows the correspondence between the layered/leveled and ring structures when a relationship like security and protection is of interest.

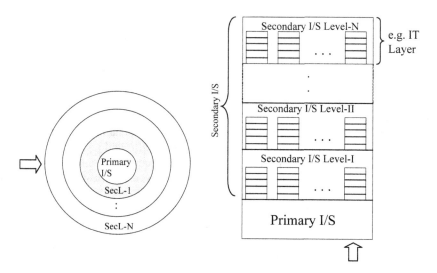

Fig. 4. Ring structured and leveled/layered I/S

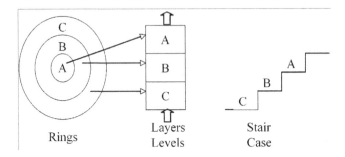

Fig. 5. Correspondence between layered/leveled and ring structured I/S

4.2 Spatial: Internal, External, and Combination

Parts of the components that make up a system's I/S may be contained within the system (internal I/S) and others could be outside the system (external I/S). For example, if we think of a personal computer, the internal I/S would be processor and its accessories. The necessary power for the computer, or the network connectivity through which the computer can communicate with other computers would be external I/S. In general, the overall I/S would contain both internal and external elements.

4.3 IT I/S Types

We classify the IT I/S into four categories: static (hardcore), dynamic, virtual, and adaptive. We caution that these categories may have overlapping features. The case of having an overlap becomes particularly common for adaptive and virtual I/Ss. Our classification is based on current engineering terminology and its implications. We will use the term static I/S and hardcore interchangeably.

The hardcore is an essential component of I/S. The dictionary defines hardcore as a dedicated completely faithful nucleus of a group or movement. It performs the 'minimum' essential functions of a system. It is also the part of the system that may be hard to change. This is not to say that hardcore never changes but rather the changes made to the hardcore are much slower and less often than other, non-hardcore, elements. I/S is built on (designed around) hardcore; I/S includes hardcore. The hardcore can include CPU, memory, bus, execution unit, etc. In the hardware (microprocessor) world, hardcore can be a subsystem that also contains a hardwired or a microprogrammed procedure for performing minimum essential functions. One such function makes the microprocessor to tests itself and if certain conditions are satisfied, it initiates tests layer by layer until the total processor system is tested. By this, the hardcore establishes the operational readiness of the system.

Dynamic I/S functions are those I/S activities that are dynamically selectable, relocatable and executable on parts of the system that may include the hard core. Hence, the dynamic I/S functions support and serve the system along with the static I/S. The static I/S only serves the dynamic I/S by providing the fundamental services.

Virtual I/S is the realistic, software directed simulation of the required I/S functions, resources, and environment. These simulations provide services provided by certain I/S functions. These may include functions served by the internal and external

I/Ss. We generally use the virtual I/Ss for short durations. They are used as "spare tires" and not for use for extremely long time durations because of power and performance issues. The important concept here is that the virtual I/S function serves as a substitute or replacement of another I/S function. When certain I/S functions fail the virtual I/S concept may come as a rescue. The virtual I/S concept may find many applications in grid and cluster computing and is a fruitful research area.

Adaptive I/Ss are configured by assembling functions and resources from the existing I/S (fixed), plus those which are dynamically assigned (variable) and/or virtually created. Adaptive I/S are provided to satisfy changing or evolving environments. Because of its flexibility, an adaptive I/S can support changes due to different system configurations, platforms, and applications. This can help to provide orderly evolutionary transitions due to product updates, upgrades, enhancements etc. Adaptivity in I/S requires careful design considerations on the I/S. Adaptive I/S resources are generally supported/provided by application service providers.

The techniques used to achieve adaptive I/Ss are similar to program relocation, indirect addressing, etc. Adaptive I/Ss can be created and formed so that the system's functions can dynamically be relocate-able, reconfigurable, substitutable, and enhance-able. This concept is reminiscent of concept of 'dynamic binding' used in computer science and software engineering.

We will cite two examples for adaptive I/Ss. Walt Disney Los Angeles Concert Hall is built such that it has a fixed and a variable I/S from an acoustic point of view. In order to produce the necessary acoustic requirements for a specific performance, movable beams and fixtures (variable I/S) within the concert hall are rearranged with the built-in acoustic environment (fixed I/S). Our second example is from the Avery Fisher Hall in New York. The adaptive acoustic I/S is created by rearranging the players, musicians, and the movable panels (variable I/S) along with the fixed acoustic environment of the hall (fixed I/S) to meet the needs of a particular concert.

IT I/S differs from other I/Ss in the sense that it can include a high number of virtual higher layers (including some elements in these higher layers) and can be adaptive. The adaptivity of IT I/S can be achieved through the dynamic I/S concepts. Inclusion of virtual I/S concepts can further increase the adaptivity of IT I/S.

4.3.1 Adaptive I/S for Computer Security

In order to motivate the applicability of the I/S notion for computer security, we will look at the I/S analogy in medicine. Medical I/S is about education, awareness, precaution and prevention, detection of diseases and infections, slowing down the progress of diseases, and finally disease elimination. The objectives of a patient include surviving as long as possible, enduring less pain, less hospitalization and expenses, and personalized therapy. The objectives of a medical doctor include patient's survival, determining the cure rate of the therapies, and obtaining new insights in preventing and curing diseases. This analogy can be applied to computer security. By using security measures we can slow down the spread of computer viruses, which corresponds, in the medical field, to the improving the chances of survival of the patients by slowing down the progress of the disease (e.g. strengthening the immune system).

Our approach of applying medical analogy in dealing with computer viruses or intrusions is different than the existing immune system analogy [6, 7] in dealing with computer viruses, worms, and intrusions. For the sake of simplicity, we shall use the term virus to include the worms, Trojan horses, etc. Most of the existing approaches recognize viruses based on samples of the instructions contained in them. Although this seems to be a good approach, such a defense mechanism can deal only with known viruses which have been studied and whose identities or signatures are available in the anti-virus programs' databases. When a new virus is out, such a detection mechanism will fail. Human communities living in isolation helped humans survive many deadly diseases. To date, isolating deadly diseases remains to be one of the basic steps in dealing with such epidemics. The connectivity created by the Internet can spread of viruses to all computers and networks connected to it, limited only by the available access and bandwidth capacity.

Security issues have become more complex to address due to existence of diverse set of machines (although, diversity has its advantages for immunity). The security problems become complex when we deal with mobile systems that often function outside the company's firewalls, and peer-to-peer systems from independent social organizations, and when users demand more functionality which may be directly opposed to security (e.g. VB macros for MS Word^{TM} documents), etc.

Some of the issues related to computer security include lack of rapid immunity support, slowness in detecting the infection or intrusion, the long delay in removing the virus and repairing the damage. Security activities can be time consuming because of the need for human interaction and support (while the virus keeps spreading!). Although the threats are generally known and the prevention methods are known, the appropriate response and remedy remain unknown. An adaptive resilient I/S should lessen the vulnerabilities and mitigate the effects of the attacks until human response is mounted.

The I/S approach to dealing with computer security departs from usual security engineering methods. Our idea is to construct the I/S such that it hampers or disrupts all attacks. Slowing an attack is simpler than stopping it. Taking this perspective, I/S can act like an immune system. Our approach of dealing with viruses and intrusions is a two-step process:

1. Automatic computer responses to detect and slow down the attacks (similar to human immune system). This functionality is performed by the system's I/S and constitutes fast response.
2. Human response to stop the attacks; similar to human nervous system and the brain. Human operator with automated intelligent support analyzes, isolates, and stops the intruders (slow follow-on).

In our approach, the I/S reduces the burden of prevention. The damage is reduced by the I/S itself. This approach is good for controlling fast spreading viruses, denial of service attacks etc. Such an I/S can complement and support the current security mechanisms.

An adaptive I/S focuses on two main points for security. Virus throttling and a responsive intrusion detection system. Virus throttling slows the speed of virus propagation before a signature for the virus is available. It can be achieved by analyzing the performance of machines. In this case, an abnormal slow down may mean a virus attack is in progress. It involves removing/isolating the infected machine, placing it under quarantine. Furthermore, the existing methods for address space randomization slow down the attacks [8] and are included among the virus throttling measures. As a result of virus throttling, the infection can be slowed down and contained. Meanwhile, a responsive intrusion detection system detects any abnormal system behavior and identifies a virus using a signature [7] table and helps the operator to remove the virus. A good research area is to develop methods that can make the system's IT I/S act as a virus immune system, actively detecting, slowing the spread of an infection and progress of an intrusion and providing valuable information to the central security system to help remove and repair the threat and remedy damage.

5   I/S Change and Evolution

I/Ss are expensive to build and maintain. Changes to I/S are due to technological advances, changes in human needs, and the evolution in products, systems, and services. Re-engineering costs can go up to three times the cost of original product development and approximately 4-% of the cost is due to I/S standards, protocols, platforms, ease of use, etc. Updating and upgrading legacy systems mostly revolve around upgrading of I/S elements in order to be compatible with new standards and protocols. Changes may be needed (a) in the I/S systems (e.g. to fit a new product), for example, upgrading a personal computer to run a new application; or (b) in the products (e.g. to be compatible with the existing I/S) such as the 110-220 voltage selection for some appliances; or (c) in both the product and its I/S to incorporate the new standards (e.g. BlueTooth, IEEE.801x, etc.).

I/S change and evolution requires tools and education. The education is to be carried out at three levels; user level, community level, and developer level. The evolution of I/S suggests that it functions as the system's foundation (creation and growth) and backbone (evolutionary structure) but also as the system's immune system (protection, security, and well-being). To put it simply, I/S design will require a vast amount of preplanning. We, as a community, have yet to develop design awareness and design principles to develop long lasting adaptive infrastructures for our IT products.

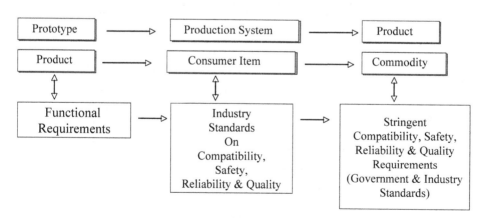

Fig. 6. Product evolution and implicit requirements

Grid computing links numerous computers, storage systems, and communication networks and creates a pool of computing power that can be accessed by different tasks and users rather than rigidly configured for a specific application (e.g., cluster computing). Grid computing can make I/S more available, accessible, automatable, and flexible. The major impact of grid computing in I/S will be to provide virtual resources and support. The virtual I/S can support strategies for fault-tolerance, performance improvement, etc. Unfortunately, grid computing needs standards to facilitate interoperability, for deploying commercial applications as well as well designed fortifications against malicious security attacks.

I/S evolution may follow the flight path of products, systems, and services. A usual product trajectory, together with its implicit requirements is seen in Fig. 6. The extended view of the product evolution is shown in Fig. 7. The industry and government standards personify a product's built-in I/S after it becomes a commodity.

The doubling of knowledge every three to seven years and semiconductor chip performance doubling every 18 months (while its price remains the same) are exponential growths. Ross Ashby's rising tide effect about consumer needs and demands for high quality products may also have an exponential growth. The question we would like to ask is that whether I/S evolution may follow a similar flight path; in other words, whether I/S evolution may be an exponential one.

Commoditization of I/S elements impacts industry standards, government standards and constraints, and intellectual property issues. I/S technology usually starts with a proprietary product, system, or service and slowly evolves into being a commodity. When it is a commodity, it is subjected to stringent industry and government standards, as seen in Fig. 7. IT products, services and functions particularly those related to software have become commodity items. What effects this commoditization can have on IT I/S design and evolution remains to be seen.

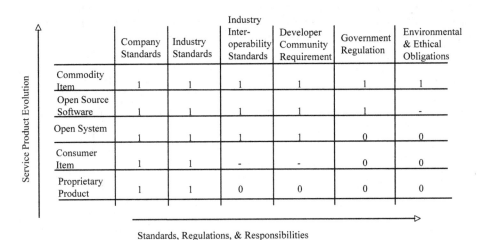

	Company Standards	Industry Standards	Industry Inter-operability Standards	Developer Community Requirement	Government Regulation	Environmental & Ethical Obligations
Commodity Item	1	1	1	1	1	1
Open Source Software	1	1	1	1	1	-
Open System	1	1	1	1	0	0
Consumer Item	1	1	-	-	0	0
Proprietary Product	1	1	0	0	0	0

Service Product Evolution (vertical axis)

Standards, Regulations, & Responsibilities

Fig. 7. Extended view of the product evolution and implicit requirements

6 Discussion, Concluding Remarks, and Future Research

We revisit I/S definition for the last time: I/S represents minimum essential resources and assets to create, design, implement, operate, sustain, and evolve activities and functions under specified environments and threats, in predictable ways. These include essential resources needed to restore essential services after abnormal events.

In summary, I/S definition is conceptually easy but vague, difficult to narrow down, and it is subjective to the intended application (user) and the environment. It is important that every system designer considers the I/S requirements at the same time as he/she considers its design. The I/S should be identified soon after the system is specified or given an I/S, the system's functional specifications will be dependent on it. In this respect, I/S can be thought of as the platform or the environment. Good I/Ss should be based on application/user needs, product-user-environment threat loop, and in general, on the system's eco-system.

Generally each system, product and service needs specialized I/S: the primary (general purpose) and the secondary (specialized). Some of the concerns are availability, security, pollution, etc. As an analogy one can consider Lubbock, Texas tap water. It is cheap, you trust in its purity, but you still prefer drinking bottled water.

Development environments (one can consider them as the 'I/S of the I/S') can be roughly classified as proprietary (cathedral, closed) and open (bazaar) environments [9]. In the proprietary environments, intellectual property issues slow down the commoditization while in open environments commoditization is rapid. To give an example, Prof. Gordon Bell observed that the reason why the computer (PC) became a commodity is that Univac did not get the computer patent, but Iowa State University, a nonprofit organization, received it due to Prof. Atanasoff, the computer pioneer. The intellectual property was, therefore, not proprietary. In general, the final system may be composed of both proprietary and open (public) I/S entities.

One can try to get the best of the two worlds (open and closed systems) in the following way. Open systems bring instant availability, continuous improvement, compatibility and interoperability. Closed systems bring proprietary and commercial systems together with trustworthiness and dependability. We conjecture that the future systems will be opportunity-based product developments, using the best of the both worlds. All these systems will live, survive, and thrive in an IT-based eco-system.

One of the major reasons for commoditizing I/S is that it may offer strong standards for availability, dependability, security, etc. We envision that there will be specialized I/S that will provide every system with its own security system for protection (e.g. specialized firewalls). All devices in the system (home, web site, portals, etc.) will be protected by their dedicated security system.

We also envision that I/Ss will be equipped with special core competencies. Such I/Ss help to create, sustain, protect and evolve new products and services that will be befitting their overall purpose and application domains. In this respect, an I/S will be a part of the IT eco-system, where the products are conceived, born, grow, live, thrive and procreate. The challenge is to identify and develop appropriate I/Ss to fit the target system into the IT eco-system.

Building survivable systems will require specifying a specialized eco-system to support I/S's for a spectrum of applications based on properties such as real time criticality, security, safety, pervasiveness etc. The eco-system, along with the I/S systems within it, can serve as a part of the system's immune system, providing instant protection, security and dependability during its lifecycle.

We may start by prioritizing the list of services and functions; identify possible product designs with their I/S needs; chart a family genealogical tree of product evolution (a road-map of future products—a la Utterback's Dominant Product concept [10]); select I/S design requirements for the family of products; use the services of application service providers to locate and utilize these needed elements/components (essentially Application Service Providers' become I/S service providers). In summary, we need to start off with a good evolutionary design of I/S system that can be evolved, adapted, and modified incrementally as we go. Then we can design our systems based on such I/S's.

Educational and research issues include disaster-hardening the I/S. That is, how we protect I/S from disasters and catastrophes. Disaster hardening of an I/S is an important area for future research. Testing I/S is going to be one of the difficult problems we will have to address since the classical testing methodologies may not apply to testing an I/S. Identification of appropriate development environments for disaster-hardened I/S is another fruitful research direction. As an educational initiative, we see it necessary to include I/S engineering and disaster engineering in today's engineering curricula so that the future engineers can build disaster free, safe and secure I/Ss.

Acknowledgement

The authors would like to express their gratefulness to Prof. Herbert Weber of Technical University of Berlin for introducing them to the area of infrastructures and to Prof. Sumit Ghosh of the University of Texas at Tyler for very constructive evaluation of the manuscript and many inspiring suggestions.

References

1. Financial Times. February 27 (2004)
2. Ramamoorthy, C. V., Seker, R., Disaster Engineering. Proceedings of the 22nd International System Safety Conference (ISSC 2004), Providence, Rhode Island (2004)
3. HP's Next Big Thing. Silicon Valley Biz Ink on October 31 (2003)
4. Grove, A., Only the Paranoid Survive, Doubleday, April (1999)
5. Ashby, W. R., Requisite Variety and its Implications for the Control of Complex Systems. Cybernetica, Vol. 1, No. 2 (1958) 1-17
6. Forrest, S., Hofmeyr, A. S., Somayaji, A., Computer Immunology. Commun. ACM, Vol. 40, No. 10, (1997) 88-96
7. Somayaji, A., How to Win and Evolutionary Arms Race. IEEE Security and Privacy, Vol. 2, No. 6, (2004) 70-72
8. Shacham, H., Page, M., Pfaff, B., Goh, E.-J., Modadugu, N., Boneh, D., On the Effectiveness of Address Space Randomization. Proceedings of the ACM Conference on Computer Security (2004)
9. Raymond, E.: The Cathedral and The Bazaar. O'Reily (2001)
10. Utterback, J. M., Suárez, F. F., Patterns of Industrial Evolution, Dominant Designs, and Firms' Survival, Robert Burgelman and Richard Rosenbloom (eds.) Research on Technological Innovation, Management and Policy, JAI Press, Vol. 6, (1993) 47-87

The Trajectory Approach for the End-to-End Response Times with Non-preemptive FP/EDF*

Steven Martin[1], Pascale Minet[2], and Laurent George[3]

[1] Université Paris 12, LIIA, 120, rue Paul Armangot, 94400 Vitry, France
steven.martin@esiee.org
[2] INRIA, Domaine de Voluceau, Rocquencourt, 78153 Le Chesnay, France
pascale.minet@inria.fr
[3] Ecole Centrale d'Electronique, LACSC, 53 rue de Grenelle, 75007 Paris, France
laurent.george@ece.fr

Abstract. We focus on non-preemptive *Fixed Priority* (FP) scheduling. Unlike the classical approach, where flows sharing the same priority are assumed to be scheduled arbitrarily, we assume that these flows are scheduled Earliest Deadline First (EDF), by considering their absolute deadline on their first visited node. The resulting scheduling is called FP/EDF*. In this paper, we establish new results for FP/EDF* in a distributed context, first when flows follow the same sequence of nodes (the same path). We then extend these results when flows follow different paths. We show how to compute an upper bound on the end-to-end response time of any flow when the packet priority is computed on the first node and left unchanged on any subsequent node. This alleviates the packet processing in core nodes. For that purpose, we use a worst case analysis based on the trajectory approach, that is less pessimistic than classical approaches. We compare our results with those provided by the holistic approach: the benefit can be very high.

Keywords: Trajectory approach, end-to-end response time, deterministic guarantee, quality of service, QoS network, fixed priority, earliest deadline first, holistic approach.

1 Context and Motivations

Fixed Priority scheduling has been extensively studied in the last years [1,2]. It exhibits interesting properties:

- The impact of a new flow τ_i is limited to flows having priorities smaller than or equal to this of τ_i;
- It is well adapted for service differentiation: flows with high priorities have smaller response times;
- It is easy to implement.

We focus on non-preemptive Fixed Priority scheduling of sporadic flows. Indeed, with regard to flow scheduling, the assumption generally admitted is that packet transmission is not preemptive. Several flows may have to share the same priority in the following cases:

W. Dosch, R.Y. Lee, and C. Wu (Eds.): SERA 2004, LNCS 3647, pp. 229–247, 2005.

- The number of priorities available on a processor is less than the number of flows considered;
- The priority of a flow is determined by external constraints and cannot be chosen arbitrarily;
- A class-based scheduling is used.

The classical analysis of Fixed Priority scheduling assumes that flows sharing the same priority are scheduled arbitrarily. The worst case response times obtained with this analysis can be improved, if the scheduling algorithm of flows sharing the same priority is accounted for. We propose to schedule such flows according to Earliest Deadline First (EDF). Indeed, EDF has been proved optimal [2,3] for a uniprocessor in both preemptive and non-preemptive context when the packets release times are not known in advance. EDF optimality means that if for a given scheduling problem, EDF fails to find a feasible solution, then there is no solution for this problem. That is why, we propose a new scheduling algorithm, called FP/EDF*, combining fixed priorities and deadlines. The star expresses the fact that the absolute deadline of a packet is computed on its first visited node and is used for arbitration by all nodes visited.

In this paper, we first focus on the worst case response time obtained with FP/EDF* when all flows follow the same sequence of nodes. Then, we extend our results to the case where flows follow different paths. These results can be used in various configurations where several flows can share the same priority. Hence the interest of FP/EDF*.

- In a *Differentiated Services* architecture [5], several classes are defined, each having its own priority. The highest priority class, that is the *Expedited Forwarding* (EF) class, is scheduled Fixed Priority with the other classes. Moreover, if packets belonging to the EF class need to be differentiated, different priorities can be assigned to these packets. Hence, a Fixed Priority scheduling can be used to provide the required differentiation.
- In an *Integrated Services* architecture [6], a priority is assigned to each flow. Fixed Priority scheduling is used to provide shorter response times to high priority flows.
- In an *hybrid* architecture, flows are managed either per class or individually.

The rest of the paper is organized as follows. Section 2 briefly discusses related work in the computation of worst case end-to-end response time. In Section 3, we present the models and notations used in our worst case analysis. In Section 4, we show how to compute an upper bound on the end-to-end response time of any flow, based on a worst case analysis, when all flows follow the same sequence of nodes. Then, in Section 5, we extend our results to the general case where flows follow different paths. In Section 6, we compare our results, obtained by applying the trajectory approach, with the exact worst case end-to-end response times and with the results provided by the holistic approach. The exact values are obtained by a validation tool we have designed. This validation tool does an exhaustive analysis. Finally, we conclude the paper in Section 7.

2   Response Time Computation in the Distributed Case

To determine the maximum end-to-end response time, several approaches can be used: a stochastic or a deterministic one. A *stochastic approach* consists in determining the mean behavior of the considered network, leading to mean, statistical or probabilistic end-to-end response times [9,10]. A *deterministic approach* is based on a worst case analysis of the network behavior, leading to worst case end-to-end response times [11,12].

In this paper, we are interested in the deterministic approach as we want to provide a deterministic guarantee of worst case end-to-end response times for any flow in the network. In this context, two different approaches can be used: the holistic approach and the trajectory approach.

• The *holistic approach* [13] considers the worst case scenario on each node visited by a flow, accounting for the maximum possible jitter introduced by the previous visited nodes. If no jitter control is done, the maximum jitter will increase throughout the visited nodes. In this case, the minimum and maximum response times on a node h induce a maximum jitter on the next visited node $h + 1$ that leads to a worst case response time and then a maximum jitter on the following node and so on. Otherwise, the jitter can be either cancelled or constrained.

  ○ the *Jitter Cancellation technique* consists in cancelling, on each node, the jitter of a flow before it is considered by the node scheduler [12]: a flow packet is held until its latest possible reception time. Hence a flow packet arrives at node $h + 1$ with a jitter depending only on the jitter introduced by the previous node h and the link between them. As soon as this jitter is cancelled, this packet is seen by the scheduler of node $h + 1$. The worst case end-to-end response time is obtained by adding the worst case response time, without jitter (as cancelled) on every node;

  ○ the *Constrained Jitter technique* consists in checking that the jitter of a flow remains bounded by a maximum acceptable value before the flow is considered by the node scheduler. If not, the jitter is reduced to the maximum acceptable value by means of traffic shaping.

As a conclusion, the holistic approach can be pessimistic as it considers worst case scenarios on every node possibly leading to impossible scenarios.

• The *trajectory approach* [14] consists in examining the scheduling produced by all the visited nodes of a flow. In this approach, only possible scenarios are examined. For instance, the fluid model (see [15] for GPS) is relevant to the trajectory approach. This approach produces the best results as no impossible scenario is considered but is somewhat more complex to use. This approach can also be used in conjunction with a jitter control (see [16] for EDF). In this paper, we adopt the trajectory approach without jitter control in a network to determine the maximum end-to-end response time of a flow.

We can also distinguish two main traffic models: the sporadic model and the token bucket model. The sporadic model has been used in the holistic approach and in the trajectory approach, while the token bucket model has been used only in the trajectory approach.

• The *sporadic model* is classically defined by three parameters: the maximum processing time, the minimum interarrival time and the maximum release jitter, (see section 3). This model is natural and well adapted for real-time applications.

• The *token bucket* [11,15,16] is defined by two parameters: σ, the bucket size and ρ, the token throughput. The token bucket can model a flow or a flow aggregate. In the first case, it requires to maintain per flow information on every visited node. This solution is not scalable. In the second case, the choice of good values for the token bucket parameters is complex when flows have different character- istics. A bad choice can lead to bad response times, as the end-to-end response times strongly depend on the choice of the token bucket parameters [16,17]. Furthermore, the token bucket parameters can be optimized for a given configu- ration, only valid at a given time. If the configuration evolves, the parameters of the token bucket should be recomputed on every node to remain optimal. This is not generally done.

In this paper, we adopt the trajectory approach with the sporadic traffic model and we establish new results that we compare with those provided by the classical holistic approach.

3   Models and Notations

3.1   Models

We investigate the problem of providing a deterministic end-to-end response time guarantee to any flow in a network, when these sporadic flows are sched- uled FP/EDF*. The end-to-end response time of a flow is defined between its ingress node and its egress node. We want to provide an upper bound on the end-to-end response time of any flow. As we make no particular assumption con- cerning the arrival times of packets in the network, the feasibility of a set of flows is equivalent to meet the requirement, whatever the arrival times of the packets in the network.

In this paper, we assume that time is discrete. [7] shows that results obtained with a discrete scheduling are as general as those obtained with a continuous scheduling when all flow parameters are multiples of the node clock tick. Then, any set of flows is feasible with a discrete scheduling if and only if it is feasible with a continuous scheduling. For lack of space reasons, proofs are not included in this paper; they can be found in [8]. Moreover, we assume the following models.

3.1.1   Network Model

We consider a network where links interconnecting nodes are supposed to be FIFO and the network delay between two nodes has known lower and upper bounds: $Lmin$ and $Lmax$. Moreover, we consider neither network failures nor packet losses.

3.1.2 Traffic Model

We consider a set $\tau = \{\tau_1, ..., \tau_n\}$ of n sporadic flows. Each flow τ_i follows a sequence of nodes whose first node (denoted $first_i$) is the ingress node of the flow and whose last node (denoted $last_i$) is the egress node of the flow. In the following, we call *path* this sequence. In this paper, we assume that the path followed by a flow is fixed. This can be obtained, for instance, with MPLS or *Source Routing*. Moreover, a sporadic flow τ_i following a path $\mathcal{P}_i$ is defined by:

- T_i, the minimum interarrival time (called period) between two successive packets of τ_i;

- C_i^h, the maximum processing time on node $h \in \mathcal{P}_i$ of a packet of τ_i;

- J_i, the maximum jitter of packets of τ_i arriving in the network. A packet is subject to a release jitter if there exists a non-null delay between its generation time and the time where it is accounted for by the scheduler;

- D_i, the end-to-end deadline of τ_i, that is the maximum end-to-end response time acceptable for any of its packets. Then, a packet of τ_i generated at time t must be delivered at time $t + D_i$.

3.1.3 Scheduling Model

We consider that all nodes in the network schedule packets according to non-preemptive FP/EDF*. Therefore, the node scheduler waits for the completion of the current packet transmission (if any) before selecting the next packet.

For any flow τ_i, when a packet of τ_i, requested at time t, arrives on node $first_i$, the first node visited, it is marked with its static priority P_i and its absolute deadline, equal to $t + D_i^{first_i}$, where $D_i^{first_i}$ is the relative deadline of flow τ_i on node $first_i$. This solution presents the additional advantage of requiring clock synchronization only in the ingress nodes to assign to each incoming packet its absolute deadline. The computation of $D_i^{first_i}$ is made from the end-to-end deadline D_i. Solution can be found in [12].

Let $D_i^{first_i}$ be the relative deadline attributed to flow τ_i on its first node visited, denoted $first_i$. The local deadline is computed from the end-to-end deadline. For instance, with a uniform assignment, the local deadline is equal to $\lfloor D_i/q \rfloor$, where q denotes the number of nodes visited by τ_i. With this assignment, a flow τ_i having an end-to-end deadline D_i but visiting few nodes has an intermediate deadline $D_i^{first_i}$ higher than a flow τ_j with the same end-to-end deadline but visiting more nodes. Other solutions exist, for instance solutions accounting for the workload of the visited nodes. The determination of the best value is out of the scope of this paper.

Each node visited by this packet schedules it according to FP/EDF* accounting for its fixed priority P_i and its absolute deadline $t + D_i^{first_i}$, computed on node $first_i$. This scheduling rule ensures that for any packet m of τ_i, requested at time t on node $first_i$, all visited nodes take their scheduling decision on exactly the same values of both the fixed priority P_i and the absolute deadline $t + D_i^{first_i}$. Notice that EDF* is applied on $t + D_i^{first_i}$ on each visited node, but the end-to-end deadline that must be met by flow τ_i is $t + D_i$.

Hence, priority of packet m belonging to flow τ_i is higher than or equal to this of packet m' belonging to flow τ_j and generated at time t' if and only if: $(P_i > P_j)$ or $(P_i = P_j$ and $t + D_i^{first_i} \geq t' + D_j^{first_j})$.

Property 1. *FP/EDF* ensures that for any packets m and m', if m has a priority higher than m' on a node, then this is true on any visited node.*

Notice that Property 1 does not imply that the scheduling order is the same on all nodes. Indeed, let us consider the case illustrated by Figure 1, where the generalized priority of a packet m' is higher than this of m. Suppose that node 1 is idle when m arrives. Packet m is then immediately processed. Packet m', arrived after, has to wait. Suppose that node 2 is busy when m and m' arrive. Packet m' is then processed before packet m according to their priorities.

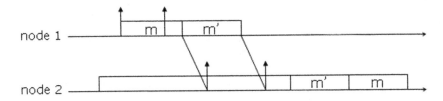

Fig. 1. The scheduling order depends on the node

3.2   Notations

We consider n real-time flows. This set of flows is denoted $\tau = \{\tau_1, \tau_2, ..., \tau_n\}$. Let $\tau_i \in \tau$ (then $i \in [1, n]$) following a path $\mathcal{P}_i$. We focus on the packet m of τ_i generated at time t. We denote P_i the fixed priority of flow τ_i. We then define the three following sets:

- $hp_i = \{j \in [1, n], \ P_j > P_i\}$;
- $sp_i = \{j \in [1, n], \ j \neq i, \ P_j = P_i\}$;
- $lp_i = \{j \in [1, n], \ P_j < P_i\}$.

Therefore, if $j \in hp_i$ (respectively lp_i), the fixed priority of flow τ_j is higher (respectively lower) than the fixed priority of flow τ_i. If $j \in sp_i$, flows τ_j and τ_i share the same fixed priority. In this case, packets are scheduled according to their dynamic priorities. We then have to distinguish two kinds of flows: (i) flows that are able to generate packets with a dynamic priority higher than this of packet m and (ii) flows that are not able to generate such packets.

Let m be the packet of any flow τ_i generated at time t. For any flow τ_j, if $j \in sp_i(t)$, then after time $t + D_i^{first_i} - D_j^{first_j}$, τ_j can no longer generate packets with a dynamic priority higher than this of m. Then, for any time $t \geq -J_i$, we denote:

- $sp_i(t) = \{j \in sp_i, \ -J_j \geq t + D_i^{first_i} - D_j^{first_j}\}$;
- $\overline{sp}_i(t) = \{j \in sp_i, \ -J_j < t + D_i^{first_i} - D_j^{first_j}\}$.

In the following, we denote $h' <_i h$ (resp. $h' >_i h$) if node h' is visited before (resp. after) node h by flow τ_i. We also denote:

- $\mathcal{P}_i = [first_i, ..., last_i]$, the path followed by flow τ_i, with $first_i$ (resp. $last_i$) the ingress node (resp. the egress node) of the flow in the network;
- $|\mathcal{P}_i|$, the cardinal of path $\mathcal{P}_i$, that is the number of nodes visited by flow τ_i;
- $slow_i$, the slowest node visited by flow τ_i on path $\mathcal{P}_i$, that is: $\forall h \in \mathcal{P}_i$, $C_i^{slow_i} \geq C_i^h$;
- $\mathcal{P}_{j,i} = [first_{j,i}, ..., last_{j,i}]$, the subpath followed by both flows τ_i and τ_j, with $first_{j,i}$ (resp. $last_{j,i}$) the first node (resp. the last node) visited by both τ_i and τ_j. Notice that $\mathcal{P}_{j,i} = \mathcal{P}_{i,j}$;
- $slow_{j,i}$, the slowest node visited by flow τ_j on subpath $\mathcal{P}_{j,i}$, that is: $\forall h \in \mathcal{P}_{j,i}$, $C_j^{slow_{j,i}} \geq C_j^h$.

Finally, we adopt the following notations:

- R_i, the worst case end-to-end response time of flow τ_i;
- R_i^h, the maximum sojourn time of flow τ_i on node h;
- $Smin_i^h$, the minimum time taken by a packet of flow τ_i to go from its source node to node h;
- $Smax_i^h$, the maximum time taken by a packet of flow τ_i to go from its source node to node h;
- $W_i^h(t)$, the latest starting time on node h of the packet of flow τ_i generated at time t.

We now recall the definition of the processor utilization factor for a set of flows.

Definition 1. *For any node h, the processor utilization factor of a set $S \subset \tau$ of flows is equal to $\sum_{j \in S}(C_j^h/T_j)$. This factor represents the fraction of processor time spent by node h to process packets belonging to S.*

4   Trajectory Approach When Flows Follow the Same Path

4.1   Methodology

We consider that all flows follow the same path $\mathcal{P}$ in the network, that is the same sequence of nodes consisting of q nodes numbered from 1 to q. We want to determine the end-to-end response time of any packet m, requested at time t and belonging to any flow τ_i. With non-preemptive scheduling, if a packet arrives on any visited node h after m starts its processing, then it cannot delay m. Hence, we compute the latest starting time of m on node q, the last node visited. The mathematical expression of this latest starting time, that is an iterative expression, is analyzed (subsection 4.2).

Finally, we deduce from this time a bound on the end-to-end response time (subsection 4.3). Moreover, we show how to get a more accurate value of the delay due to packets with a priority less than m (subsection 4.4).

To determine the latest starting time of packet m, we identify the busy periods of level corresponding to m's priority[1] that affect the delay of m. For this, we consider the busy period of level corresponding to m's priority, denoted $bp_{i,t}^q$, in which m is processed on node q and we define $f(q)$ as the first packet processed in $bp_{i,t}^q$ with a priority greater than or equal to m'priority. Due to the non-preemptive effect, the execution of $f(q)$ can be delayed once by a packet with a priority less than m'priority. Hence, any packet between $f(q)$ and m has a priority greater than or equal to m'priority.

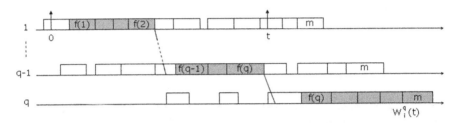

Fig. 2. Busy periods of level corresponding to m'priority

The packet $f(q)$ has been processed in a busy period on node $q-1$ at least of level $P_{i,t+D_i^1}$. Let bp_i^{q-1} be this busy period. We then define $f(q-1)$ as the first packet processed in bp_i^{q-1} with a priority less than or equal to m'priority. And so on until the busy period of node 1 in which the packet $f(1)$ is processed (see Figure 2).

Lemma 1. *When all flows follow the same path $\mathcal{P}$ consisting of q nodes numbered from 1 to q and are scheduled according to FP/EDF*, then the maximum delay incurred by the packet belonging to any flow τ_i, requested at time t on node 1, due to packets with a higher generalized priority is bounded by the maximum workload generated by:*

- *flows $\tau_j \in hp_i$ in $[-J_j, \max(0\,;\,W_i^q(t) - M_j^{1,q})]$;*
- *flows $\tau_j \in sp_i(t)$ in $[-J_j, max(0; min(W_i^q(t) - M_j^{1,q}; t + D_i^1 - D_j^1))]$;*
- *flow τ_i in $[-J_i, t]$.*

4.2   Latest Starting Time

We now compute the latest starting time of any packet m belonging to τ_i, requested at time t, as explained in the previous section.

Lemma 2. *When all flows follow the same path $\mathcal{P}$ consisting of q nodes numbered from 1 to q and are scheduled according to FP/EDF*, then for any packet*

---

[1] A busy period of level $\mathcal{L}$ is defined by an interval $[t, t')$ such that t and t' are both idle times of level $\mathcal{L}$ and there is no idle time of level $\mathcal{L}$ in (t, t'). An idle time t of level $\mathcal{L}$ is a time such that all packets with a priority greater than or equal to $\mathcal{L}$ generated before t have been processed at time t.

belonging to any flow τ_i, requested at time t on node 1, its latest starting time in node q is given by:

$$W_i^q(t) = \sum_{j \in hp_i} \left(1 + \left\lfloor \frac{\max\left(0; W_i^q(t) - M_j^{1,q}\right) + J_j}{T_j} \right\rfloor\right) \cdot C_j^{slow}$$

$$+ \sum_{j \in sp_i(t)} \left(1 + \left\lfloor \frac{\max(0; \min(W_i^q(t) - M_j^{1,q}; t + D_i^1 - D_j^1)) + J_j}{T_j} \right\rfloor\right) \cdot C_j^{slow}$$

$$+ \left(1 + \left\lfloor \frac{t + J_i}{T_i} \right\rfloor\right) \cdot C_i^{slow}$$

$$+ \sum_{\substack{h=1 \\ h \neq slow}}^{q} \max_{j \in hp_i \cup sp_i(t) \cup \{i\}} \left\{C_j^h\right\} - C_i^q + \varepsilon_i(t) + (q-1) \cdot Lmax.$$

As we can see in Lemma 2, the latest starting time of packet m is an iterative formula. Then, we consider the following series, denoted $\mathcal{W}_i^q(t)$ and establish Condition 1 that proves the existence of $W_i^q(t)$, solution of the equation given in Lemma 2.

$$\begin{cases} \mathcal{W}_i^{q\,(0)}(t) = \sum_{j \in hp_i \cup sp_i(t)} C_j^{slow} + \left(1 + \left\lfloor \frac{t + J_i}{T_i} \right\rfloor\right) \cdot C_i^{slow} + \sum_{\substack{h=1 \\ h \neq slow}}^{q} \max_{j \in hp_i \cup sp_i(t) \cup \{i\}} \left\{C_j^h\right\} \\ \qquad - C_i^q + \varepsilon_i(t) + (q-1) \cdot Lmax \\[2ex] \mathcal{W}_i^{q\,(p+1)}(t) = \sum_{j \in hp_i} \left(1 + \left\lfloor \frac{\max\left(0; \mathcal{W}_i^{q\,(p)}(t) - M_j^{1,q}\right) + J_j}{T_j} \right\rfloor\right) \cdot C_j^{slow} \\[2ex] \qquad + \sum_{j \in sp_i(t)} \left(1 + \left\lfloor \frac{\max(0; \min(\mathcal{W}_i^{q\,(p)}(t) - M_j^{1,q}; t + D_i^1 - D_j^1)) + J_j}{T_j} \right\rfloor\right) \cdot C_j^{slow} \\[2ex] \qquad + \left(1 + \left\lfloor \frac{t + J_i}{T_i} \right\rfloor\right) \cdot C_i^{slow} + \sum_{\substack{h=1 \\ h \neq slow}}^{q} \max_{j \in hp_i \cup sp_i(t) \cup \{i\}} \left\{C_j^h\right\} \\[2ex] \qquad - C_i^q + \varepsilon_i(t) + (q-1) \cdot Lmax. \end{cases}$$

Condition 1. *For any flow τ_i, for any time $t \geq -J_i$ where a packet of τ_i is requested on node 1, if $U_{hp_i \cup sp_i(t)}^{slow} < 1$, where $U_{hp_i \cup sp_i(t)}^{slow}$ denotes the utiliza- tion factor on node slow for the flows belonging to $hp_i \cup sp_i(t)$, then $\mathcal{W}_i^q(t)$ is convergent.*

We recall that a necessary condition for the feasibility of a set of flows is: $\forall h \in \mathcal{L}, U^h \leq 1$, where $U^h = \sum_{j=1}^{n} C_j^h / T_j$ denotes the utilization factor on node h. Hence, Condition 1 is not restrictive. Indeed, if $U^{slow} \leq 1$, then $U_{hp_i \cup sp_i(t)}^{slow} < 1$.

4.3 Worst Case End-to-End Response Time

The worst case end-to-end response time of flow τ_i is equal to the maximum of the worst case end-to-end response times of its packets. Then, we have:

$R_i = \max_{t \geq -J_i} \{W_i^q(t) + C_i^q - t\}$. The three following lemmas show that only a limited set of arrival times in the network has to be tested to obtain R_i.

Lemma 3. *Let $\mathcal{T}$ be the ordered set of times t such that $t = k \cdot T_j - J_j - D_i^1 + D_j^1 \geq -J_i$, where $k \in \mathbb{N}$ and $j \in sp_i \cup \{i\}$. Let t_1 and t_2 be two consecutive times of $\mathcal{T}$. Then, $\forall\, t' \in [t_1, t_2)$, $W_i^q(t') = W_i^q(t_1)$.*

Lemma 4. *For any flow $\tau_i \in \tau$, for any t greater than or equal to $\max_{k \in sp_i}\{D_k^1\} - D_i^1 - \min_{k \in sp_i}\{J_k\}$, we have: $\overline{sp}_i(t) = \emptyset$.*

Lemma 5. *For any flow $\tau_i \in \tau$, for any time t greater than or equal to: $\max_{k \in sp_i}\{D_k^1\} - D_i^1 - \min_{k \in sp_i}\{J_k\}$, we have: $W_i^q(t + B_i^{slow}) \leq W_i^q(t) + B_i^{slow}$, with: $B_i^{slow} = \sum_{j \in hp_i \cup sp_i \cup \{i\}} \lceil B_i^{slow}/T_j \rceil \cdot C_j^{slow}$.*

Hence, to compute this worst case response time, we have only to consider times $t \geq -J_i$ such that: $t = k \cdot T_j - J_j - D_i^1 + D_j^1$ and $t < \max_{k \in sp_i}\{D_k^1\} - D_i^1 - \min_{k \in sp_i}\{J_k\} + B_i^{slow}$, with $k \in \mathbb{N}$ and $j \in sp_i \cup \{i\}$.

Property 2. *When all flows follow the same path $\mathcal{P}$ consisting of q nodes numbered from 1 to q and are scheduled according to FP/EDF*, the worst case end-to-end response time of any flow τ_i meets:*
$R_i = \max_{t \in \mathcal{T}'}\{W_i^q(t) + C_i^q - t\}$, *where:*

$$W_i^q(t) = \sum_{j \in hp_i}\left(1 + \left\lfloor \frac{\max(0\,;\,W_i^q(t) - M_j^{1,q}) + J_j}{T_j} \right\rfloor\right) \cdot C_j^{slow}$$

$$+ \sum_{j \in sp_i(t)}\left(1 + \left\lfloor \frac{max(0\,;\,min(W_i^q(t) - M_j^{1,q}\,;\,t + D_i^1 - D_j^1)) + J_j}{T_j} \right\rfloor\right) \cdot C_j^{slow}$$

$$+ \left(1 + \left\lfloor \frac{t + J_i}{T_i} \right\rfloor\right) \cdot C_i^{slow}$$

$$+ \sum_{\substack{h=1 \\ h \neq slow}}^{q} \max_{j \in hp_i \cup sp_i(t) \cup \{i\}}\{C_j^h\} - C_i^q + \varepsilon_i(t) + (q-1) \cdot Lmax.$$

and $\mathcal{T}'$ denotes the ordered set of times $t \geq -J_i$ such that: $t = k \cdot T_j - J_j - D_i^1 + D_j^1$ and $t < \max_{k \in sp_i}\{D_k^1\} - D_i^1 - \min_{k \in sp_i}\{J_k\} + B_i^{slow}$, with $k \in \mathbb{N}$ and $j \in sp_i \cup \{i\}$.

It is important to notice that the cardinal of set $\mathcal{T}'$ only depends on flow τ_i and flows having the same priority. We can also notice that in the single node case, this bound is exact.

Property 3. *In the single node case, the bound given by property 2 is this given in [8] in the uniprocessor context. Indeed, we get:*
$R_i = \max_{t \in \mathcal{T}'}\{W_i^1(t) + C_i^1 - t\}$, *where:*

$$W_i^1(t) = \sum_{j \in hp_i}\left(1 + \left\lfloor \frac{W_i^1(t) + J_j}{T_j} \right\rfloor\right) \cdot C_j^1$$

$$+ \sum_{j \in sp_i(t)}\left(1 + \left\lfloor \frac{min(W_i^1(t)\,;\,t + D_i^1 - D_j^1) + J_j}{T_j} \right\rfloor\right) \cdot C_j^1$$

$$+ \left\lfloor \frac{t + J_i}{T_i} \right\rfloor \cdot C_i^1 + \max\left(0\,;\,\max_{j \in lp_i \cup \overline{sp}_i(t)}\{C_j^1\}\right),$$

and $\mathcal{T}'$ denotes the ordered set of times $t \geq -J_i$ such that: $t = k \cdot T_j - J_j - D_i^1 + D_j^1$ and $t < \max_{k \in sp_i}\{D_k^1\} - D_i^1 - \min_{k \in sp_i}\{J_k\} + B_i^1$, with $k \in \mathbb{N}$ and $j \in sp_i \cup \{i\}$.

4.4   Non-preemptive Effect

With non-preemptive scheduling on any node h, any packet m of flow τ_i, requested at time t on node 1, can be delayed by a packet m' with a smaller priority if m' has started its processing before the arrival on node h of m. The following lemma gives an upper bound on the maximum delay incurred by m and directly due to packets belonging to $lp_i \cup \overline{sp}_i(t)$.

Lemma 6. *When all flows are scheduled FP/EDF* and follow the same path $\mathcal{P}$ consisting of q nodes numbered from 1 to q, the maximum delay incurred by the packet m of any flow τ_i, requested at time t on node 1, directly due to packets belonging to $lp_i \cup \overline{sp}_i(t)$ meets: $\varepsilon_i(t) \leq \sum_{h=1}^{q} \max(0; \max_{j \in lp_i \cup \overline{sp}_i(t)}\{C_j^h\} - 1)$.*

Proof: By definition, no packet of flows belonging to $lp_i \cup \overline{sp}_i(t)$ can be processed in a busy period of level corresponding to m'priority, except the first packet of this busy period (see Section 4.2). Hence, the maximum delay incurred by any packet m of flow τ_i directly due to packets belonging to $lp_i \cup \overline{sp}_i(t)$ cannot be greater than $\max(0; \max_{j \in lp_i \cup \overline{sp}_i(t)}\{C_j^h\} - 1)$ on each node h visited. ∎

We now improve the bound given in Lemma 6 on the maximum delay incurred by a packet of τ_i, requested at time t on node 1, directly due to packets belonging to $lp_i \cup \overline{sp}_i(t)$.

Property 4. *When all flows are scheduled FP/EDF* and follow the same path $\mathcal{P}$ consisting of q nodes numbered from 1 to q, the maximum delay incurred by the packet m of any flow τ_i, requested at time t on node 1, directly due to packets belonging to $lp_i \cup \overline{sp}_i(t)$ meets:*
$$\varepsilon_i(t) \leq \max\left(0; \max_{j \in lp_i \cup \overline{sp}_i(t)}\left\{C_j^1\right\} - 1\right)$$
$$+ \sum_{h \in (1,q]} \max\left(0; \delta_i \cdot \left(\max_{j \in lp_i \cup \overline{sp}_i(t)}\left\{C_j^h\right\} - C_i^{h-1} + Lmax - Lmin\right)\right),$$

where $\forall h \in \mathcal{P}$, $\max_{j \in lp_i \cup \overline{sp}_i(t)}\{C_j^h\} = 0$ *if* $lp_i \cup \overline{sp}_i(t) = \emptyset$
and $\delta_i = 1$ *if* $lp_i \cup \overline{sp}_i(t) \neq \emptyset$ *and 0 otherwise.*

Proof: See [18]. ∎

5   Trajectory Approach When Flows Follow Different Paths

5.1   Methodology

When flows follow different paths, we proceed in two steps to compute their worst case end-to-end response times. Indeed, for the sake of simplicity, we first adopt Assumption 1: With regard to any flow τ_i, we consider that any flow τ_j following path $\mathcal{P}_j$ with $\mathcal{P}_j \neq \mathcal{P}_i$ and $\mathcal{P}_j \cap \mathcal{P}_i \neq \emptyset$ never visits a node of path

$\mathcal{P}_i$ after having left this path. In the second step, we show how to remove this assumption (see Subsection 5.4).

Assumption 1. *Let τ_i be a flow of $\mathbb{H}$ following path $\mathcal{P}_i$. For any flow $\tau_j \in hp_i \cup sp_i$ following path $\mathcal{P}_j$ with $\mathcal{P}_j \neq \mathcal{P}_i$ and $\mathcal{P}_j \bigcap \mathcal{P}_i \neq \emptyset$, if there exists a node $h \in \mathcal{P}_j \bigcap \mathcal{P}_i$ such that the node visited by τ_j immediately after h is not the one visited by τ_i, then τ_j never visits a node h'' belonging to $\mathcal{P}_i$ after.*

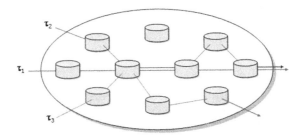

Fig. 3. Assumption 1

On Figure 3, if flow τ_2 belongs to $hp_1 \cup sp_1$, Assumption 1 is not met. We will see in Section 5.4 how to remove this assumption and extend our results to the general case.

5.2   Worst Case End-to-End Response Time

In [18], the worst case end-to-end response time of any flow $\tau_i \in \tau_H$ has been established. We recall this result in the following property. We denote $\lfloor x \rfloor^+ = \max(0; \lfloor x \rfloor)$ and $pre_i(h)$ the node visited before node h by flow τ_i.

Property 5. *When flows are scheduled FP/EDF*, if $\sum_{j \in hp_i \cup sp_i(t)} U_j^{first_{j,i}} < 1$, then the worst case end-to-end response time of any flow τ_i is bounded by:*

$$R_i = \max_{t \in \mathcal{T}_i} \left\{ W_i^{last_i}(t) - t \right\} + C_i^{last_i}, \text{ with :}$$

$$W_i^{last_i}(t) = \sum_{j \in hp_i} \left(1 + \left\lfloor \frac{W_i^{last_{j,i}}(t) - Smin_j^{last_{j,i}} - M_j^{first_{j,i}}(t) + Smax_j^{first_{j,i}} + J_j}{T_j} \right\rfloor^+ \right) \cdot C_j^{slow_{j,i}};$$

$$+ \sum_{j \in sp_i(t)} \left(1 + \left\lfloor \frac{\min\left(t + D_i^{first_i} - D_j^{first_j}; W_i^{last_{j,i}}(t) - Smin_j^{last_{j,i}} \right) - M_i^{first_{j,i}}(t) + Smax_j^{first_{j,i}} + J_j}{T_j} \right\rfloor^+ \right) \cdot C_j^{slow_{j,i}}$$

$$+ \left(1 + \left\lfloor \frac{t + J_i}{T_i} \right\rfloor \right) \cdot C_i^{slow_i} - C_i^{last_i} + \sum_{\substack{h \in \mathcal{P}_i \\ h \neq slow_i}} \max_{j \in hp_i \cup sp_i(t) \cup \{i\}} \left\{ C_j^h \right\} + \varepsilon_i(t) + (|\mathcal{P}_i| - 1) \cdot Lmax,$$

$$M_i^{first_{j,i}} = \sum_{h=first_i}^{pre_i(first_{j,i})} \left(\min_{j \in hp_i \cup sp_i(t) \cup \{i\}} \{ C_j^h \} + Lmin \right)$$

and $\mathcal{T}_i$ the set of times t such that:

- $-J_i \leq t < \bar{t}_i^0 + B_i^{slow_i}$, where $\bar{t}_i^0$ is the first time t such that $\overline{sp}_i(t) = \emptyset$ and
$B_i^{slow_i} = \sum_{j \in hp_i \cup sp_i(t) \cup \{i\}} \left\lceil \frac{B_i^{slow_i}}{T_j} \right\rceil \cdot C_j^{slow_{j,i}}$;

- $\exists j$ and l belonging to $sp_i(t) \cup \{i\}$ such that $t = -J_j + k_j \cdot T_j + M_i^{first_{j,i}}(t) - Smax_j^{first_{j,i}} + D_i^{first_i} - D_l^{first_{l,i}}$, $k_j \in \mathbb{N}$.

Proof: See [18]. ∎

Explanations

In Property 5, if m denotes the packet of flow τ_i generated at time t, we have:
- The first term of $W_i^{last_i}(t)$ represents the maximum delay incurred by m due to packets having higher fixed priorities;
- The second term represents the maximum delay incurred by packet m due to packets having the same fixed priority but higher dynamic priorities;
- The difference between the third term and the fourth one represents the maximum delay incurred by packet m due to previous packets of flow τ_i;
- $\varepsilon_i(t)$ represents the delay directly due to the non-preemptive effect;
- The last term represents the maximum transmission delay.

Worst case end-to-end response time algorithm

To compute the worst case end-to-end response time of any flow $\tau_i \in \tau$ when Assumption 1 is met, we apply the following algorithm:
- We first determine the set S_i of flows belonging to $hp_i \cup sp_i$ crossing directly or indirectly flow τ_i. τ_j belongs to S_i iff $\tau_j \in hp \cup sp_i$ and directly crosses either τ_i or a flow $\tau_k \in S_i$.
- We then initialize for the iteration $q = 1$ the value of $Smax_j^{first_{j,k}}(q)$ for any flow $\tau_k \in S_i$ and for any flow τ_j crossing τ_k. We have:
$Smax_j^{first_{j,k}}(1) = \sum_{h=first_j}^{pre(first_{j,k})}(C_j^h + Lmax)$.
- We then proceed iteratively as follows:

```
q = 0
Repeat
    q=q+1
    for any flow τk ∈ Si
        for h from firstk to lastk
            if (h = lastk) or (∃τj crossing τk such that
            h = lastj,k or h = prek(firstk,j)) then
                compute Wkʰ(t)
                if ∃j such that h = prek(firstk,j) then
                    Smaxk^firstk,j(q + 1) = maxt(Wkʰ(t) − t) + Ckʰ + Lmax
                if h = lastk then
                    compute Rk = maxt(Wkʰ(t) − t) + Ckʰ
Until (∃τk ∈ Si, Rk > Dk)
    or (∀τk ∈ Si, ∀h = prek(firstk,j) Smaxk^firstk,j(q + 1) = Smaxk^firstk,j(q))
```

5.3   Non-preemptive Effect

We recall that packet scheduling is non-preemptive. Hence, despite the high priority of any packet m, released at time t, a packet with a lower priority can delay m processing due to non-preemption. Indeed, if a packet m of any flow τ_i arrives on node h while a packet m' belonging to $lp_i \cup \overline{sp}_i(t)$ is being processed, m has to wait until m' completion.

It is important to notice that the non-preemptive effect is not limited to this waiting time. The delay incurred by packet m on node h directly due to m' may lead to consider packets belonging to $hp_i \cup sp_i(t)$, arrived after m on the node but before m starts its execution. Then, we denote $\varepsilon_i(t)$ the maximum delay incurred by packet m while following its path directly due to the non-preemptive effect.

Property 6. *Let $\tau_i \in \tau$, be a flow following path $\mathcal{P}_i = [first_i, ..., last_i]$. When flows are scheduled FP/EDF*, the maximum delay incurred by the packet of τ_i generated at time t directly due to packets having a smaller priority meets:*

$$\varepsilon_i(t) \leq \max\left(0\,;\max_{j \in lp_i \cup \overline{sp}_i(t)}\left\{C_j^{first_i}\right\} - 1\right)$$
$$+ \sum_{\substack{h \in \mathcal{P}_i \\ h \neq first_i}} \max\left(0\,;\max_{\substack{j \in lp_i \cup \overline{sp}_i(t) \\ first_{j,i}=h}}\left\{C_j^h\right\} - 1\,;\delta_i \cdot \left(\max_{\substack{j \in lp_i \cup \overline{sp}_i(t) \\ first_{j,i}\neq h}}\left\{C_j^h\right\} - C_i^{h-1} + Lmax - Lmin\right)\right),$$

where $\forall\, h \in \mathcal{P}_i$, $\max_{j \in lp_i \cup \overline{sp}_i(t)}\{C_j^h\} = 0$ if $lp_i \cup \overline{sp}_i(t) = \emptyset$ and $\delta_i = 1$ if $lp_i \cup \overline{sp}_i(t) \neq \emptyset$ and 0 otherwise.

Proof: See [18].   ∎

5.4   Generalization

Property 5, giving the worst case end-to-end response time of any flow $\tau_i \in \tau$ following path $\mathcal{P}_i$, can be extended to the general case (i.e. by removing Assumption 1). To achieve that, the idea is to consider any flow $\tau_j \in hp_i \cup sp_i$ crossing path $\mathcal{P}_i$ after it left $\mathcal{P}_i$ as a new flow. We proceed by iteration until meeting Assumption 1. We then apply Property 5 considering all these flows.

For example, in Figure 4, to compute the worst case end-to-end response time of flow τ_i following path $\mathcal{P}_i = \{1, 3, 4, 5, 6, 8, 10, 11, 12\}$, flow τ_j following path $\mathcal{P}_j = \{2, 3, 4, 5, 7, 9, 10, 11, 12\}$ has to be decomposed in two flows to meet Assumption 1, that is:

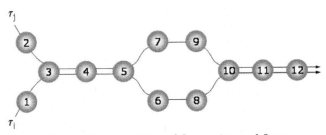

Fig. 4. Decomposition of flow τ_j into subflows

- τ_{j1}, following path $\mathcal{P}_{j1} = [2, 3, 4, 5]$;
- τ_{j2}, following path $\mathcal{P}_{j2} = [7, 9, 10, 11, 12]$.

Then, each of these two flows crosses path $\mathcal{P}_i$ only once. It is important to notice that the release jitter of flow τ_{j2} is equal to the output jitter of flow τ_{j1} on node $last_{j1,i} = 5$ plus $Lmax - Lmin$.

6   Comparative Evaluation

We now propose to compare the trajectory approach with the holistic one and with the exact values obtained by a validation tool we have developed. We first recall the computation principle of the worst case end-to-end response time in the distributed case when applying the holistic approach. Then, we give several examples that illustrate how close our results based on the trajectory approach are to the exact results. We also compare our results to these obtained by the holistic approach.

6.1   Worst Case End-to-End Response Time by the Holistic Approach

We now apply the holistic approach to compute the worst case end-to-end response time of any flow τ_i, when all flows follow the same path $\mathcal{P}$. We denote $Rmax_j^h$ (resp. $Rmin_j^h$) the maximum (resp. the minimum) response time experienced by packets of flow τ_j in node h and J_j^h its worst case jitter when entering node h.

The holistic approach proceeds iteratively and starts with node 1. Knowing the value of J_j^1 for any $j \in [1, n]$, we compute $Rmax_j^1$ using Property 3 and $Rmin_j^1 = C_j^1$. We proceed in the same way for any node h, $h \in (1, q]$.

Knowing the value of $J_j^h = \sum_{k=1..h-1}(Rmax_j^k - Rmin_j^k) + (h - 1) \cdot (Lmax - Lmin)$, $\forall j \in [1, n]$, we compute $Rmax_j^h$ using Property 3 and $Rmin_j^h = C_j^h$. Then, a bound on the end-to-end response time of flow τ_i is given by:
$\sum_{h=1}^{q} Rmax_i^h - \sum_{h=2}^{q} J_i^h + (q - 1) \cdot Lmax$.

6.2   Examples

In this section, we give examples of bounds on the end-to-end response times of flows in a network. We successively consider two cases:

- All flows follow the same path (Subsection 6.2.1);
- Flows follow different paths (Subsection 6.2.2).

We assume that $\tau = \{\tau_1, \tau_2, \tau_3, \tau_4, \tau_5\}$, all flows having a period equal to 36 and entering the network without jitter. Moreover, we assume that $Lmax = Lmin = 1$. We have developed a simulation tool providing the exhaustive solution of a real-time scheduling problem in a network. Indeed, once the different parameters have been specified, all the possible scenarios are generated and feasibility of the flow set is checked for each of them. The simulation result is a file containing the exact worst case end-to-end response time of each flow.

6.2.1 Examples with a Single Path

In this subsection, all flows follow the same path consisting of 5 nodes ($q = 5$).
For any flow τ_i, we have $D_i^1 = \lfloor D_i/q \rfloor$. Table 1 gives the priority and the end-to-end deadline of each flow we consider.

Table 1. Priorities and end-to-end deadlines

	τ_1	τ_2	τ_3	τ_4	τ_5
P_i	1	1	2	2	3
D_i	47	50	44	45	39

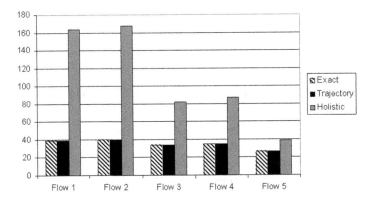

Fig. 5. Worst case end-to-end response times

We first consider that all packets have a maximum processing time equals to 4 on each visited node, that is: $\forall i \in [1,5], \forall h \in [1,5], C_i^h = 4$. Figure 5 gives for any flow τ_i the exact value of its worst case end-to-end response time and the value computed according to the trajectory approach. To show the improvement of our results compared with those obtained by the classical technique, we also include the value computed according to the holistic approach. Notice that the values given by the trajectory approach are exact for all flows, whereas those provided by the holistic approach are up to 5.5 times the exact values.

We now consider a more general case, by assuming that the maximum processing time of a flow is not the same on each visited node. More precisely, we consider ten configurations, numbered from 1 to 10 in Table 2. In each of them, the load is equal to 83.3%.

Figure 6 gives for flow τ_4 the exact value of its worst case end-to-end response time and the value computed according to the trajectory approach in each configuration. The value computed according to the holistic approach is also given. We observe that the values provided by the trajectory approach are exact or very close to the exact values (maximum deviation of +7.14%). Concerning the bounds provided by the holistic approach, they are very pessimistic. Indeed, these values are about two times the exact ones, whatever the configuration.

Table 2. Processing time of any flow τ_i on each node for 10 configurations

	Configurations									
	1	2	3	4	5	6	7	8	9	10
C_i^1	6	2	5	4	3	4	5	5	2	6
C_i^2	2	6	3	2	5	6	4	3	6	2
C_i^3	5	4	6	6	2	2	3	4	3	3
C_i^4	3	3	2	3	6	5	2	6	5	4
C_i^5	4	5	4	5	4	3	6	2	4	5

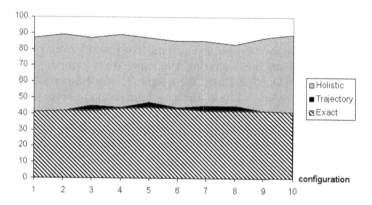

Fig. 6. End-to-end response time of flow τ_4

Table 3. Priorities and end-to-end deadlines

	τ_1	τ_2	τ_3	τ_4	τ_5
P_i	10	10	11	11	12
D_i	47	50	49	49	39

6.2.2   Example with Different Paths

In this subsection, we give an example of bounds on the end-to-end response times of real-time flows in a network, when these flows are scheduled according to FP/EDF*. We consider that the network meets: $Lmax = Lmin = 1$. Moreover, we assume that: $\tau = \{\tau_1, \tau_2, \tau_3, \tau_4, \tau_5\}$. All these flows have a period equal to 36 and enter the network without jitter. The maximum processing time of any packet of flow τ_i on node $h \in \mathcal{P}_i$ is assumed to be equal to 4. Moreover, for any flow τ_i, we have $D_i^{first_i} = \lfloor D_i / |\mathcal{P}_i| \rfloor$. Table 3 gives the fixed priority and the end-to-end deadline of each real-time flow.

The path taken by each flow is defined as follows:

- $\mathcal{P}_1 = \{1, 3, 4, 5\}$;
- $\mathcal{P}_2 = \{9, 10, 7, 6\}$;
- $\mathcal{P}_3 = \{2, 3, 4, 7, 10, 11\}$;

- $\mathcal{P}_4 = \{2, 3, 4, 7, 10, 11\}$;
- $\mathcal{P}_5 = \{2, 3, 4, 7, 8\}$.

Table 4. End-to-end response times of real-time flows

	τ_1	τ_2	τ_3	τ_4	τ_5
Exact	31	31	43	43	33
Trajectory	31	37	46	46	33
Holistic	43	91	64	64	36

Applying Properties 5 and 6, we obtain Table 4 giving the worst case end-to-end response time of any real-time flow.

7 Conclusion

In this paper, we have focused on non-preemptive Fixed Priority scheduling of sporadic flows, where all flows sharing the same fixed priority are scheduled according to Earliest Deadline First. We assume that all flows follow the same sequence of nodes. With our solution, the scheduling is non-preemptive FP/EDF*: packets are scheduled first according to their static priorities and second according to their absolute deadlines computed on the first node visited and used for arbitration by all nodes visited. This solution ensures that if a packet m has a priority higher than a packet m' on a node, this is true on any visited node.

We have shown how to compute an upper bound on the end-to-end response time of any flow with a worst case analysis using the trajectory approach. We have compared these results with the exact values and those provided by the holistic approach. We have shown that the bound given by the trajectory approach is reached in various configurations, whereas the holistic approach provides a bound that can be very pessimistic.

References

1. K. Tindell, A. Burns, A. J. Wellings, *Analysis of hard real-time communications*, Real-Time Systems, Vol. 9, pp. 147-171, 1995.
2. J. Liu, *Real-time systems*, Prentice Hall, New Jersey, 2000.
3. K. Jeffay, D. F. Stanat, C. U. Martel, *On non-preemtive scheduling of periodic and sporadic tasks*, IEEE Real-Time Systems symposium, pp. 129-139, San Antonio, USA, December 1991.
4. L. George, N. Rivierre, M. Spuri, *Preemptive and non-preemptive scheduling real-time uniprocessor scheduling*, INRIA Research Report No 2966, September 1996.
5. S. Blake, D. Black, M. Carlson, E. Davies, Z. Wang, W. Weiss, *An architecture for Differentiated Services*, RFC 2475, December 1998.
6. R. Braden, D. Clark, S. Shenker, *Integrated services in the Internet architecture: An overview*, RFC 1633, June 1994.
7. S. Baruah, R. Howell, L. Rosier, *Algorithms and complexity concerning the preemptive scheduling of periodic real-time tasks on one processor*, Real-Time Systems, 2, p 301-324, 1990.
8. S. Martin, P. Minet, L. George, *FP/EDF, a non-preemptive scheduling combining fixed priorities and deadlines: Uniprocessor and distributed cases*, INRIA Research Report No 5112, *http://www.inria.fr/rrrt/rr-5112.html*, Feb. 2004.

9. V. Sivaraman, F. Chiussi, M. Gerla, *End-to-end statistical delay service under GPS and EDF scheduling: A comparaison study*, INFOCOM'2001, Anchorage, April 2001.

10. M. Vojnovic, J. Le Boudec, *Stochastic analysis of some expedited forwarding networks*, INFOCOM'2002, New York, June 2002.

11. F. Chiussi, V. Sivaraman, *Achieving high utilization in guaranteed services networks using early-deadline-first scheduling*, IWQoS'98, Napo, California, May 1998.

12. L. George, D. Marinca, P. Minet, *A solution for a deterministic QoS in multimedia systems*, International Journal on Computer and Information Science, Vol.1, N3, September 2001.

13. K. Tindell, J. Clark, *Holistic schedulability analysis for distributed hard real-time systems*, Microprocessors and Microprogramming, Euromicro Journal, Vol. 40, 1994.

14. J. Le Boudec, P. Thiran, *Network calculus: A theory of deterministic queuing systems for the Internet*, Springer Verlag, LNCS 2050, September 2003.

15. A. Parekh, R. Gallager, *A generalized processor sharing approach to flow control in integrated services networks: The multiple node case*, IEEE ACM Transactions on Networking, Vol. 2, 1994.

16. L. Georgiadis, R. Guérin, V. Peris, K. Sivarajan, *Efficient network QoS provisioning based on per node traffic shaping*, IEEE/ACM Transactions on Networking, Vol. 4, No. 4, August 1996.

17. V. Sivaraman, F. Chiussi, M. Gerla, *Traffic shaping for end-to-end delay guarantees with EDF scheduling*, IWQoS'2000, Pittsburgh, June 2000.

18. S. Martin, *Maîtrise de la dimension temporelle de la qualité de service dans les réseaux*, Ph.D. thesis, University of Paris 12, France, July 2004.

Web Service Based Inter-AS Connection Managements for QoS-Guaranteed DiffServ Provisioning*

Young-Tak Kim and Hyun-Ho Shin

Advanced Networking Technology Lab, Yeungnam University,
Gyeongsan-Si, Gyeongbuk, 712-749, Korea
ytkim@yu.ac.kr, srobic@hanmail.net

Abstract. In this paper, we propose a Web service based inter-AS (autonomous system) connection management architecture for QoS-guaranteed DiffServ provisioning. In the proposed architecture, the interaction between customer network management (CNM) and network management system (NMS), and the interactions among multiple NMSs are designed and implemented based on Web service architecture with WSDL, SOAP/XML and UDDI. The proposed architecture can be easily implemented in the early stage of MPLS network employment where the MPLS signaling is not mature yet, and provides efficient internetworking among multiple Internet Service Providers (ISPs) that is requested to provide end-to-end QoS-guaranteed differentiated services.

1   Introduction

In Next Generation Internet (NGI), the most important issue is how to provide efficiently QoS-guaranteed realtime multimedia services with maximized network utilization. DiffServ-aware-MPLS traffic engineering has been developed as the most promising solution to provide QoS-guaranteed broadband differentiated services[1,2,3]. In the DiffServ-aware-MPLS traffic engineering, separated policing (metering & marking) and queuing are applied to each DiffServ class-type to guarantee the requested bandwidth and QoS [4,5].

In order to deploy the QoS-guaranteed end-to-end DiffServ-aware-MPLS traffic engineering functions in Internet environment, several conditions must be solved : (i) MPLS signaling must be fully supported to establish MPLS LSP (label switched path) with traffic engineering function, (ii) multiple MPLS networks must be interconnected to provide end-to-end DiffServ-aware-MPLS connections for realtime multimedia services, and (iii) an efficient end-user's on-demand service request for QoS-guaranteed end-to-end connection establishment that should be handled dynamically with proper Service Level Agreement (SLA) processing.

---

* This work has been supported by Yeungnam University IT Research Center (ITRC) Project.

W. Dosch, R.Y. Lee, and C. Wu (Eds.): SERA 2004, LNCS 3647, pp. 248–260, 2005.

The inter-domain MPLS signaling, however, has not been fully standardized and developed to be used in the inter-networking among MPLS LSRs (label switched routers) from multiple vendors, and in the internetworking among multiple domain networks of different network operators[6]. Especially, the MPLS NNI (network-node interface) signaling has not been well matured. Since the customer network is usually deployed with Gigabit Ethernet technology, it may not be able to support connection-oriented MPLS networking functions.

To provide an efficient way to support on-demand QoS-guaranteed differentiated multimedia services dynamically based on semi-permanent MPLS LSPs before the wide deployment of well-established MPLS signaling, there must be (i) service access interaction between user terminal (or customer network) and MPLS network provider, and (ii) inter-domain networking interactions among multiple subnetworks.

Recently, Web service architecture has been proposed to provide a single uniform software infrastructure to support a wide range of distributed services, thereby reducing training and software development costs [7,8]. Since Web services are expected to become standard components of future operating systems, it is expected to be integrated within common office applications [7,8]. For the efficient provisioning of end-to-end QoS-guaranteed networking services, the Web service architecture is a good candidate operational model for inter-networking and network service access, especially when the unified network signaling technology is not supported well.

In this paper we propose a Web service based distributed connection management architecture to provide end-to-end QoS-guaranteed DiffServ-aware-MPLS services across multiple MPLS domain networks. The distributed connection management function is designed and implemented with WSDL, SOAP/XML and UDDI. We designed an on-line network service access scheme between user terminal and MPLS provider network with SLA function for detailed negotiation on the requirements on QoS parameters, traffic parameters, and application specific features. We also designed the inter-domain connection management function among multiple MPLS domain networks.

The rest of this paper is organized as follows. In section 2, some related works are introduced, and in section 3 the Web service based distributed connection management architecture is designed in detail. In section 4, the implementation of NMS and EMS are explained in detail, and finally in section 5, we conclude this paper.

2   Related Work

2.1   QoS-Guaranteed Service Provisioning with DiffServ-Aware-MPLS Traffic Engineering

Differentiated Service (DiffServ) technology has been developed to provide differentiated quality-of-service (QoS) according to the user's requirements and traffic & QoS parameters of multimedia data flow[1]. The main objective of DiffServ is to protect the higher-priority premium IP traffic from the lower-priority best-effort traffic under network congestion. DiffServ by itself, however, only provides per-hop-based differentiated packet processing with relative priority or weight; it cannot guarantee QoS or bandwidth.

DiffServ-aware-MPLS has been developed to provide QoS-guaranteed differentiated services by using DiffServ packet processing with connection-oriented MPLS traffic engineering [2,3]. In DiffServ-aware-MPLS traffic engineering, up to 8 class-types (ordered aggregates) are defined with different priority or weight, and the mapping of DiffServ class-types into MPLS LSP is implemented in either E-LSP or L-LSP model. In E-LSP model, multiple class-types are mapped onto an MPLS LSP, and the EXP field of the MPLS Shim header conveys the per-hop-behavior (PHB) (i.e., packet scheduling treatment and packet drop precedence) to be applied to the packet at each LSR[4].

In order to establish LSPs with guaranteed bandwidth and QoS level to carry DiffServ traffic, MPLS signaling is required. Currently, two MPLS signaling standards are under development: RSVP-TE [9] and CR-LDP [10]. Even though the basic interoperability test of L2VPN and L3VPN among multiple MPLS switches from various vendors has been demonstrated in MPLS world congress 2003, the MPLS signaling interoperability test over RSVP-TE tunnel has shown some unresolved configuration issues in a couple of cases [6]. The interoperability of MPLS signaling with RSVP-TE and CR-LDP will generate further more complicated interoperability problems.

In order to request QoS-guaranteed service, the end user application must send a QoS request to the Internet service provider (ISP), as shown in Fig. 1[11]. The admission control agent of ISP network determines the admission of the requested service/connection provision according to the current network resource availability and network operation policy. In the case of inter-networking environment [12], the QoS request must be delivered to multiple MPLS domain networks, along the selected shortest route that can provide the requested network resource for the guaranteed QoS provisioning.

The current status of MPLS control plane for admission control and resource control, however, is usually configured within a domain network without inter-domain NNI (network-node-interface) signaling function. Also, there is no MPLS signaling function between customer premises network (CPN) domain and MPLS edge router of provider network. As a result, we need to devise an efficient on-line interactive service provisioning mechanism for inter-networking multiple MPLS domain networks which may easily cooperate with different MPLS signaling capabilities and their own routing and connection management functions. Web service architecture can be used to interconnect multiple distributed processing components, such as multiple MPLS domain network management systems (NMSs).

In this paper, we propose a Web service based distributed connection management architecture for QoS-guaranteed DiffServ-aware-MPLS networking. The proposed architecture can be easily implemented in the early stage of MPLS network deployment where the MPLS signaling is not mature yet, and provides inter-

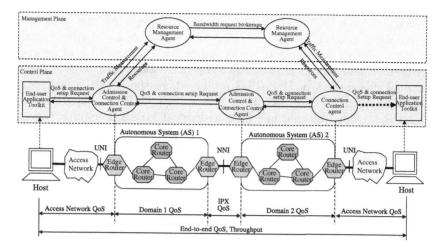

Fig. 1. Internetworking of MPLS network

networking among multiple MPLS networks of Internet Service Providers (ISPs) for end-to-end QoS-guaranteed differentiated service (DiffServ) provisioning.

2.2 Service Level Agreement (SLA) and Related QoS Parameters

In Next Generation Internet, the service description with related parameters for QoS-guaranteed service will be negotiated between user (client) and the network operator (server), and will be specified by service level agreement (SLA) [13]. SLA will be translated into detailed service level specification (SLS) that defines the detailed operational parameters for the requested service provision. SLA/SLS

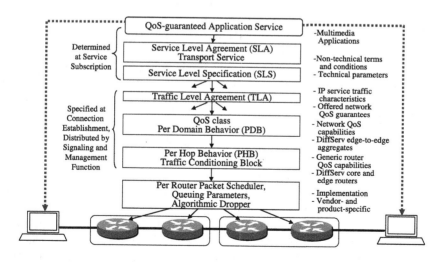

Fig. 2. SLA and its implementation

defines the required QoS level, such as end-to-end packet transfer delay, limit of
delay variations (jitter), packet loss ratio, packet error ratio, service availability,
and fault restoration capability. As shown in Fig. 2, the SLS is interpreted
to per-domain behavior (PDB) and per-hop behavior (PHB) to determine the
operational parameters of IP/MPLS router where the packet scheduler, per-
class-type queue and algorithmic dropper is configured. When the MPLS service
provision is provided by multiple inter-networked MPLS domain network, the
PDB is defined for each domain network, and within each domain network PHB
is defined for each IP/MPLS node. The interaction between PHB and IP/MPLS
router can be implemented in SNMP, CLI (command line interface) or COPS
(Common Open Policy Service) protocol [14,15].

2.3   Web Service Architecture

Web services are Extensible Markup Language (XML) applications mapped to
programs, objects, databases and business functions [18]. Web service architecture enables the Internet-based applications to find, access, and automatically
interact with other Internet based applications; Web service provides efficient
mechanism for software-oriented interactions. Web service standards define the
format of the message, specify the interface to which a message is sent, describe conventions for mapping the contents of the message into and out of the
programs implementing the service, and define mechanisms to publish and to
discover Web services interfaces [18].

Web service is being standardized by the World Wide Web Consortium
(W3C), and promises to provide a single uniform software infrastructure to support a wide range of distributed services, thereby reducing training and software
development costs [7,8]. In Web service architecture, Web Service Description
Language (WDSL) is used to define the actual Web services, where WSDL is
similar to the IDL (Interface Description Language) of CORBA (Common Object Request Broker Architecture) that defines the interface among distributed
computing components; WSDL files include the operations supported by a particular service, the parameters of these operations, the type of the returned value,
the protocol binding (usually SOAP), and the location of the service (expressed
in the form of a Uniform Resource Identifier, URI)[7,8]. Simple Object Access
Protocol (SOAP) messages can be exchanged over different underlying transfer
protocol, where most people currently envision using SOAP over HTTP/1.1[7]. A
companion standard, Universal Description, Discovery, and Integration (UDDI),
is used to register Web services described in WDSL, and to help the discovery
of WSDL files.

Although Web services have not been specifically designed for management
purposes, we can find it attractive to develop management applications [7], especially when the local domain network management systems are implemented
by various programming language (i.e. C++ and Java) with different platform
(i.e., C# on MS-Windows, STL on UNIX, and J2EE). Also, we can use the Web
Service architecture to implement following two kinds of inter-domain networking: (i) DiffServ-aware-MPLS service access from the customer network manager

(CNM) to the MPLS network service provider, where MPLS signaling is not available, and (ii) among MPLS domain networks where MPLS NNI signaling is not fully mature yet.

3   Web Service Based Distributed Connection Management Architecture

3.1   Inter-AS (Autonomous System) Traffic Engineering

The provisioning of inter-AS traffic engineering is required to support inter-AS bandwidth guarantees, inter-AS resource optimization, and fast recovery across ASs [12]. The inter-AS MPLS traffic engineering must be supported in both (i) within one SP (service provider) administrative domain, and (ii) across multiple SP administrative domains. The provisioning of QoS-guaranteed VPN (virtual private network) in the initial stage of DiffServ-aware-MPLS network deployment requires inter-AS traffic engineering.

In an intra-AS (autonomous system) MPLS domain network that is operated by a network operator, the link status and the available network resources with routing information in the AS can be collected by interior gateway protocol (IGP), such as ISIS-TE [16] or OSPF-TE [17]. Since the whole intra-AS domain network is operated and managed by a network operator, the network/link status information and policy of resource allocation can be unified, and the whole network can be operated as a single AS. When the network size becomes large to cover one nation or to cross continent, however, the network should be divided into multiple AS domains to solve the scalability problems of IGP link status flooding and path computations.

As shown in Fig. 3, when multiple MPLS domain networks are inter-networked, and the end-to-end service provisioning requires MPLS LSP setup across multiple MPLS domain networks of different AS's [11], the reachability information with the specified bandwidth and QoS requirement of each domain network must be collected and used in the constraint routed shortest path computation. In IP-based Internet, BGP (Border Gateway Protocol) provides basic inter-networking information, such as reachability [18]. The detailed parameters for the DiffServ-aware-MPLS traffic engineering is not supported yet. For inter-AS DiffServ provisioning, bandwidth broker model, called BGRP (Board Gateway Reservation Protocol), has been proposed, but not standardized[11].

As an alternative implementation method of the inter-AS traffic engineering, the Web service architecture with per-domain network management functions can be used. Each domain MPLS network is equipped with its own network management functions to configure the MPLS LSRs, to establish traffic engineering tunnels, and to setup backup path of TE tunnels for fast restoration. Since the network management functions of each MPLS domain network may be implemented with different programming languages and development platforms, Web service architecture that can interconnect heterogeneous distributed computing modules is a good solution for the implementation technology for inter-AS traffic engineering.

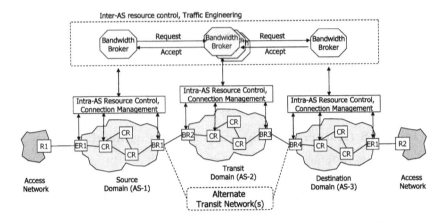

Fig. 3. Inter-AS Traffic Engineering

3.2   Distributed Connection Management in Multi-domain DiffServ-Aware-MPLS Service Provision

Fig. 4 shows the overall interaction architecture of distributed connection management for DiffServ-aware-MPLS service provisioning across multiple domain networks. The customer premises network (CPN) is managed by a customer network management (CNM) system. CNM contains end-user application management functions that initiates QoS-guaranteed service request. Since there is no MPLS signaling support between the CPN and the edge IP/MPLS router of ISP network, the interaction between CNM and the NMS with resource management and admission control function should be implemented separately to support on-demand service request and resource allocation function. For flexible online service request and management function, we propose a Web Service based distributed connection management architecture for DiffServ-aware-MPLS.

An MPLS domain network may contain multiple subnetworks, where each subnetwork is controlled and managed by an EMS (element management system). The interaction between NMS and EMS can be implemented by SOAP or RMI. Each EMS must register its available services and resources to NMS. The interaction between EMS and the network element (NE), such as IP/MPLS router and transmission system is usually implemented by SNMP or CLI. More detailed functions among NMS, EMS and NE in Web service architecture will be given in following subsections.

3.3   Web Service Based Inter-AS Traffic Engineering and Connection Management Architecture

The most important function of inter-AS traffic engineering on multiple MPLS domain networks is (i) how to configure bandwidth guaranteed traffic engineering tunnels across multiple domain networks, (ii) how to optimize the resource utilization, and (iii) how to provide efficient fast recovery of traffic engineering

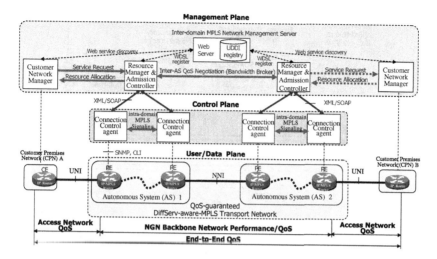

Fig. 4. Web service based QoS-guaranteed internetworking of DiffServ-aware-MPLS network

tunnels across ASs. For efficient inter-AS traffic engineering and connection management, the connection reachability and availability of resource in each domain network must be provided to network management systems (NMSs).

As shown in Fig. 4, the NMS of each MPLS domain registers WSDL that describes its network service to the inter-domain MPLS network management server. The registered information for inter-AS traffic engineering must include available bandwidth and QoS among edge routers of the domain network, connectivity to neighbor AS, and reachability to other ISPs. When the inter-AS traffic engineering is operated among ASs of different ISP, the detailed information of available network resource may not be provided because of network security or internal policy; but even in this case, the contact information to request an inter-domain LSP connection setup will be registered and provided to other domain networks.

Each NMS can discover its neighbor domain network, the delegate NMS for the neighbor domain network, connectivity, and available bandwidth & QoS. Using the UDDI repository, the CNM can find the NMS to which it can send a service request. The ingress NMS evaluates the connection admission condition, and makes decision. When a connection request is accepted, the required network resource must be allocated. If the requested connection reaches beyond an ISP's domain network, multiple MPLS domains must collaborate with internetworking function to find the shortest path to the destination while guaranteeing the requested QoS and bandwidth.

3.4   Interactions Between NMS and EMS

For each domain network, an NMS may control multiple EMSs (element management systems) where each EMS controls a sub-domain MPLS network. EMS

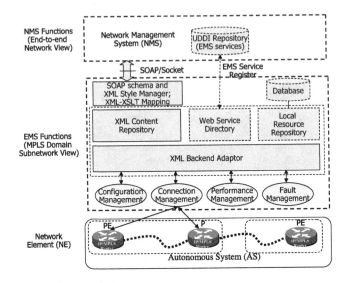

Fig. 5. Interactions between NMS and EMS

provides basic network configuration, traffic engineering tunnel establishment, node/link protection mode setup, and configuration of fault notification and fast restoration. The EMS is tightly integrated with the signaling module of control plane for on-demand dynamic connection establishment. In the initial stage of MPLS network provisioning, where MPLS signaling function is not fully mature, the EMS is used to provide traffic engineering tunnel (TE-LSP) establishments.

The EMS may be implemented by various programming language and platforms. Usually, the network element(NE, i.e. MPLS LSR) is developed together with its related EMS function for local management and test purpose. In order to provide interactions among EMS functions and the NMS function, the basic EMS functions must be registered in the UDDI repository of the NMS as shown in Fig. 5. The NMS, that is responsible for the network, can discover the EMS functions for the management of subnetwork connection setup via SOAP/HTTP protocol.

Since the Web Service architecture is currently supported by only Microsoft .NET and SUN J2EE, if the EMS has been implemented on UNIX platform, the legacy EMS function modules programmed in C++ must be adapted to JAVA J2EE. The XML backend adapter module in Fig. 5 provides the adaptation for legacy EMS modules.

4   Implementations and Analysis

4.1   Implementations of Web Service Based Inter-AS Distributed Connection Management

Fig. 6 shows the overall interactions among CNM, NMS, EMS, and Web server with UDDI registry. When CNM receives a user's request to establish a DiffServ-

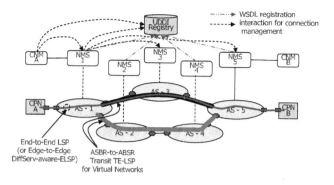

Fig. 6. Interactions among NMS, EMS and CNM

aware-MPLS connection, it discovers available services from the Web server, locating the specific NMS to which the CPN is subscribed. The CNM then requests the connection establishment to the NMS providing required parameters such as destination address, bandwidth, and QoS. The ingress NMS then performs routing to find the QoS-guaranteed shortest path to the destination customer edge. When the specified destination is not within the same AS of the ingress NMS, the ingress NMS must discover a possible shortest route to the destination, the ASs along the route, and the transit NMSs.

By discovering the transit ASs and NMSs, the ingress NMS can also get the access methods of the transit NMS, by which it can request to establish a DiffServ-aware-MPLS LSP segment across the AS. The connection setup requests are delivered via SOAP/HTTP protocol. If multiple transit ASs must be interconnected for the end-to-end LSP, the same operation is repeated for each domain until the LSP reaches at the egress NMS. Each transit NMS then establishes the required subnetwork connection by interactions with EMS.

4.2   Implementation of EMS

EMS (element management system) configures, controls and manages each network element (NE) node. EMS has been implemented with C++ STL on UNIX platform. Since current Java 1.4 environment supports SOAP 1.1 specification, there is no easy way to directly interact C++ module and Java module through SOAP protocol. When Java 1.5 supports SOAP 1.2 specification, C++ based EMS and Java based NMS can be inter-connected through SOAP, easily. Currently, we are using XML/socket protocol to deliver connection request messages to EMS, and reply messages to NMS.

The LSP_Setup operation of the EMS is registered to the managing NMS that establishes a subnetwork connection (SNC). The requested arguments of bandwidth and QoS parameters are passed by XML string. Since the EMS should be implemented as a single network management system on UNIX operating system that provides node protection for fault tolerance, the interaction of NMS and EMS with Web service architecture should be implemented based on J2EE platform with security. The XML backend adapter will be designed and implemented to map the SOAP/XML based LSP setup request to the C++ based connection management module.

4.3 Implementation of NMS

Fig. 7 shows the architecture of NMS with Web Service functions. Each NMS contains the network management functions for the AS domain network, such as admission control, SLA/SLS/TLS policy management, virtual topology network configuration for QoS-guaranteed DiffServ provisioning, bandwidth negotiation for transit network configuration, configuration management, connection management, performance management and fault management.

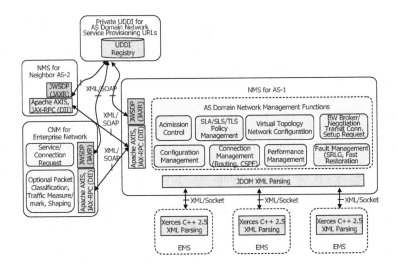

Fig. 7. NMS Functional Architecture

Currently, Apache AXIS and JAX-RPC(DII) are used to provide XML/SOAP based interactions among NMSs and CNM-NMS. JDOM is used in NMS and Xerces C++ 2.5 XML parsing is used in EMS which is implemented with C++/Solaris. JWSDP with JAXR is used to provide interactions between UDDI registry and NMS/EMS.

5   Conclusion

In this paper, we proposed a Web service based inter-AS distributed connection management architecture for QoS-guaranteed DiffServ-aware-MPLS networking. In the proposed architecture, the interaction between customer network management (CNM) and network management system (NMS), and the interaction among multiple NMSs are designed and implemented based on Web service architecture with WSDL, SOAP/XML and UDDI registry.

Currently we are developing the proposed inter-AS distributed DiffServ-aware-MPLS connection management system with Web service architecture, based on J2EE platform. The basic operations to setup a DiffServ-aware-MPLS LSP has been tested on a small scale testbed network that composed of 5 Cisco 7200 series MPLS routers for PE (Provider Edge), P (Provider node) and 4 Cisco 3620 series IP/MPLS routers for CE (Customer Edge). The performance evaluations of the connection setup delay, scalability and hierarchical connection management are under development.

The proposed architecture can be easily implemented in the early stage of MPLS network employment where the MPLS signaling is not mature yet, and provides internetworking among multiple Internet Service Providers (ISPs) that is required for end-to-end QoS-guaranteed service provisioning.

References

1. IETF mpls working group, "Multi-protocol Label Switching Architecture," IETF Internet Draft, draft-ietf-mpls-arch-05,(1999).
2. RFC 2475, "An Architecture of Differentiated Services," December 1998.
3. RFC 3031, "Multiprotocol Label Switch (MPLS) Architecture," April 2002.
4. RFC 3270, "Multiprotocol Label Switching (MPLS) support of Differentiated Services," April 2002.
5. RFC 3564, "Requirements for support of Differentiated Service aware MPLS traffic engineering," July 2003.
6. Youngtak Kim and Chul Kim, "QoS-guaranteed DiffServ-aware-MPLS Traffic Engineering with Controlled Bandwidth Borrowing," Proc. of ACIS International Conference on Software Engineering Research & Applications (SERA'03), San Francisco, U.S.A., June 25-27, 2003, pp. 112-117.
7. MPLS World Congress 2003, http://www.upperside.fr/mplswc2003/mplswc03pro.htm, MPLS Forum.
8. Jurgen Schonwalder, Aiko Pras and Jean-Philippe Martin-Flatin, "On the Future of Internet Management Technologies," IEEE Communication Magazine, Oct. 2003, pp. 90-97.
9. Eric Newcomer, Understanding Web Services, Addison Wesley professional, 2002.
10. RFC 3209, "RSVP-TE: Extensions to RSVP for LSP tunnels," December 2001.
11. IETF Draft, "Constraint-Based LSP Setup using LDP," Feb. 2001.
12. Thomas Engel et. al, "AQUILA: Adaptive Resource Control for QoS using an IP-based Layered Architecture," IEEE Communication Mag., Jan. 2003, pp. 46-53.
13. IETF Draft, "MPLS Inter-AS Traffic Engineering requirements," draft-ietf-tewg-interas-mpls-te-req-05.txt, 2000.
14. Eleni Mykoniati et. al, "Admission Control for Providing QoS in DiffServ IP Networks: The TEQUILA Approach," IEEE Communication Mag., Jan. 2003, pp. 38-44.
15. J. Boyle et al., "The COPS (Common Open Policy Service) Protocol," RFC 2748, Jan. 2000.
16. K. Chan et al., "COPS Usage for Policy Provisioning," RFC 3084, Mar. 2001.

17. IETF Internet Draft, "IS-IS extensions for Traffic Engineering,"draft-ietf-isis-traffic-05.txt, Aug. 2003 (work in progress).
18. IETF Internet Draft, "Traffic Engineering Extensions to OSPF," draft-ietf-ospf-ospfv3-traffic-01.txt, June 2001 (work in progress).
19. IETF RFC 3107, "Carrying Label Information in BGP-4," May 2001.

Author Index

Lecture Notes in Computer Science

For information about Vols. 1–3770

please contact your bookseller or Springer